# German

*Phrase book & dictionary*

COLLINS

*Glasgow & London*

First published 1990

Copyright © William Collins Sons & Company Limited
Published by William Collins Sons & Company Limited
Printed in Hong Kong
ISBN 0 00-435868-6

Your *Collins Traveller Phrase Book and Dictionary* is a handy, quick-reference guide that will help you make the most of your stay abroad. Its clear layout, with direct alphabetical access to the relevant information, will save you valuable time when you need that crucial word or phrase.

There are two main sections in this book:

• 70 practical topics arranged in A-Z order from **ACCIDENTS** to **WINTER SPORTS** via such subjects as **MENUS, ROOM SERVICE** and **TAXIS**. Each topic gives you the basic phrases you will need along with clear but simple pronunciation guidelines. In many cases, there's the added bonus of our 'Streetwise' travel tips – practical and often invaluable travel information.

And, if you've found the right phrase but still need a vital word, you're sure to find it in the final topic, **WORDS**, a brief but rigorously practical list of English words and their translations, chosen for their relevance to the needs of the general traveller.

• A 4000-word foreign vocabulary; the key to all those mystifying but important notices, traffic signs, menus, etc which confront the traveller at every turn. This mini-dictionary will help you enjoy to the full the country's cuisine, save you time with asking directions, and perhaps prevent you getting into one or two tricky situations!

So, just flick through the pages to find the information you require. Why not start with a quick look at the **GRAMMAR, ALPHABET** and **PRONUNCIATION** topics? From there on the going is easy with your *Collins Traveller Phrase Book and Dictionary*.

*Gute Reise!*

*Streetwise*

*Third party insurance is obligatory. It is best to carry an international Green Card which you should be able to obtain from your insurers. Always call the police after an accident. For a traffic offence, German police have the power to fine you on the spot.*

| | |
|---|---|
| There's been an accident | **Ein Unfall ist passiert**<br>*ine oonfal ist paseert* |
| I've crashed my car | **Ich habe gerade einen Autounfall gehabt**<br>*ikh hah-be gerah-de ine-en owto-oonfal gehapt* |
| Can I see your insurance certificate please? | **Kann ich Ihre Versicherungspapiere sehen?**<br>*kan ikh ee-re fer-zikh-eroongs-papee-re zay-en* |
| We will have to report it to the police | **Wir müssen das der Polizei melden**<br>*veer moo-sen das der poli-tsy melden* |
| He ran into me | **Er ist in mich hineingefahren**<br>*er ist in mikh hin-ine-gefah-ren* |
| He was driving too fast | **Er ist zu schnell gefahren**<br>*er ist tsoo shnel gefah-ren* |
| He was too close behind | **Er ist zu dicht aufgefahren**<br>*er ist tsoo dikht owf-gefah-ren* |
| He did not give way | **Er hat die Vorfahrt nicht beachtet**<br>*er hat dee forfart nikht be-akh-tet* |
| The car number was … | **Die Autonummer war …**<br>*dee owto-noomer var …* |
| He was coming from my right/left | **Er kam von rechts/links**<br>*er kahm fon rekhts/links* |

# ACCIDENTS – INJURIES

*Streetwise*

*Before you set off, it is always advisable to obtain proper insurance.
Ambulances have to be paid for. In most areas the number for
emergency services is 110, but the number will in any case be
displayed under the heading NOTRUF inside phone boxes. Carry
your passport and your E111 (or other) medical insurance form at all
times. There are first aid posts at most motorway service stations.*

| | |
|---|---|
| There has been an accident | **Ein Unfall ist passiert**<br>*ine oonfal ist paseert* |
| Call an ambulance/ a doctor | **Rufen Sie einen Krankenwagen/einen Arzt**<br>*roofen zee ine-en kranken-vahgen/ine-en artst* |
| He has hurt himself | **Er hat sich verletzt**<br>*er hat zikh fer-letst* |
| He is seriously injured/bleeding | **Er ist schwer verletzt/Er blutet**<br>*er ist shvayr fer-letst/er bloo-tet* |
| He can't breathe/ move | **Er kann nicht atmen/sich nicht bewegen**<br>*er kan nikht aht-men/zikh nikht be-vay-gen* |
| I can't move my arm/ leg | **Ich kann meinen Arm/mein Bein nicht bewegen**<br>*ikh kan mine-en arm/mine bine nikht be-vay-gen* |
| Cover him up | **Decken Sie ihn zu**<br>*decken zee een tsoo* |
| Don't move him | **Bewegen Sie ihn nicht**<br>*be-vay-gen zee een nikht* |
| He has cut himself | **Er hat sich geschnitten**<br>*er hat zikh ge-shnit-en* |

See also **EMERGENCIES**

*Streetwise*

*Hotels are officially graded from 1 to 5 stars. If you stay in a Hotel Garni there will be no meals served except for breakfast and possibly snacks and drinks. In addition to hotels, look for signs saying Pension or Privatpension (boarding house) – these are generally cheaper. Always check whether or not the price quoted includes breakfast. Fremdenzimmer or Zimmer frei are rooms in private houses. Inclusive rates are Vollpension (full board) and Halbpension (half board). Most German towns have an agency called a Zimmernachweis where you can book accommodation.*

| | |
|---|---|
| We're looking for a hotel/an apartment | **Wir suchen ein Hotel/eine Wohnung**<br>*veer **zoo**-khen ine ho**tel**/ine-e **voh**-noong* |
| I want to reserve a single/double room | **Ich möchte ein Einzelzimmer/ Doppelzimmer reservieren**<br>*ikh mur'kh-te ine **ine**-tsel-tsimmer/ **dop**el-tsimmer ray-zer-**vee**ren* |
| Do you have facilities for the disabled? | **Haben Sie hier Einrichtungen für Behinderte?**<br>***hah**-ben zee heer **ine**-rikh-toongen foor be-**hin**-der-te* |
| I want bed and breakfast/full board | **Ich möchte ein Zimmer mit Frühstück/ Vollpension**<br>*ikh mur'kh-te ine tsimmer mit **froo**-shtook/ **fol**pen-syohn* |
| What is the daily/ weekly rate? | **Was kostet es für einen Tag/eine Woche?**<br>*vas kostet es foor ine-en tahk/ine-e **vo**-khe* |
| I want to stay three nights/from … till … | **Ich möchte drei Nächte bleiben/vom … bis zum … bleiben**<br>*ikh mur'kh-te dry **nekh**-te **bly**-ben/fom … bis tsoom … **bly**-ben* |

See also **HOTEL DESK, ROOM SERVICE, SELF-CATERING**

| | |
|---|---|
| Where do I check in for the flight to Munich? | **Wo ist die Abfertigung für den Flug nach München?**<br>*voh ist dee **ap**-fer-tigoong foor dayn flook nakh **moon**-khen* |
| I'd like an aisle/a window seat | **Ich hätte gern einen Gangsitz/Fenstersitz**<br>*ikh het-te gern ine-en **gang**-zits/**fen**-ster-zits* |
| Will a meal be served on the plane? | **Wird im Flugzeug ein Essen serviert?**<br>*veert im **flook**-tsoyk ine **es**-en zer-**veert*** |
| Where is the snack bar/duty-free shop? | **Wo ist die Cafeteria/der Duty-free-Shop?**<br>*voh ist dee ka-fe-**tay**-ree-a/der duty-free shop* |
| Where can I change some money? | **Wo kann ich Geld wechseln?**<br>*voh kan ikh gelt **vek**-seln* |
| Where do I get the bus to town? | **Wo fährt ein Bus in die Stadt ab?**<br>*voh fayrt ine boos in dee **shtat** ap* |
| Where are the taxis/telephones? | **Wo sind die Taxis/Telefone?**<br>*voh zint dee taxis/tay-lay-**foh**-ne* |
| I want to hire a car/reserve a hotel room | **Ich möchte gern ein Auto mieten/ein Hotelzimmer reservieren**<br>*ikh mur'kh-te gern ine **ow**to meeten/ine ho**tel**-tsimmer ray-zer-**vee**ren* |
| I am being met | **Ich werde abgeholt**<br>*ikh vayr-de **ap**-ge-hohlt* |

# ALPHABET

The German alphabet is the same as the English alphabet except for **ä**, **ö** and **ü** (**a**, **o** and **u** with an *Umlaut*) and **s** and **z** together which is written **ß**. The pronunciation of each letter except **y** is given below, together with the word normally used for clarification when spelling something out.

| | | | | | |
|---|---|---|---|---|---|
| **A** *ah* | **wie** *vee* | **Anton** *anto* | **N** *en* | **wie** *vee* | **Nordpol** *nort-pol* |
| **B** *bay* | **for** | **Berta** *berta* | **O** *oh* | **for** | **Otto** *o-toh* |
| **C** *tsay* | | **Caesar** *tsay-zar* | **P** *pay* | | **Paula** *pow-la* |
| **D** *day* | | **Dora** *do-rah* | **Q** *koo* | | **Quelle** *kwe-le* |
| **E** *ay* | | **Emil** *ay-meel* | **R** *ayr* | | **Richard** *rikh-art* |
| **F** *ef* | | **Friedrich** *freed-rikh* | **S** *es* | | **Siegfried** *zeekfreet* |
| **G** *gay* | | **Gustav** *goos-tahf* | **T** *tay* | | **Theodor** *tay-o-dor* |
| **H** *hah* | | **Heinrich** *hine-rikh* | **U** *oo* | | **Ulrich** *ool-rikh* |
| **I** *ee* | | **Ida** *eedah* | **V** *fow* | | **Victor** *viktor* |
| **J** *yot* | | **Julius** *yoo-lee-oos* | **W** *vay* | | **Wilhelm** *vilhelm* |
| **K** *kah* | | **Konrad** *konrat* | **X** *iks* | | **Xanten** *ksan-ten* |
| **L** *el* | | **Ludwig** *lood-vikh* | **Y** *oopsi-lon* | | |
| **M** *em* | | **Martin** *martin* | **Z** *tset* | | **Zeppelin** *tse-peleen* |

**ä, ö, ü** are read as *ah, o, oo*, umlaut (*oom-lowt*)
**ß** is read as **Eszett** (*es-tset*)

# ASKING QUESTIONS

*Streetwise*

*When addressing someone you are not on familiar terms with you should always use the pronoun Sie and the third person plural form of the verb. Thus 'Are you from Munich?' translates as 'Sind Sie aus München?'.*

| | |
|---|---|
| Is it far/expensive? | **Ist es weit/teuer?**<br>*ist es vite/**toy**-er* |
| Are you Herr Braun? | **Sind Sie Herr Braun?**<br>*zint zee hayr **brown*** |
| Do you understand? | **Verstehen Sie mich?**<br>*fer-**shtay**-en zee mikh* |
| Can you help me? | **Können Sie mir bitte helfen?**<br>***kur'**-nen zee meer **bi**-te helfen* |
| Where is the nearest chemist's? | **Wo ist die nächste Apotheke?**<br>*voh ist dee **nekh**-ste apoh-**tay**-ke* |
| Where are the toilets? | **Wo sind die Toiletten?**<br>*voh zint dee twa-**le**-ten* |
| How do I get there? | **Wie komme ich dorthin?**<br>*vee **ko**-me ikh **dort**-hin* |
| How far/big is it? | **Wie weit/groß ist es?**<br>*vee vite/grohs ist es* |
| What is this? | **Was ist das?**<br>*vas ist das* |
| How much is it? | **Wieviel kostet das?**<br>*vee**feel** kostet das* |

*Northern Germany has many fine beaches. On many of them you can rent a Strandkorb (beach chair). Topless bathing is permitted and there are special areas for nudists, indicated by the sign FKK-Strand (Freikörperkultur).*

| | |
|---|---|
| Is it safe to swim here? | **Kann man hier bedenkenlos schwimmen?**<br>*kan man heer be-**deng**-ken-lohs **shvim**men* |
| When is high/low tide? | **Wann ist Flut/Ebbe?**<br>*van ist floot/**e**-be* |
| How deep is the water? | **Wie tief ist das Wasser hier?**<br>*vee teef ist das vasser heer* |
| Are there strong currents? | **Gibt es hier starke Strömungen?**<br>*gipt es heer shtar-ke **shtrur'**-moongen* |
| Is it a private/quiet beach? | **Ist das ein privater/ruhiger Strand?**<br>*ist das ine pree**vah**-ter/**roo**-ig-er shtrant* |
| Where do we change? | **Wo können wir uns umziehen?**<br>*voh **kur'**-nen veer uns **oom**-tsee-en* |
| Can I hire a deck chair/a boat? | **Kann ich hier einen Liegestuhl/ein Boot mieten?**<br>*kan ikh heer ine-en **lee**-ge-shtool/ine **boht** meeten* |
| Can I go fishing/windsurfing? | **Kann ich hier angeln/windsurfen?**<br>*kan ikh heer **ang**-eln/**vint**-zoorfen* |
| Is there a children's pool? | **Gibt es hier ein Kinderbecken?**<br>*gipt es heer ine **kin**der-becken* |

*Streetwise*

*There are orange-coloured emergency call boxes on the motorways at 1 km intervals. These put you through to the the ADAC (Allgemeiner Deutscher Automobil Club) which is affiliated to the AA and the RAC. Ask for Straßenwachthilfe (**shtrah**-sen-vakht-hilfe – road service assistance). Motorists must carry a triangular warning sign and a medical kit.*

| | |
|---|---|
| My car has broken down? | **Mein Auto hat eine Panne**<br>*mine **ow**to hat ine-e **pa**-ne* |
| There is something wrong with the brakes/the electrics | **Mit den Bremsen/der elektrischen Anlage stimmt etwas nicht**<br>*mit dayn **brem**-zen/der e**lek**-trishen **an**-lah-ge shtimt **et**vas nikht* |
| I have run out of petrol | **Ich habe kein Benzin mehr**<br>*ikh **hah**-be kine ben**tseen** mayr* |
| There is a leak in the petrol tank/radiator | **Der Tank/Der Kühler ist leck**<br>*der tank/der **koo**ler ist leck* |
| The windscreen has shattered | **Die Windschutzscheibe ist zersplittert**<br>*dee **vint**shoots-shy-be ist tser-**shpli**-tert* |
| The engine is overheating | **Der Motor wird zu heiß**<br>*dayr **moh**tor veert tsoo hice* |
| Can you tow me to a garage? | **Könnten Sie mich bitte bis zu einer Werkstatt abschleppen?**<br>***kur'n**-ten zee mikh **bi**-te bis tsoo ine-er **verk**-shtat **ap**-shleppen* |
| Can you send a mechanic/a breakdown van? | **Könnten Sie bitte ein Mechaniker/einen Abschleppwagen herschicken?**<br>***kur'n**-ten zee **bi**-te ine-en **mekha**-nicker/ine-en **ap**-shlep-vahgen **hayr**-shicken* |

*Streetwise*

*Office hours vary but most offices will be open from 0830 to 1230
and then from 1330 to 1730, Mon.-Fri.*

| | |
|---|---|
| I have an appointment with Herr Braun | **Ich habe einen Termin mit Herrn Braun**<br>*ikh hah-be ine-en ter-meen mit hayrn brown* |
| He is expecting me | **Er erwartet mich**<br>*er er-vartet mikh* |
| Can I leave a message with his secretary? | **Kann ich eine Nachricht für ihn bei seiner Sekretärin hinterlassen?**<br>*kan ikh ine-e nakh-rikht foor een by zine-er zekray-tayrin hinter-lassen* |
| I am free tomorrow morning/for lunch | **Ich habe morgen früh/zum Mittagessen Zeit**<br>*ikh hah-be morgen froo/tsoom mitak-essen tsite* |
| Here is my business card | **Hier ist meine Visitenkarte**<br>*heer ist mine-e vizeeten-kar-te* |
| Can I send a telex from here? | **Kann ich von hier aus ein Telex schicken?**<br>*kan ikh fon heer ows ine taylex shicken* |
| Where can I get some photocopying done? | **Wo kann ich Fotokopien machen lassen?**<br>*voh kan ikh fohtoh-ko-pee-en ma-khen lassen* |
| I want to send this by courier | **Ich möchte das per Eilboten schicken lassen**<br>*ikh mur'kh-te das per ile-boh-ten shicken lassen* |
| Have you a catalogue/ some literature? | **Haben Sie einen Katalog/ Informationsmaterial?**<br>*hah-ben zee ine-en ka-talohg/ infor-matsyohns-matay-ree-al* |

# BUYING

| | |
|---|---|
| Do you sell stamps? | **Verkaufen Sie Briefmarken?**<br>*fer-**kow**fen zee **breef**-mark-en* |
| How much is that? | **Wieviel kostet das?**<br>*vee**feel** kostet das* |
| Have you anything smaller/bigger? | **Haben Sie etwas Kleineres/Größeres?**<br>*hah-ben zee etvas **kline**-er-es/**grur'**-se-res* |
| Have you got any bread/matches? | **Haben Sie Brot/Streichhölzer?**<br>*hah-ben zee broht/**shtrykh**-hur'l-tser* |
| I'd like a newspaper/ five apples | **Ich hätte gern eine Zeitung/fünf Äpfel**<br>*ikh het-te gern ine-e **tsy**-toong/foonf epfel* |
| A packet of cigarettes, please | **Eine Schachtel Zigaretten bitte**<br>*ine-e **shakh**-tel tsiga-**ret**ten **bi**-te* |
| I'd like to see the dress in the window | **Ich würde gern das Kleid im Schaufenster sehen**<br>*ikh **voor**-de gern das klite im **show**-fenster **zay**-en* |
| I'll take this one/that one there | **Ich nehme das hier/das dort**<br>*ikh **nay**-me das **heer**/das **dort*** |
| Could you wrap it up for me, please? | **Könnten Sie es mir bitte einpacken?**<br>***kur'n**-ten zee es meer **bi**-te **ine**-packen* |
| I think you've given me the wrong change | **Ich glaube Sie haben mir falsch herausgegeben**<br>*ikh glow-be zee **hah**-ben meer falsh her-**ows**-ge-**gay**ben* |

See also **PAYING, SHOPPING**

# CAMPING

*Never camp without permission in fields or on common land, as penalties can be severe. There are numerous official campsites with excellent facilities, sometimes including a restaurant and a shop. Local tourist offices will provide details of the facilities in their area.*

We are looking for
a campsite

**Wir suchen einen Campingplatz**
*veer **zoo**-khen ine-en **kemp**ing-plats*

Do you have any
vacancies?

**Haben Sie noch freie Plätze?**
*hah-ben zee nokh **fry**-e **plet**-se*

How much is it per
night?

**Wieviel kostet es pro Nacht?**
*vee**feel** kostet es pro **nakht***

We want to stay
one night

**Wir möchten eine Nacht bleiben**
*veer **mur'kh**-ten ine-e nakht **bly**-ben*

May we camp here?

**Dürfen wir hier campen?**
*doorfen veer **heer** kempen*

Can we park our
caravan there?

**Können wir unseren Wohnwagen dort hinstellen?**
*kur'n-en veer oon-ze-ren **vohn**-vahgen **dort hin**-shtellen*

Is there a shop/a
restaurant?

**Gibt es einen Laden/ein Restaurant?**
*gipt es ine-en **lah**-den/ine restoh-**rong***

Where is the
washroom/drinking
water?

**Wo ist der Waschraum/Wo gibt es Trinkwasser?**
*voh ist der **vash**rowm/voh gipt es **trink**-vasser*

What facilities do
you have here?

**Welche Einrichtungen haben Sie hier?**
***vel**-khe **ine**rikh-toongen **hah**-ben zee heer*

# CAR HIRE

*Streetwise*

Cars can be hired in most towns and at airports. You must be over 21 and have held a full licence for at least two years. Make sure that the price includes comprehensive insurance and that you know on what basis you will be charged.

I want to hire a car
**Ich möchte ein Auto mieten**
*ikh mur'kh-te ine **ow**to meeten*

I need a car with a chauffeur
**Ich brauche ein Auto mit Chauffeur**
*ikh brow-khe ine **ow**to mit sho-**fur***

I want a large/small car
**Ich möchte ein großes/kleines Auto**
*ikh mur'kh-te ine **groh**-ses/**kline**-es owto*

Is there a charge per kilometre?
**Verlangen Sie eine Kilometergebühr?**
*fer-**lang**en zee ine-e keelo-**may**ter-ge**boor***

How much extra is the comprehensive insurance cover?
**Wieviel mehr kostet die Vollkaskoversicherung?**
*vee**feel** mayr **ko**stet dee **fol**-kasko-fer**zikh**-eroong*

I would like to leave the car in Cologne
**Ich möchte gern das Auto in Köln lassen**
*ikh mur'kh-te gern das **ow**to in **kur'ln** lassen*

My husband/My wife will be driving as well
**Mein Mann/Meine Frau wird auch das Auto fahren**
*mine **man**/mine-e **frow** veert owkh das **ow**to **fah**-ren*

Is there a radio/radio-cassette?
**Ist ein Radio/Radio mit Kassettenrecorder im Auto?**
*ist ine **rah**-dyo/**rah**-dyo mit ka-**se**tten-ray-**kor**der im **ow**to*

How do I operate the controls?
**Wie bediene ich die Schalter?**
*vee be-**dee**-ne ikh dee shalter*

# CHEMIST'S

*Streetwise*

Note that at an Apotheke *(pharmacy)* you can buy medicines with and without prescriptions and toiletries, while at a Drogerie *you can buy toiletries, household cleaners, babyfood, camera supplies etc. An Apotheke will always be indicated by a sign bearing a red A on a white background. There are now a number of chemists' shops called Drogeriemarkt which (like Boots in the UK) are a type of department store. A Reformhaus is a health food store.*

| | |
|---|---|
| I want something for a headache/a sore throat/toothache | **Ich möchte etwas gegen Kopfschmerzen/ Halsschmerzen/Zahnschmerzen**<br>*ikh mur'kh-te etvas gay-gen kopf-shmertsen/ hals-shmertsen/tsahn-shmertsen* |
| I would like some aspirin/sticking plaster | **Ich hätte gern Aspirin/Heftpflaster**<br>*ikh het-te gern aspi-reen/heft-pflaster* |
| Have you anything for insect bites/ sunburn/diarrhoea? | **Haben Sie etwas gegen Insektenstiche/ Sonnenbrand/Durchfall?**<br>*hah-ben zee etvas gay-gen inzek-ten-shtikh-e/ zonnen-brant/doorkh-fal* |
| I have a cough/a cold | **Ich habe Husten/eine Erkältung**<br>*ikh hah-be hoosten/ine-e er-kel-toong* |
| How much do I take? | **Wieviel soll ich einnehmen?**<br>*veefeel zol ikh ine-naymen* |
| How often do I take it? | **Wie oft soll ich es einnehmen?**<br>*vee oft zol ikh es ine-naymen* |
| Is it safe for children? | **Kann man es bedenkenlos Kindern geben?**<br>*kan man es be-deng-ken-lohs kindern gayben* |

# CHILDREN

*Streetwise*

*Children are allowed in public bars if accompanied by an adult. There are reductions for children of around 50% on public transport, at swimming pools, in museums, theatres and cinemas.*

I have a small baby/ two children
**Ich habe ein kleines Baby/zwei Kinder**
*ikh hah-be ine kline-es baby/tsvy kinder*

Do you have a special rate for children?
**Gibt es eine Ermäßigung für Kinder?**
*gipt es ine-e er-may-sigoong foor kinder*

Do you have facilities/ activities for children?
**Gibt es hier Einrichtungen/ Veranstaltungen für Kinder?**
*gipt es heer ine-rikh-toongen/feran-shtal-toongen foor kinder*

Have you got a cot for the baby?
**Haben Sie ein Kinderbett für das Baby?**
*hah-ben zee ine kinder-bet foor das baby*

Do you have a special menu for children?
**Haben Sie ein spezielles Kindermenü?**
*hah-ben zee ine shpe-tsee-el-es kinder-me-noo*

Where can I feed/ change the baby?
**Wo kann ich das Baby füttern/wickeln?**
*voh kan ikh das baby footern/vikeln*

Where can I warm the baby's bottle?
**Wo kann ich die Babyflasche warm machen?**
*voh kan ikh dee baby-fla-she varm makh-en*

Is there a playroom?
**Gibt es hier ein Spielzimmer?**
*gipt es heer ine shpeel-tsimmer*

Is there a babysitting service?
**Gibt es hier einen Babysitterdienst?**
*gipt es heer ine-en baby-zitter-deenst*

*Streetwise*

*Churches are normally open all day. Sunday services are at various times and these can be checked in the local papers. They are also often indicated on signs either at the church or along roads into the town. As a result of historical developments, Northern Germany is primarily Protestant while the South and West are primarily Catholic.*

| | |
|---|---|
| Where is the nearest church? | **Wo ist die nächste Kirche?**<br>*voh ist dee **nekh**-ste **kir**-khe* |
| Where is there a Protestant/Catholic church? | **Wo ist hier eine evangelische/katholische Kirche?**<br>*voh ist heer ine-e ayvan-**gay**lish-e/ka**toh**-lish-e **kir** khe* |
| I want to see a priest | **Ich möchte gern einem Pfarrer sprechen**<br>*ikh mur'kh-te gern ine-em **pfar**rer **shpre**-khen* |
| What time is the service? | **Um wieviel Uhr ist der Gottesdienst?**<br>*oom vee**feel** oor ist der **go**-tes-deenst* |
| I want to go to confession | **Ich möchte zur Beichte gehen**<br>*ikh mur'kh-te tsoor **bykh**-te gayen* |

# CITY TRAVEL

## Streetwise

*Most cities have excellent bus, underground, train and sometimes tram services. Tickets are often interchangeable. Zeitkarten (travel passes) are used by regular travellers and there is generally a separate entrance to the bus or train for holders of such tickets. If a seat bears the sign Schwerbeschädigte, it means that it is reserved for invalids. Never travel on public transport without a ticket as fines are heavy.*

Does this bus/train go to ...?
**Fährt dieser Bus/Zug nach ...?**
*fayrt deezer boos/tsook nakh ...*

Where do I get a bus for the cathedral?
**Wo fährt der Bus zum Dom ab?**
*voh fayrt der boos tsoom **dohm** ap*

Which bus do I take for the museum?
**Mit welchem Bus komme ich zum Museum?**
*mit **vel**-khem boos **ko**-me ikh tsoom moo-**zay**-oom*

Where do I change/ get off?
**Wo muß ich umsteigen/aussteigen?**
*voh moos ikh **oom**-shty-gen/**ows**-shty-gen*

How frequent are the buses/trains to town?
**Wie oft fahren die Busse/Züge in die Stadt?**
*vee oft **fah**-ren dee **boo**-se/**tsoo**-ge in dee **shtat***

What is the fare to the town centre?
**Wieviel kostet eine Fahrt ins Stadtzentrum?**
*vee**feel** kostet ine-e fahrt ins **shtat**-tsen-troom*

Where do I buy a ticket?
**Wo kann ich eine Fahrkarte kaufen?**
*voh kan ikh ine-e **fahr**kar-te kowfen*

What time is the last bus?
**Wann fährt der letzte Bus?**
*van fayrt der **lets**-te boos*

*A dry cleaner's is called a* Reinigung *or* chemische Reinigung. *A* Schnellreinigung *provides a fast service whereby you can collect your items within an hour or two of handing them in. Sometimes a dry cleaner's is combined with a laundry – a* Wäscherei. *Launderettes are called* Waschsalons.

| | |
|---|---|
| Is there a laundry service? | **Gibt es hier einen Wäschedienst?**<br>*gipt es heer ine-en **we**-she-deenst* |
| Is there a launderette/dry cleaner's nearby? | **Gibt es hier in der Nähe einen Waschsalon/eine chemische Reinigung?**<br>*gipt es heer in der **nay**-e ine-en **vash**-zalong/ine-e **kay**-mish-e **ry**-nigoong* |
| Where can I get this skirt cleaned/ironed? | **Wo kann ich diesen Rock reinigen/bügeln lassen?**<br>*voh kan ikh deezen **rok ry**-ni-gen/**boo**geln lassen* |
| I need to wash this off immediately | **Ich muß das sofort auswaschen**<br>*ikh moos das zoh-**fort ows**-vashen* |
| Where can I do some washing? | **Wo kann ich ein paar Sachen waschen?**<br>*voh kan ikh ine par **za**-khen vashen* |
| I need some soap and water | **Ich brauche etwas Seife und Wasser**<br>*ikh **brow**-khe etvas **zy**-fe oont vasser* |
| Where can I dry my clothes? | **Wo kann ich meine Kleider trocknen?**<br>*voh kan ikh mine-e **kly**-der **trok**nen* |
| This stain is coffee/blood | **Das ist ein Kaffeefleck/Blutfleck**<br>*das ist ine **ka**fay-flek/**bloot**flek* |
| Can you remove this stain? | **Können Sie diesen Fleck entfernen?**<br>***kur'n**-en zee deezen flek ent-**fer**nen* |

# CLOTHES

| | |
|---|---|
| I take a continental size 40 | **Ich trage Größe vierzig** <br> *ikh trah-ge grur'-se **feer**-tsikh* |
| Can you measure me please? | **Können Sie bitte bei mir Maß nehmen?** <br> ***kur'n**-en zee **bi**-te by meer **mahs** naymen* |
| May I try on this dress? | **Kann ich dieses Kleid anprobieren?** <br> *kan ikh deezes klite **an**proh-beeren* |
| May I take it over to the light? | **Kann ich es ans Licht nehmen?** <br> *kan ikh es ans likht naymen* |
| Where are the changing rooms? | **Wo sind die Ankleideräume?** <br> *voh zint dee **an**-kly-der-**roy**-me* |
| Is there a mirror? | **Gibt es hier einen Spiegel?** <br> *gipt es heer ine-en **shpee**gel* |
| It's too big/small | **Es ist zu groß/klein** <br> *es ist tsoo grohs/kline* |
| What is the material? | **Aus welchem Material ist es?** <br> *ows **vel**-khem matay-ree-**al** ist es* |
| Is it washable? | **Ist es waschbar?** <br> *ist es **vash**bar* |
| I don't like it | **Mir gefällt es nicht** <br> *meer ge**felt** es nikht* |
| I don't like the colour | **Mir gefällt die Farbe nicht** <br> *meer ge**felt** dee **far**-be nikht* |

| | |
|---|---|
| Is there a bus to ...? | **Fährt hier ein Bus nach ...?** <br> *fayrt heer ine boos nakh ...* |
| Which bus goes to ...? | **Welcher Bus fährt nach ...?** <br> ***vel**-kher boos fayrt nakh ...* |
| Where do I catch the bus for ...? | **Wo fährt der Bus nach ... ab?** <br> *voh fayrt der boos nakh ... ap* |
| What are the times of the buses to ...? | **Wann fahren die Busse nach ... ab?** <br> *van **fah**-ren dee **boo**-se nakh ... ap* |
| Does this bus go to ...? | **Fährt dieser Bus nach ...?** <br> *fayrt deezer boos nakh ...* |
| Where do I get off? | **Wo muß ich aussteigen?** <br> *voh moos ikh **ows**-shty-gen* |
| Is there a toilet on board? | **Gibt es eine Toilette im Bus?** <br> *gipt es ine-e twa-**le**-te im boos* |
| What time does the bus leave? | **Um wieviel Uhr fährt der Bus ab?** <br> *oom vee**feel** oor fayrt der boos ap* |
| What time does the bus arrive? | **Um wieviel Uhr kommt der Bus an?** <br> *oom vee**feel** oor komt der boos an* |
| Will you tell me where to get off? | **Sagen Sie mir bitte, wo ich aussteigen muß?** <br> *zagen zee meer **bi**-te voh ikh **ows**-shty-gen moos* |
| Let me off here, please | **Lassen Sie mich bitte hier aussteigen** <br> *lassen zee mikh **bi**-te heer **ows**-shty-gen* |

# COMPLAINTS

| | |
|---|---|
| This does not work | **Das funktioniert nicht**<br>*das foonk-tsyoh-**neert** nikht* |
| I can't turn the heating off/on | **Ich kann die Heizung nicht abstellen/ anstellen**<br>*ikh kan dee **hy**-tsoong nikht **ap**-shtellen/ **an**-shtellen* |
| The lock is broken | **Das Schloß ist kaputt**<br>*das shloss ist ka**poot*** |
| I can't open the window | **Ich kann das Fenster nicht öffnen**<br>*ikh kan das fenster nikht **ur'f**-nen* |
| The toilet won't flush | **Die Toilettenspülung funktioniert nicht**<br>*dee twa-**le**-ten-shpooloong foonk-tsyoh-**neert** nikht* |
| There is no hot water/ toilet paper | **Es gibt kein heißes Wasser/Toilettenpapier**<br>*es gipt kine **hy**-ses vasser/twa-**le**-ten-pa**peer*** |
| The washbasin is dirty | **Das Waschbecken ist schmutzig**<br>*das **vash**-becken ist **shmoo**-tsig* |
| My coffee is cold | **Mein Kaffee ist kalt**<br>*mine **ka**fay ist kalt* |
| We are still waiting to be served | **Wir wurden noch nicht bedient**<br>*veer voorden nokh nikht be**deent*** |
| I bought this here yesterday | **Ich habe das gestern hier gekauft**<br>*ikh **hah**-be das **ge**-stern heer ge**kowft*** |
| It has a flaw/hole in it | **Es hat einen Fehler/ein Loch**<br>*es hat ine-en fayler/ine lokh* |

## Streetwise

*When you are introduced to somebody, you either say angenehm ('pleased to meet you') if you wish to be formal or just guten Morgen/Tag/Abend ('good morning/afternoon/evening'). Germans normally shake hands when they meet or leave each other.*

| | |
|---|---|
| How do you do/ Hello/Goodbye | **Guten Tag!/Hallo!/Auf Wiedersehen!** *goo*ten **tahk**/*halo*/owf **vee**der-zayn |
| Do you speak English? | **Sprechen Sie Englisch?** **shpre**-khen zee **eng**-lish |
| I don't speak German | **Ich spreche kein Deutsch** ikh **shpre**-khe kine doytch |
| What's your name? | **Wie heißen Sie?** vee **hy**-sen zee |
| My name is … | **Ich heiße …** ikh **hy**-se … |
| Is this seat taken? | **Ist dieser Platz besetzt?** ist deezer plats be**zetst** |
| I'm English/Scottish | **Ich komme aus England/Schottland** ikh **ko**-me ows **eng**-lant/**shot**lant |
| Are you German/ Austrian? | **Kommen Sie aus Deutschland/ Österreich?** kommen zee ows **doytch**-lant/**ur'**-ste-rykh |
| Would you like to come out with me? | **Hätten Sie Lust mit mir auszugehen?** hetten zee loost mit meer **ows**-tsoo-gayen |
| Yes, I should like to | **Ja gern!** ya gern |

# CONVERSATION 2

Yes please/No thank you
**Ja bitte!/Nein danke!**
*ya **bi**-te/nine **dang**-ke*

Thank you (very much)
**Danke! (Vielen Dank!)**
***dang**-ke (feelen dank)*

Don't mention it
**Bitte!**
***bi**-te*

I'm sorry
**Entschuldigung!**
*ent**shool**-digoong*

I'm on holiday here
**Ich bin hier auf Urlaub**
*ikh bin heer owf **oor**lowp*

This is my first trip to ...
**Das ist meine erste Reise nach ...**
*das ist mine-e **er**-ste **ry**-ze nakh ...*

Do you mind if I smoke?
**Macht es Ihnen etwas aus wenn ich rauche?**
*makht es **ee**-nen **et**vas ows ven ikh **row**-khe*

Would you like a drink?
**Hätten Sie gern etwas zu trinken?**
*hetten zee gern **et**vas tsoo trinken*

Have you ever been to Britain?
**Waren Sie schon einmal in Großbritannien?**
***vah**-ren zee shohn **ine**-mal in grohs-bri**tah**-nee-en*

Did you like it there?
**Hat es Ihnen gefallen?**
*hat es ee-nen ge-**fal**-en*

What part of Germany are you from?
**Woher kommen Sie aus Deutschland?**
*voh-**hayr** kommen zee ows **doytch**-lant*

In the weight and length charts the middle figure can be either metric or imperial. Thus 3.3 feet = 1 metre, 1 foot = 0.3 metres, and so on.

| feet | | metres | inches | | cm | lbs | | kg |
|---|---|---|---|---|---|---|---|---|
| 3.3 | 1 | 0.3 | 0.39 | 1 | 2.54 | 2.2 | 1 | 0.45 |
| 6.6 | 2 | 0.61 | 0.79 | 2 | 5.08 | 4.4 | 2 | 0.91 |
| 9.9 | 3 | 0.91 | 1.18 | 3 | 7.62 | 6.6 | 3 | 1.4 |
| 13.1 | 4 | 1.22 | 1.57 | 4 | 10.6 | 8.8 | 4 | 1.8 |
| 16.4 | 5 | 1.52 | 1.97 | 5 | 12.7 | 11 | 5 | 2.2 |
| 19.7 | 6 | 1.83 | 2.36 | 6 | 15.2 | 13.2 | 6 | 2.7 |
| 23 | 7 | 2.13 | 2.76 | 7 | 17.8 | 15.4 | 7 | 3.2 |
| 26.2 | 8 | 2.44 | 3.15 | 8 | 20.3 | 17.6 | 8 | 3.6 |
| 29.5 | 9 | 2.74 | 3.54 | 9 | 22.9 | 19.8 | 9 | 4.1 |
| 32.9 | 10 | 3.05 | 3.9 | 10 | 25.4 | 22 | 10 | 4.5 |
| | | | 4.3 | 11 | 27.9 | | | |
| | | | 4.7 | 12 | 30.1 | | | |

| °C | 0 | 5 | 10 | 15 | 17 | 20 | 22 | 24 | 26 | 28 | 30 | 35 | 37 | 38 | 40 | 50 | 100 |
|---|---|---|---|---|---|---|---|---|---|---|---|---|---|---|---|---|---|
| °F | 32 | 41 | 50 | 59 | 63 | 68 | 72 | 75 | 79 | 82 | 86 | 95 | 98.4 | 100 | 104 | 122 | 212 |

| Km | 10 | 20 | 30 | 40 | 50 | 60 | 70 | 80 | 90 | 100 | 110 | 120 |
|---|---|---|---|---|---|---|---|---|---|---|---|---|
| Miles | 6.2 | 12.4 | 18.6 | 24.9 | 31 | 37.3 | 43.5 | 49.7 | 56 | 62 | 68.3 | 74.6 |

**Tyre pressures**

| lb/sq in | 15 | 18 | 20 | 22 | 24 | 26 | 28 | 30 | 33 | 35 |
|---|---|---|---|---|---|---|---|---|---|---|
| kg/sq cm | 1.1 | 1.3 | 1.4 | 1.5 | 1.7 | 1.8 | 2 | 2.1 | 2.3 | 2.5 |

**Liquids**

| gallons | 1.1 | 2.2 | 3.3 | 4.4 | 5.5 |
|---|---|---|---|---|---|
| litres | 5 | 10 | 15 | 20 | 25 |

| pints | 0.44 | 0.88 | 1.76 |
|---|---|---|---|
| litres | 0.25 | 0.5 | 1 |

# CUSTOMS & PASSPORTS

I have nothing to declare

**Ich habe nichts zu verzollen**
*ikh hah-be nikhts tsoo fer-tsolen*

I have the usual allowances of alcohol/tobacco

**Ich habe die zollfreie Menge an Alkohol/ Tabak**
*ikh hah-be dee tsol-fry-e meng-e an al-kohol/ tabak*

I have two bottles of wine/a bottle of spirits to declare

**Ich habe zwei Flaschen Wein/eine Flasche Branntwein zu verzollen**
*ikh hah-be tsvy flashen vine/ine-e fla-she brant-vine tsoo fer-tsolen*

My wife/My husband and I have a joint passport

**Meine Frau/Mein Mann und ich haben einen gemeinsamen Paß**
*mine-e frow/mine man oont ikh hah-ben ine-en gemine-zahmen pahs*

The children are on this passport

**Dieser Paß gilt auch für die Kinder**
*deezer pahs gilt owkh foor dee kinder*

I shall be staying in this country for three weeks

**Ich werde drei Wochen in diesem Land bleiben**
*ikh vayr-de dry vo-khen in deezem lant bly-ben*

We are here on holiday

**Wir sind hier auf Urlaub**
*veer zint heer owf oorlowp*

I am here on business

**Ich bin geschäftlich hier**
*ikh bin gesheft-likh heer*

I have an entry visa

**Ich habe ein Einreisevisum**
*ikh hah-be ine ine-ry-ze-veezoom*

| | | |
|---|---|---|
| What is the date today? | **Der wievielte ist heute?** | *der vee**feel**-te ist **hoy**-te* |
| It's the … | **Heute ist der …** | *hoy-te ist der* |
| 1st of March | **der erste März** | *der **er**-ste mayrts* |
| 2nd of June | **der zweite Juni** | *der **tsvy**-te **yoo**nee* |
| We will arrive on the 29th of August | **Wir werden am neunundzwanzigsten August ankommen** | *veer vayrden am noyn-oont-**tsvan**-tsikh-sten ow**goost an**-kommen* |
| 1984 | **neunzehnhundert- vierundachtzig** | *noyntsayn-hoondert- **feer**-oont-**akh**-tsikh* |
| Monday | **Montag** | *mohntakh* |
| Tuesday | **Dienstag** | *deenstakh* |
| Wednesday | **Mittwoch** | *mitvokh* |
| Thursday | **Donnerstag** | *donners-takh* |
| Friday | **Freitag** | *fry-takh* |
| Saturday | **Samstag** | *zamstakh* |
| Sunday | **Sonntag** | *zontakh* |
| January | **Januar** | *yanoo-ar* |
| February | **Februar** | *faybroo-ar* |
| March | **März** | *mayrts* |
| April | **April** | *april* |
| May | **Mai** | *my* |
| June | **Juni** | *yoonee* |
| July | **Juli** | *yoolee* |
| August | **August** | *owgoost* |
| September | **September** | *zep-tember* |
| October | **Oktober** | *ok-tohber* |
| November | **November** | *noh-vember* |
| December | **Dezember** | *day-tsember* |

# DENTIST

*Streetwise*

*If you want to see a Zahnarzt (dentist), you will have to pay for the treatment immediately and in full. A number of dentists are closed on Wednesday afternoons. The standard of treatment is generally very high. Form E111 (available from the DSS) entitles you to a refund.*

| | |
|---|---|
| I need to see a dentist (urgently) | **Ich muß (dringend) zum Zahnarzt**<br>*ikh moos (**dring**ent) tsoom **tsahn**-artst* |
| I have toothache | **Ich habe Zahnschmerzen**<br>*ikh **hah**-be **tsahn**-shmertsen* |
| I've broken a tooth | **Mir ist ein Zahn abgebrochen**<br>*meer ist ine tsahn **ap**-gebro-khen* |
| A filling has come out | **Eine Füllung ist herausgefallen**<br>*ine-e **foo**loong ist her-**ows**-ge-falen* |
| My gums are bleeding/are sore | **Mein Zahnfleisch blutet/tut mir weh**<br>*mine **tsahn**-flysh blootet/toot meer **vay*** |
| Please give me an injection | **Geben Sie mir bitte eine Spritze**<br>*gayben zee meer **bi**-te ine-e **shprit**-se* |
| My dentures need repairing | **Mein Gebiß muß repariert werden**<br>*mine ge**biss** moos ray-pa-**reert vayr**den* |

## THE DENTIST MAY SAY:

**Ich werde den Zahn ziehen müssen**
*ikh vayr-de dayn tsahn **tsee**-en moossen*

I shall have to take the tooth out

**Sie brauchen eine Füllung**
*zee **brow**-khen ine-e **foo**loong*

You need a filling

**Das kann ein bißchen weh tun**
*das kan ine **bis**-khen **vay** toon*

This might hurt a bit

# DIRECTIONS

| | |
|---|---|
| Where is the nearest post office? | **Wo ist das nächste Postamt?** *voh ist das **nekh**-ste **post**amt* |
| How do I get to the airport? | **Wie komme ich zum Flughafen?** *vee **ko**-me ikh tsoom **flook-hah**fen* |
| Can you please tell me the way to the station? | **Können Sie mir bitte sagen, wie ich zum Bahnhof komme?** *kur'-nen zee meer **bi**-te **zah**gen vee ikh tsoom **bahn**-hohf **ko**-me* |
| Is this the right way to the cathedral? | **Ist das der richtige Weg zum Dom?** *ist das der **rikh**-ti-ge vayk tsoom dohm* |
| I am looking for the tourist information office | **Ich suche das Fremdenverkehrsamt** *ikh **zoo**-khe das fremden-fer-**kayrs**-amt* |
| Is it far to walk/by car? | **Ist es weit zu Fuß/mit dem Auto?** *ist es vite tsoo **foos**/mit daym **ow**to* |
| Which road do I take for ...? | **Welche Straße führt nach ...?** ***vel**-khe **shtrah**-se foort nakh …* |
| Is this the turning for ...? | **Ist das die Abzweigung nach ...?** *ist das dee **ap**-tsvy-goong nakh …* |
| How do I get onto the motorway? | **Wie komme ich auf die Autobahn?** *vee **ko**-me ikh owf dee **ow**to-bahn* |
| I have lost my way | **Ich habe mich verlaufen** *ikh **hah**-be mikh fer-**low**fen* |
| Can you please show me on the map? | **Können Sie es mir bitte auf der Karte zeigen?** *kur'-nen zee es meer **bi**-te owf der kar-te **tsy**-gen* |

# DOCTOR

*If you visit a doctor you will have to pay at once so make sure that you are adequately insured. Before leaving the UK, obtain form E111 (from the DSS) which entitles you to reimbursement.*

| | |
|---|---|
| I need a doctor | **Ich brauche einen Arzt**<br>*ikh **brow**-khe ine-en artst* |
| Can I please have an appointment with the doctor? | **Können Sie mir bitte einen Termin geben?**<br>***kur'**-nen zee meer **bi**-te ine-en ter-**meen** gayben* |
| My son/My wife is ill | **Mein Sohn/Meine Frau ist krank**<br>*mine **zohn**/mine-e **frow** ist krank* |
| I have a sore throat/ a stomach upset | **Ich habe Halsschmerzen/eine Magenverstimmung**<br>*ikh **hah**-be **hals**-shmertsen/ine-e **mah**-gen-fer-shtimoong* |
| He has diarrhoea/ earache | **Er hat Durchfall/Ohrenschmerzen**<br>*er hat **doorkh**-fall/**oh**-ren-shmertsen* |
| I have a pain here/ in my chest | **Ich habe hier/in der Brust Schmerzen**<br>*ikh **hah**-be **heer**/in der broost **shmayr**-tsen* |
| She has a temperature | **Sie hat Fieber**<br>*zee hat **fee**ber* |
| He has been stung/ bitten | **Er ist gestochen/gebissen worden**<br>*er ist ge-**shto**-khen/ge-bissen vorden* |
| He can't breathe/ walk | **Er kann nicht atmen/laufen**<br>*er kan nikht **aht**men/**low**fen* |
| I feel dizzy | **Mir ist schwindlig**<br>*meer ist **shvin**-delikh* |

| | |
|---|---|
| I can't sleep/swallow | **Ich kann nicht schlafen/schlucken**<br>*ikh kan nikht **shlah**-fen/shlooken* |
| She has been sick | **Sie hat sich übergeben**<br>*zee hat zikh **oo**ber-gayben* |
| I am diabetic/<br>pregnant | **Ich bin zuckerkrank/schwanger**<br>*ikh bin **tsoo**ker-krank/**shvang**er* |
| I am allergic to<br>penicillin | **Ich bin gegen Penizillin allergisch**<br>*ikh bin **gay**-gen peni-tsi-**leen** a-**ler**-gish* |
| I have high blood<br>pressure | **Ich habe hohen Blutdruck**<br>*ikh **hah**-be hoh-en **bloot**-drook* |
| My blood group is<br>A positive/O<br>negative | **Ich habe Blutgruppe A positiv/O negativ**<br>*ikh **hah**-be **bloot**groo-pe ah po-zee **teef**/oh nega-**teet*** |

**THE DOCTOR MAY SAY:**

**Sie müssen im Bett bleiben**
*zee moossen im **bet bly**-ben*

You must stay in bed

**Er muß ins Krankenhaus**
*er moos ins **krank**en-hows*

He will have to go to hospital

**Sie müssen operiert werden**
*zee moossen opay-**reert vayr**-den*

You will need an operation

**Nehmen Sie das dreimal am Tag**
*naymen zee das **dry**-mal am tahk*

Take this three times a day

**Nehmen Sie zwei Tabletten zweimal am Tag**
*naymen zee tsvy ta**ble**-ten **tsvy**-mal am tahk*

Take two tablets twice a day

# DRINKS

*The most popular drinks are beer and wine. During the week most
bars close at 0100, although opening hours vary from place to place.
If you want a snack, look out for the sign* Imbiss *or* Imbissstube. *Tea is
usually served in a glass with a wedge of lemon. If you want milk you
will have to ask for it separately – make sure you get* Frischmilch
*(fresh milk). Coffee is ordered by the cup or pot.*

| | |
|---|---|
| A black/white coffee, please | **Einen Kaffee ohne Milch/mit Milch bitte!**<br>*ine-en **ka**fay **oh**-ne milkh/mit milkh **bi**-te* |
| Two cups of coffee | **Zwei Tassen Kaffee**<br>*tsvy tassen **ka**fay* |
| A pot of coffee | **Ein Kännchen Kaffee**<br>*ine **ken**-khen **ka**fay* |
| A tea with milk, please | **Tee mit Frischmilch, bitte!**<br>*tay mit **frish**-milkh **bi**-te* |
| A glass of lemonade with ice | **Ein Glas Limonade mit Eis**<br>*ine glass leemo-**nah**-de mit ice* |
| A bottle of mineral water | **Eine Flasche Mineralwasser**<br>*ine-e **fla**-she mi-ner-**ahl**-vasser* |
| Do you have ...? | **Haben Sie ...?**<br>***hah**-ben zee ...* |
| Another coffee, please | **Noch einen Kaffee bitte!**<br>*nokh ine-en **ka**fay **bi**-te* |
| A draught beer, please | **Ein Faßbier bitte!**<br>*ine **fass**-beer **bi**-te* |

See also **WINES & SPIRITS**

# DRIVING

*Streetwise*

Drive on the right-hand side of the road and give priority to traffic
coming from your right. Speed limits are 50km/h in towns and
villages, and 100km/h on ordinary roads. In general, there is no speed
limit on motorways. However, there are high penalties for speeding
elsewhere and for other traffic offences. Seat belts are compulsory.

| | |
|---|---|
| What is the speed limit on this road? | **Was ist die Höchstgeschwindigkeit auf dieser Straße?**<br>*vas ist dee **hur'khst**-ge**shvin**-dikh-kite owf deezer **shtrah**-se* |
| Is there a toll on this motorway? | **Muß man für diese Autobahn eine Mautgebühr zahlen?**<br>*moos man foor dee-ze **ow**to-bahn ine-e **mowt**-geboor **tsah**len* |
| Is there a short-cut? | **Gibt es eine Abkürzung?**<br>*gipt es ine-e **ap**-kuortsoong* |
| Where can I park? | **Wo kann ich parken?**<br>*voh kan ikh **par**ken* |
| Is there a car park nearby? | **Gibt es hier in der Nähe einen Parkplatz?**<br>*gipt es heer in der **nay**-e ine-en **park**plats* |
| Can I park here? | **Darf ich hier parken?**<br>*darf ikh **heer par**ken* |
| Do I need a parking disc? | **Brauche ich hier eine Parkscheibe?**<br>***brow**-khe ikh heer ine-e **park**-shy-be* |

# EATING OUT

*Streetwise*

*Even small restaurants can provide superb meals. Most restaurants offer special set-price menus called* Tagesmenü, *which are good value. You will also find* Kinderteller *(children's menus) and* Seniorteller *(senior citizens' menus).*

Is there a café/a restaurant near here?
: **Gibt es hier in der Nähe ein Café/ein Restaurant?**
*gipt es heer in der **nay**-e ine kafay/ine restoh-**rong***

A table for four, please
: **Einen Tisch für vier bitte!**
*ine-en tish foor feer **bi**-te*

May we see the menu?
: **Können wir bitte die Speisekarte haben?**
***kur'**-nen veer **bi**-te dee **shpy**-ze-kar-te **hah**-ben*

We'll take the set menu please
: **Wir hätten gern das Tagesmenü**
*veer hetten gern das **tahg**es-me**noo***

Do you have a menu for children?
: **Haben Sie eine Kinderkarte?**
***hah**-ben zee ine-e **kin**der-kar-te*

Could we have some more bread/water?
: **Können wir bitte noch etwas Brot/Wasser haben?**
***kur'**-nen veer **bi**-te nokh **et**vas broht/vasser **hah**-ben*

We'd like a dessert
: **Wir hätten gern einen Nachtisch**
*veer hetten gern ine-en **nakh**-tish*

The bill, please
: **Die Rechnung bitte!**
*dee **rekh**-noong **bi**-te*

Is service included?
: **Ist die Bedienung inbegriffen?**
*ist dee be-**dee**noong **in**-be-griffen*

See also DRINKS, ORDERING, PAYING

*Streetwise*

*In most areas you should dial 110 for emergency services, but the number will always be displayed on or by the phone under the heading NOTRUF.*

| | |
|---|---|
| Call a doctor/an ambulance! | **Rufen Sie einen Arzt/Krankenwagen!**<br>*roofen zee ine-en **artst**/**krank**en-vahgen* |
| We must get him to hospital | **Wir müssen ihn ins Krankenhaus bringen**<br>*veer moossen een ins **kranken**-hows bringen* |
| Fetch help quickly! | **Holen Sie schnell Hilfe!**<br>***hoh**-len zee shnel **hil**-fe* |
| Get the police! | **Holen Sie die Polizei!**<br>***hoh**-len zee dee poli-**tsy*** |
| Where's the nearest police station/hospital? | **Wo ist die nächste Polizeiwache/das nächste Krankenhaus?**<br>*voh ist dee **nekh**-ste poli-**tsy**-va-khe/das **nekh**-ste **kranken**-hows* |
| I've lost my credit card/wallet | **Ich habe meine Scheckkarte/Brieftasche verloren**<br>*ikh **hah**-be mine-e **shek**-kar-te/**breef**-ta-she fer**loh**-ren* |
| My child/My handbag is missing | **Mein Kind/Meine Handtasche ist verschwunden**<br>*mine kint/mine-e **hand**-ta-she ist fer-**shvoon**den* |
| My passport/My watch has been stolen | **Mein Paß/Meine Armbanduhr ist gestohlen worden**<br>*mine pahs/mine-e **arm**bant-oor ist ge**shtoh**-len vorden* |

See also **ACCIDENTS, BREAKDOWNS, DENTIST, DOCTOR**

# ENTERTAINMENT

| | |
|---|---|
| Can you recommend something for the children? | **Können Sie mir etwas für die Kinder empfehlen?**<br>*kur'-nen zee meer **et**vas foor dee kinder emp-**fay**len* |
| What is there to do in the evenings? | **Was kann man hier abends unternehmen?**<br>*vas kan man heer **ah**-bents oonter-**nay**men* |
| Where is there a cinema/theatre? | **Wo gibt es hier ein Kino/Theater?**<br>*voh gipt es heer ine **kee**no/tay-**ah**ter* |
| Where can we go to a concert? | **Wo gibt es hier ein Konzert?**<br>*voh gipt es heer ine kon-**tsert*** |
| Can you book the tickets for us? | **Können Sie bitte für uns die Karten reservieren?**<br>*kur'-nen zee **bi**-te foor oons dee karten ray-zer-**vee**ren* |
| Are there any night clubs/discos? | **Gibt es hier Nachtclubs/Discos?**<br>*gipt es heer **nakht**-kloops/diskos* |
| Is there a swimming pool? | **Gibt es hier ein Schwimmbad?**<br>*gipt es heer ine **shvim**-baht* |
| Can we go fishing/ riding? | **Können wir hier angeln/reiten?**<br>*kur'-nen veer heer **ang**-eln/**ry**-ten* |
| Where can we play tennis/golf? | **Wo können wir hier Tennis/Golf spielen?**<br>*voh **kur'**-nen veer heer tennis/golf shpeelen* |
| Can we hire the equipment? | **Können wir die Ausrüstung leihen?**<br>*kur'-nen veer dee **ows**-roostoong **ly**-en* |

See also **NIGHTLIFE, SIGHTSEEING**

| | |
|---|---|
| What time is the next sailing? | **Um wieviel Uhr fährt die nächste Fähre?** *oom veefeel oor fayrt dee nekh-ste fay-re* |
| A return ticket for one car, two adults and two children | **Eine Rückfahrkarte für ein Auto, zwei Erwachsene und zwei Kinder bitte!** *ine-e rookfahr-kar-te foor ine owto tsvy er-vak-se-ne oont tsvy kinder bi-te* |
| How long does the crossing take? | **Wie lange dauert die Überfahrt?** *vee lang-e dow-ert dee oober-fart* |
| Are there any cabins/reclining seats? | **Gibt es hier Kabinen/Liegesitze?** *gipt es heer ka-beenen/lee-ge-zit-se* |
| Is there a TV lounge/bar? | **Gibt es hier einen Fernsehraum/eine Bar?** *gipt es heer ine-en fern-zayrowm/ine-e bar* |
| Where are the toilets? | **Wo sind die Toiletten?** *voh zint dee twa le-ten* |
| Where is the duty-free shop? | **Wo ist der Duty-free-Shop?** *voh ist der duty-free shop* |
| Can we go out on deck? | **Können wir an Deck gehen?** *kur'-nen veer an dek gay-en* |
| Is the sea rough today? | **Ist die See heute stürmisch?** *ist dee zay hoy-te shtur-mish* |

# GIFTS & SOUVENIRS

Where can we buy
souvenirs of the
cathedral?

**Wo können wir Souvenirs vom Dom
kaufen?**
*voh kur'-nen veer zoo-veneers fom dohm
kowfen*

Where is the nearest
gift shop?

**Wo kann man hier in der Nähe
Geschenkartikel kaufen?**
*voh kan man heer in der nay-e
ge-shenk-artee-kel kowfen*

I want to buy a
present for my
husband/my wife

**Ich möchte gern ein Geschenk für meinen
Mann/meine Frau kaufen**
*ikh mur'kh-te gern ine ge-shenk foor mine-en
man/mine-e frow kowfen*

Have you anything
typical of this town/
region?

**Haben Sie etwas Typisches von dieser
Stadt/Gegend?**
*hah-ben zee etvas toopish-es fon deezer shtaht/
gaygent*

Is this hand-made?

**Ist das Handarbeit?**
*ist das hant-arbite*

Have you anything
suitable for a young
child?

**Haben Sie etwas Geeignetes für ein
kleines Kind?**
*hah-ben zee etvas ge-ige-ne-tes foor ine kline-es
kint*

I want something
cheaper/more
expensive

**Ich möchte gern etwas Billigeres/Teureres**
*ikh mur'kh-te gern etvas bilig-e-res/toy-re-res*

Do you have any
postcards?

**Haben Sie Ansichtskarten?**
*hah-ben zee an-zikhts-karten*

**Nouns**

In German all nouns begin with a capital letter.
The plural form of nouns varies from noun to noun – there is no universal plural as in English (cat – cats, dog – dogs), e.g.

| **Mann – Männer** | **Frau – Frauen** | **Tisch – Tische** |
|---|---|---|
| man – men | woman – women | table – tables |

(In the dictionary, plural forms appear where they may be useful.)

All German nouns are masculine, feminine or neuter, and this is shown by the words for 'the' and 'a' used before them:

| *masculine* | *feminine* | *neuter* |
|---|---|---|
| **der** Stuhl the chair | **die** Frau the woman | **das** Kind the child |
| **ein** Stuhl a chair | **eine** Frau a woman | **ein** Kind a child |
| | *plural (all genders)* | |
| | **die** Stühle the chairs | |
| | (no '**ein**' form) | |

These forms are used before a verb, when the noun carries out the action of the verb, e.g. **der Mann steht auf** (the man is standing up). Masculine singular nouns have a different form of 'the' and 'a' when they *undergo* the action of the verb:

| **ich sehe *den* Mann** | I see the man |
|---|---|
| **ich sehe *einen* Mann** | I see a man |

The following forms show possession, like -'s in English:

| *masculine* | *feminine* | *neuter* | *plural (all genders)* |
|---|---|---|---|
| **des** Stuhls | **der** Frau | **des** Kinds | **der** Stühle |
| **eines** Stuhls | **einer** Frau | **eines** Kinds | |

e.g. **das Haus *der Frau*** the woman's house

The following forms express 'to the/to a ...'

| **dem** Stuhl | **der** Frau | **dem** Kind | **den** Stuhlen |
|---|---|---|---|
| **einem** Stuhl | **einer** Frau | **einem** Kind | |

# GRAMMAR 2

e.g. **ich gebe es** *der* **Frau**   I'm giving it to the woman
**ich gebe es** *einer* **Frau**   I'm giving it to a woman

Several other words used before nouns have similar endings to **der** and **ein** (see also below). Those like **der** are:

**dieser** (**diese, dieses,** etc) this; **jener** (**jene, jenes,** etc) that; **jeder** (**jede, jedes,** etc) each; **welcher** (**welche, welches,** etc) which

## Adjectives

When used *before* a noun, adjectives vary like words for 'the' and 'a' (see p.41), depending on the gender and number of the noun, and how the noun is used in the sentence. Adjectives also depend on what word *precedes* them (the 'the'-word, or the 'a'-word), thus:

| | | |
|---|---|---|
| *der* **klug**e **Mann** | *die* **klug**e **Frau** | *das* **klug**e **Kind** |
| the clever man | the clever woman | the clever child |
| *ein* **klug**er **Mann** | *eine* **klug**e **Frau** | *ein* **klug**es **Kind** |
| a clever man | a clever woman | a clever child |

After all other forms of 'the' and 'a' the adjective ends in **-en**, e.g.

| | | |
|---|---|---|
| *des* **klug**en **Mann** | *einer* **klug**en **Frau** | *den* **klug**en **Männern** |
| of the clever man | to the clever woman | to the clever men |

When used after the noun, adjectives do not have endings:
**der Mann/die Frau/das Kind ist** *klug*
the man/ the woman/the child is clever

## 'My', 'Your', 'His', 'Her'

These words all take endings like those of the words for 'a' (see p.41), depending on the number, gender and function of the noun:

**mein**   my

| | |
|---|---|
| *mein* **Mann kommt** | my husband is coming |
| **ich liebe** *meinen* **Mann** | I love my husband |

| das Auto *meines* Manns | my husband's car |
| ich gebe es *meinem* Mann | I'm giving it to my husband |

| *meine* Kinder kommen | my children are coming |
| ich liebe *meine* Kinder | I love my children |
| die Spielsachen *meiner* Kinder | my children's toys |
| ich gebe es *meinen* Kindern | I'm giving it to my children |

Other forms are exactly as for **ein** (see p.41).

Other words which take these endings are:

| **Ihr** | your | **unser** | our |
| **sein** | his | **euer** | their |
| **ihr** | her | | |

## Pronouns

SUBJECT

| I | **ich** | *ikh* |
| you | **Sie** | *zee* |
| he/it* | **er** | *ayr* |
| she/it* | **sie** | *zee* |
| it (neuter) | **es** | *es* |
| we | **wir** | *veer* |
| they | **sie** | *zee* |

OBJECT

| me | **mich** | *mikh* |
| you | **Sie** | *zee* |
| him/it* | **ihn** | *een* |
| her/it* | **sie** | *zee* |
| it (neuter) | **es** | *es* |
| us | **uns** | *oons* |
| them | **sie** | *zee* |

INDIRECT OBJECT

| to me | **mir** | *meer* |
| to you | **Ihnen** | *eenen* |
| to him/it* | **ihm** | *eem* |
| to her/it* | **ihr** | *eer* |
| to it (neuter) | **ihm** | *eem* |
| to us | **uns** | *oons* |
| to them | **ihnen** | *eenen* |

OTHERS

| who? | **wer?** | *vayr* |
| whom? | **wen?** | *vayn* |
| whose? | **wessen?** | *vessen* |
| to whom? | **wem?** | *vaym* |

*As nouns in German are either masculine, feminine or neuter, the

# GRAMMAR 4

masculine and feminine pronouns can mean *it* as well as *he/she, him/her*.

e.g.
**Ich** (I) **sehe ihn** (him/it)
I see him/it

**er** (he) **gibt es** (it) **ihr** (to her)
he gives it to her

**gib ihm** (to him) **das Buch**
give him the book

**hör sie** (her) **zu**
listen to her

## Verbs

There are two main types of verbs in German – 'weak' and 'strong'. Here are the patterns for each type:

|  | WEAK | STRONG |
|---|---|---|
|  | **spielen** (to play) | **helfen** (to help) |
| **ich**<br>I ... | **spiele** *(shpee-le)*<br>... play | **helfe** *(hel-fe)*<br>... help |
| **Sie/wir/sie**<br>you/we/they ... | **spielen** *(shpee-len)*<br>... play | **helfen** *(hel-fen)*<br>... help |
| **er/sie/es**<br>he/she/it ... | **spielt** *(shpeelt)*<br>... plays | **hilft*** *(hilft)*<br>... helps |

And in the past:

|  | WEAK | STRONG |
|---|---|---|
| **ich/er/sie/es**<br>I/he/she/it ... | **spielte** *(shpeel-te)*<br>... played | **half**** *(half)*<br>... helped |
| **Sie/wir/sie**<br>you/we/they ... | **spielten** *(shpeel-ten)*<br>... played | **halfen**** *(hal-fen)*<br>... helped |

Another past form corresponds to the English 'have done' and uses the verb **haben** (to have):

**ich habe** *(hah-be)*
I have …

**Sie/wir/sie haben** *(hah-ben)*   **gespielt**        **geholfen***
you/we/they have …      … played       … helped

**er/sie/es hat** *(hat)*
he/she/it has …

\* The vowel often changes here.
\*\* The vowel always changes here.

The verbs **sein** (to be) and **haben** (to have) are irregular in the present. **Haben** was shown in the second past tense above. Here is **sein**:

**ich bin** *(bin)*
I am

**Sie/wir/sie sind** *(zint)*
you/we/they are

**er/sie/es ist** *(ist)*
he/she/it is

# GREETINGS

*In German there are two forms of addressing people. Du is used when speaking to close friends and relatives. Sie is the usual way of addressing strangers. Germans will shake hands on greeting someone and when leaving. Females over 18 are addressed as 'Frau ...'. The use of 'Fräulein' is restricted to under-18s and to calling a waitress.*

| | |
|---|---|
| Hello | **Guten Tag!** (in S. Germany, Austria: **Grüß Gott!**)<br>*gooten tahk (groos got)* |
| Good morning/Good afternoon/Good evening | **Guten Morgen!/Guten Tag!/Guten Abend!**<br>*gooten morgen/gooten tahk/gooten ahbent* |
| Goodbye/Cheerio | **Auf Wiedersehen!/Tschüs!**<br>*owf veeder-zayn/tshoos* |
| Good night | **Gute Nacht!**<br>*goo-te nakht* |
| How do you do? | **Guten Tag!**<br>*gooten tahk* |
| Pleased to meet you | **Freut mich!**<br>*froyt mikh* |
| How are you? | **Wie geht es Ihnen?**<br>*vee gayt es ee-nen* |
| Fine, thank you | **Gut danke!**<br>*goot dang-ke* |
| See you soon | **Bis bald!**<br>*bis balt* |

*Streetwise*

*A lot of hairdressers' in small towns and villages are closed on Mondays. Don't forget to give a tip to the person who did your hair.*

| | |
|---|---|
| I'd like to make an appointment | **Ich hätte gern einen Termin**<br>*ikh het-te gern ine-en ter-meen* |
| A cut and blow-dry, please | **Schneiden und Fönen bitte!**<br>*shny-den oont fur'-nen bi-te* |
| A shampoo and set | **Waschen und Legen**<br>*vashen oont laygen* |
| Not too short | **Nicht zu kurz**<br>*nikht tsoo koorts* |
| I'd like it layered | **Ich hätte gern einen Stufenschnitt**<br>*ikh het-te gern ine-en shtoofen-shnit* |
| Not too much off the back/the fringe | **Hinten/Den Pony nicht zu kurz**<br>*hinten/dayn pony nikht tsoo koorts* |
| Take more off the top/the sides | **Schneiden Sie oben/an den Seiten mehr weg**<br>*shny-den zee oh-ben/an dayn zy-ten mayr vek* |
| My hair is permed/tinted | **Ich habe eine Dauerwelle/gefärbte Haare**<br>*ikh hah-be ine-e dower-ve-le/gefayrp-te hah-re* |
| My hair is naturally curly/straight | **Meine Haare sind von Natur aus lockig/glatt**<br>*mine-e hah-re zint fon natoor ows lock-ikh/glat* |
| I'd like a conditioner, please | **Ich hätte gern eine Haarschnellkur**<br>*ikh het-te gern ine-e har-shnelkoor* |

# HOTEL DESK

| I have reserved a room in the name of … | **Ich habe ein Zimmer auf den Namen … reserviert**<br>*ikh **hah**-be ine tsimmer owf dayn **nah**-men … ray-zer-**veert*** |
|---|---|
| I confirmed my booking by letter | **Ich habe meine Reservierung schriftlich bestätigt**<br>*ikh **hah**-be mine-e ray-zer-**vee**roong **shrift**-likh be-**shtay**-tikht* |
| Could you have my luggage taken up? | **Könnten Sie bitte mein Gepäck hinaufbringen lassen?**<br>***kur'n**-ten zee **bi**-te mine ge**pek** hin**owf**-bringen lassen* |
| What time is breakfast? | **Wann gibt es Frühstück?**<br>*van gipt es **froo**-shtook* |
| Can we have breakfast in our room? | **Können wir in unserem Zimmer frühstücken?**<br>***kur'n**-en veer in **oon**-ze-rem tsimmer **froo**-shtoo-ken* |
| Please call me at … | **Bitte wecken Sie mich um …** (*see* TIME)<br>***bi**-te vecken zee mikh oom …* |
| Can I have my key? | **Kann ich meinen Schlüssel haben?**<br>*kan ikh mine-en **shloo**-sel **hah**-ben* |
| I want to stay an extra night | **Ich möchte noch eine Nacht bleiben**<br>*ikh mur'kh-te **nokh** ine-e nakht **bly**-ben* |
| I shall be leaving at … | **Ich reise morgen früh um … ab** (*see* TIME)<br>*ikh ry-ze **mor**gen **froo** oom … ap* |

See also ACCOMMODATION, ROOM SERVICE, PAYING

*You will always find a left-luggage office – Gepäckaufbewahrung – and lockers – Schliessfächer – at airports and railway stations.*

| | |
|---|---|
| Where do I check in my luggage? | **Wo kann ich mein Gepäck abfertigen lassen?**<br>*voh kan ikh mine gepek ap-fer-ti-gen lassen* |
| Where is the luggage from the London flight/train? | **Wo ist das Gepäck vom Flug/Zug aus London?**<br>*voh ist das gepek fom flook/tsook ows London* |
| Our luggage has not arrived | **Unser Gepäck ist nicht angekommen**<br>*oonzer gepek ist nikht an-ge-kommen* |
| My suitcase was damaged in transit | **Mein Koffer wurde beim Transport beschädigt**<br>*mine koffer voor-de bime tran-sport be-shay-dikht* |
| Where is the left-luggage office? | **Wo ist hier die Gepäckaufbewahrung?**<br>*voh ist heer dee gepek-owf-bevah-roong* |
| Are there any luggage trolleys? | **Gibt es hier Kofferkulis?**<br>*gipt es heer koffer-kooleez* |
| Can you help me with my bags, please? | **Können Sie mir bitte mit meinem Gepäck helfen?**<br>*kur'-nen zee meer bi-te mit mine-em gepek helfen* |
| Please take my luggage to a taxi | **Bitte tragen Sie mein Gepäck zu einem Taxi**<br>*bi-te trah-gen zee mine gepek tsoo ine-em taxi* |
| I sent my luggage on in advance | **Ich habe mein Gepäck vorausgeschickt**<br>*ikh hah-be mine gepek forows-geshikt* |

# MAPS & GUIDES

## Streetwise

Maps and guides can be bought in bookshops and at most newspaper kiosks. Street maps are normally displayed on a board in the town/city centre.

Where can I buy a map of the area?
**Wo kann ich eine Landkarte von dieser Gegend kaufen?**
*voh kan ikh ine-e **lant**kar-te fon deezer **gay**gent kowfen*

Have you got a town plan?
**Haben Sie einen Stadtplan?**
*hah-ben zee ine-en **shtat**-plan*

I want a street map of the city
**Ich hätte gern einen Stadtplan**
*ikh het-te gern ine-en **shtat**-plan*

I need a road map of …
**Ich brauche eine Straßenkarte von …**
*ikh **brow**-khe ine-e **shtrah**-sen-kar-te fon …*

Can I get a map at the tourist office?
**Kann ich im Verkehrsamt einen Stadtplan bekommen?**
*kan ikh im fer-**kayrz**-amt ine-en **shtat**-plan be-**ko**mmen*

Can you show me on the map?
**Können Sie es mir bitte auf der Karte zeigen?**
*kur'-nen zee es meer **bi**-te owf der **kar**-te **tsy**-gen*

Do you have a guidebook in English?
**Haben Sie einen Reiseführer auf englisch?**
*hah-ben zee ine-en **ry**-ze-foorer owf **eng**-lish*

Do you have a guidebook to the cathedral?
**Haben Sie einen Führer vom Dom?**
*hah-ben zee ine-en foorer fom **dohm***

See also **DIRECTIONS**

# MEASUREMENTS

a pint of…
**einen halben Liter …**
*ine-en halben leeter*

a litre of…
**einen Liter …**
*ine-en leeter*

a kilo of …
**ein Kilo …**
*ine keelo*

a pound of …
**ein Pfund …**
*ine pfoont*

100 grammes of …
**100 Gramm …**
*hoondert gram*

half a kilo of …
**ein halbes Kilo …**
*ine halbes keelo*

a half-bottle of …
**eine halbe Flasche**
*ine-e hal-be fla-she*

a slice of …
**eine Scheibe …**
*ine-e shy-be*

a portion of …
**eine Portion …**
*ine-e por-tsy-ohn*

a dozen
**ein Dutzend**
*ine doo-tsent*

20 Marks worth of …
**für 20 Mark …**
*foor tsvan-tsikh mark*

a third
**ein Drittel**
*ine drittel*

two thirds
**zwei Drittel**
*tsvy drittel*

a quarter
**ein Viertel**
*ine feertel*

three quarters
**dreiviertel**
*dry-feer-tel*

ten per cent
**zehn Prozent**
*tsayn pro-tsent*

more …
**noch etwas …**
*nokh etvas*

less …
**weniger …**
*vayni-ger*

enough …
**genug …**
*ge-nook*

double
**doppelt**
*dop-elt*

twice
**zweimal/doppelt**
*tsvy-mal/dop-elt*

three times
**dreimal**
*dry-mal*

See also **BUYING, NUMBERS, PAYING**

# MENUS

In Germany most people eat three meals a day:

**Frühstück** (breakfast) of bread or bread rolls, butter, jam, cheese and coffee or tea;

**Mittagessen** (lunch), which is normally the main meal of the day, and **Abendessen** (evening meal) consisting of bread and various cold meats and cheeses.

In addition, a lot of people also enjoy **Kaffeetrinken** (equivalent to afternoon tea), either in a café or, especially on Sunday afternoons, at home.

In a restaurant there is often a set-price menu (*Tagesmenü* or *Menü*), which is usually good value, and most restaurants also offer *Senioren-* and *Kinderteller* (special dishes for senior citizens and children). The main items on a German menu would be:

| | |
|---|---|
| **Vorspeisen (kalt/warm)** | Starters (cold/hot) |
| **Suppen** | Soups |
| **Hauptgerichte** | Main dishes |
| **Eierspeisen** | Egg dishes |
| **Fischgerichte** | Fish |
| **Fleischgerichte** | Meat |
| **Wildgerichte (in der Saison)** | Game (when in season) |
| **Käse** | Cheese |
| **Nachspeisen** | Desserts |
| **Getränke** | Drinks |

| | |
|---|---|
| What is the chef's speciality? | **Was ist die Spezialität des Hauses?** |
| | *vas ist dee shpe-tsee-ali-**tayt** des howses?* |
| What is the soup of the day? | **Welche Tagessuppe gibt es?** |
| | ***vel**-khe **tah**-ges-zoo-pe gipt es?* |
| How is this dish cooked? | **Wie ist das Gericht zubereitet?** |
| | *vee ist das gerikht **tsoo**-berytet?* |
| Enjoy your meal! | **Guten Appetit!** |
| | ***goo**-ten apay-**teet*** |

German coins come in denominations of 1, 2, 5, 10, 50 Pfennigs and 1, 2, 5 Marks, while notes come in denominations of 10, 20, 50, 100, 500 and 1,000 Marks. If you want to change money in a bank you will need your passport for identification purposes.

| | |
|---|---|
| Have you any change? | **Haben Sie Kleingeld?**<br>*hah-ben zee kline-gelt* |
| Can you change a 50 Mark note? | **Können Sie einen Fünfzigmarkschein wechseln?**<br>*kur'-nen zee ine-en foonf-tsikh-mark-shine vek-seln* |
| I'd like to change these traveller's cheques | **Ich möchte gern diese Reiseschecks einlösen**<br>*ikh mur'kh-te gern dee-ze ry-ze sheks ine-lur'-zen* |
| I want to change some D-Mark into pounds | **Ich möchte gern D-Mark in Pfund wechseln**<br>*ikh mur'kh-te gern day-mark in pfoont vek-seln* |
| What is the rate for sterling/dollars? | **Wie steht der Kurs für das Pfund Sterling/ den Dollar?**<br>*vee shtayt der koors foor das pfoont shter-ling/ dayn dollar* |
| Can I get a cash advance with my credit card? | **Kann ich auf meine Kreditkarte Bargeld bekommen?**<br>*kan ikh owf mine-e kredeet-kar-te bar-gelt be-kommen* |
| I should like to transfer some money from my account | **Ich möchte gern Geld von meinem Konto überweisen**<br>*ikh mur'kh-te gern gelt fon mine-em konto oober-vy-zen* |

What is there to do in the evenings?

**Was kann man hier abends unternehmen?**
*vas kan man heer **ah**bents oonter-**nay**men*

Where can we go to see a cabaret/go to dance?

**Wo gibt es hier ein Variété/Wo können wir hier tanzengehen?**
*voh gipt es heer ine varee-ay**tay**/voh **kur'**-nen veer heer **tan**tsen-gay-en*

Are there any good night clubs/discos?

**Gibt es hier gute Nachtclubs/Discos?**
*gipt es heer **goo**-te **nakht**-kloops/diskos*

How do we get to the casino?

**Wie kommen wir zum Spielkasino?**
*vee kommen veer tsoom **shpeel**-kazee-no*

Do we need to be members?

**Müssen wir Mitglieder sein?**
*moossen veer **mit**-gleeder zine*

How much does it cost to get in?

**Wieviel kostet der Eintritt?**
*vee**feel** kostet der **ine**-trit*

We'd like to reserve two seats for tonight

**Wir möchten gern zwei Plätze für heute abend reservieren**
*veer mur'kh-ten gern tsvy **plet**-se foor **hoy**-te **ah**bent ray-zer-**vee**ren*

Is there a bar/a restaurant?

**Gibt es eine Bar/ein Restaurant?**
*gipt es ine-e bar/ine restoh-**rong***

What time does the show/concert begin?

**Wann beginnt die Aufführung/das Konzert?**
*van be**gint** dee **owf**-fooroong/das kon-**tsert***

How long does the performance last?

**Wie lange dauert die Aufführung?**
*vee lang-e **dow**-ert dee **owf**-fooroong*

Which film is on at the cinema?

**Welcher Film läuft im Kino?**
*vel-kher film loyft im **kee**no*

See also **EATING OUT, ENTERTAINMENT**

| | | | | | | |
|---|---|---|---|---|---|---|
| 0 | **Null**<br>*nool* | 13 | **dreizehn**<br>*dry-tsayn* | 50 | **fünfzig**<br>*foonf-tsikh* |
| 1 | **eins**<br>*ines* | 14 | **vierzehn**<br>*feer-tsayn* | 60 | **sechzig**<br>*zekh-tsikh* |
| 2 | **zwei**<br>*tsvy* | 15 | **fünfzehn**<br>*foonf-tsayn* | 70 | **siebzig**<br>*zeep-tsikh* |
| 3 | **drei**<br>*dry* | 16 | **sechzehn**<br>*yekh-tsayn* | 80 | **achtzig**<br>*akh-tsikh* |
| 4 | **vier**<br>*feer* | 17 | **siebzehn**<br>*zeep-tsayn* | 90 | **neunzig**<br>*noyn-tsikh* |
| 5 | **fünf**<br>*foonf* | 18 | **achtzehn**<br>*akh-tsayn* | 100 | **hundert**<br>*hoondert* |
| 6 | **sechs**<br>*zekhs* | 19 | **neunzehn**<br>*noyn-tsayn* | 101 | **hunderteins**<br>*hoondert-ines* |
| 7 | **sieben**<br>*zeeben* | 20 | **zwanzig**<br>*tsvan-tsikh* | 200 | **zweihundert**<br>*tsvy-hoondert* |
| 8 | **acht**<br>*akht* | 21 | **einundzwanzig**<br>*ine-oont-tsvan-tsikh* | 300 | **dreihundert**<br>*dry-hoondert* |
| 9 | **neun**<br>*noyn* | 22 | **zweiundzwanzig**<br>*tsvy-oont-tsvan-tsikh* | 500 | **fünfhundert**<br>*foonf-hoondert* |
| 10 | **zehn**<br>*tsayn* | 23 | **dreiundzwanzig**<br>*dry-oont-tsvan-tsikh* | 1,000 | **tausend**<br>*towzent* |
| 11 | **elf**<br>*elf* | 30 | **dreißig**<br>*dry-sikh* | 2,000 | **zweitausend**<br>*tsvy-towzent* |
| 12 | **zwölf**<br>*tsvur'lf* | 40 | **vierzig**<br>*feer-tsikh* | 1,000,000 | **eine Million**<br>*ine-e milee-ohn* |

| | | | | | |
|---|---|---|---|---|---|
| 1st | **erste**<br>*erst-e* | 5th | **fünfte**<br>*foonf-te* | 9th | **neunte**<br>*noyn-te* |
| 2nd | **zweite**<br>*tsvy-te* | 6th | **sechste**<br>*zekhs-te* | 10th | **zehnte**<br>*tsayn-te* |
| 3rd | **dritte**<br>*drit-te* | 7th | **siebte**<br>*zeep-te* | | |
| 4th | **vierte**<br>*feer-te* | 8th | **achte**<br>*akh-te* | | |

See also **MEASUREMENTS**

# ORDERING

| | |
|---|---|
| Do you have a set menu? | **Haben Sie ein Tagesgericht?**<br>*hah-ben zee ine **tah**-ges-ge-**rikht*** |
| We will have the menu at ... Marks | **Wir hätten gern das Menü um ...** (*see* NUMBERS) **Mark?**<br>*veer hetten gern das me**noo** oom ... mark* |
| May we see the wine list, please? | **Können wir bitte die Weinliste haben?**<br>*kur'-nen veer **bi**-te dee **vine**-lis-te **hah**-ben* |
| What do you recommend? | **Was können Sie uns empfehlen?**<br>*vas **kur'**-nen zee oons emp-**fay**len* |
| Is there a local speciality? | **Gibt es eine Spezialität dieser Gegend?**<br>*gipt es ine-e shpe-tsee-ali-**tayt** deezer **gay**gent* |
| How is this dish served? | **Wie wird dieses Gericht serviert?**<br>*vee veert deezez ge-**rikht** zer-**veert*** |
| What is in this dish? | **Was ist das für ein Gericht?**<br>*vas ist das foor ine ge-**rikht*** |
| Are the vegetables included? | **Ist Gemüse dabei?**<br>*ist ge-**moo**-ze da-**by*** |
| Rare/Medium/Well done, please | **Englisch/Halbdurch/Durchgebraten bitte!**<br>***eng**-lish/halp**doorkh**/**doorkh**-ge-brah-ten **bi**-te* |
| We'd like a dessert/ some coffee | **Wir hätten gern einen Nachtisch/Kaffee**<br>*veer hetten gern ine-en **nakh**-tish/**ka**fay* |

See also **COMPLAINTS, EATING OUT, PAYING, WINES & SPIRITS**

## Streetwise

*Credit cards are not as widely used as they are in Great Britain, but Eurocheques are accepted almost everywhere. In Germany VAT (MwSt) is charged on books.*

| | |
|---|---|
| Can I have the bill, please? | **Kann ich bitte die Rechnung haben?**<br>*kan ikh **bi**-te dee **rekh**-noong **hah**-ben* |
| Is service/VAT included? | **Ist Bedienung/die Mehrwertsteuer inbegriffen?**<br>*ist be-**dee**noong/dee **mayr**-vayrt-shtoy-er **in**-be-griffen* |
| What does that come to? | **Wieviel macht das zusammen?**<br>*vee**feel** makht das tsoo-**zam**men* |
| How much is that? | **Wieviel kostet das?**<br>*vee**feel** kostet das* |
| Do I pay in advance? | **Muß ich im voraus zahlen?**<br>*moos ikh im fo-**rows** tsah-len* |
| Can I pay by credit card/cheque? | **Kann ich mit Kreditkarte/Scheck zahlen?**<br>*kan ikh mit kre**deet**-kar-te/shek **tsah**-len* |
| Do you accept traveller's cheques? | **Nehmen Sie Reiseschecks an?**<br>*naymen zee **ry**-ze-sheks an* |
| You've given me the wrong change | **Sie haben mir falsch herausgegeben**<br>*zee **hah**-ben meer falsh her-**ows**-ge-**gay**ben* |
| I'd like a receipt, please | **Ich hätte gern eine Quittung**<br>*ikh het-te gern ine-e **kvi**-toong* |
| Can I have an itemized bill? | **Kann ich eine ausführliche Rechnung haben?**<br>*kan ikh ine-e **ows**foor-likh-e **rekh**-noong **hah**-ben* |

# PERSONAL DETAILS

| | |
|---|---|
| My name is ... | **Ich heiße ...**<br>*ikh **hy**-se ...* |
| My date of birth is ... | **Mein Geburtsdatum ist der ...**<br>*mine ge**boorts**-dah-toom ist der ...* |
| My address is ... | **Meine Anschrift lautet ...**<br>*mine-e **an**shrift **low**-tet ...* |
| I come from Britain | **Ich komme aus Großbritannien**<br>*ikh **ko**-me ows grohs-brit**ah**-nee-en* |
| I live in ... | **Ich wohne in ...**<br>*ikh **voh**-ne in ...* |
| My passport/driving licence number is ... | **Meine Paßnummer/Führerscheinnummer ist ...**<br>*mine-e **pahs**-noomer/**foo**rer-shine-noomer ist ...* |
| My blood group is ... | **Ich habe Blutgruppe ...**<br>*ikh **hah**-be **bloot**groo-pe ...* |
| I work in an office/a factory | **Ich arbeite in einem Büro/einer Fabrik**<br>*ikh **ar**-by-te in ine-em boo**roh**/ine-er fa**breek*** |
| I am a secretary/ manager | **Ich bin Sekretärin/Geschäftsführer**<br>*ikh bin zekray-**tay**rin/ge**shefts**-foorer* |
| I'm here on holiday/ business | **Ich bin hier auf Urlaub/Ich bin geschäftlich hier**<br>*ikh bin heer owf **oor**-lowp/ikh bin ge**sheft**-likh heer* |
| There are four of us altogether | **Wir sind zu viert**<br>*veer zint tsoo feert* |

*Streetwise*

Most petrol stations are self-service. You will have the option of
Normalbenzin *(three-star petrol)*, Super *(four-star)*, bleifrei *(unleaded)*,
and Diesel. *Not all petrol stations accept credit cards, so make sure
you have enough cash.*

| | |
|---|---|
| 20 litres of 2 star | **Zwanzig Liter Normalbenzin**<br>*tsvan-tsikh leeter normal-ben-tseen* |
| 30 Marks (worth) of<br>4 star | **Für dreißig Mark Super bitte!**<br>*foor dry-sikh mark zooper bi-te* |
| Fill it up, please | **Voll bitte!**<br>*fol bi-te* |
| Can you check the<br>oil/water? | **Können Sie nach dem Öl/Wasser sehen?**<br>*kur'-nen zee nakh daym ur'l/vasser zay-en* |
| Top up the windscreen<br>washers | **Können Sie die Scheibenwaschanlage<br>auffüllen?**<br>*kur'-nen zee dee shy-ben-vash-anlah-ge<br>owf-foolen* |
| Could you clean<br>the windscreen? | **Könnten Sie die Windschutzscheibe<br>sauber machen?**<br>*kur'n-ten zee dee vint-shoots-shy-be zowber<br>makh-en* |
| Where's the air-<br>line? | **Wo ist der Reifendruckmesser?**<br>*voh ist der ry-fen-drook-messer* |
| A can of oil,<br>please | **Eine Dose Öl bitte!**<br>*ine-e doh-ze ur'l bi-te* |
| How do I use the<br>car wash? | **Wie bediene ich die Autowaschanlage?**<br>*vee bedee-ne ikh dee owto-vash-anlah-ge* |

See also **DRIVING, PAYING**

# PHOTOGRAPHY

*Streetwise*

*Photographic equipment and films are best bought at a photographer's, though you can also buy them in some department stores. Films are cheaper in Germany than in the UK.*

I need a colour/black and white film for this camera
**Ich brauche einen Farbfilm/ Schwarzweißfilm für diese Kamera**
*ikh **brow**-khe ine-en **farp**film/**shvarts**-vice-film foor dee-ze **ka**mera*

It is for prints/slides
**Es ist für Bilder/Dias**
*es ist foor bilder/**dee**-az*

The film/shutter has jammed
**Der Film/Verschluß klemmt**
*der film/fer-**shloos** klemt*

The rewind mechanism does not work
**Der Rückmechanismus funktioniert nicht**
*der **rook**-mayka-nismoos foonk-tsyoh-**neert** nikht*

Can you develop this film?
**Können Sie diesen Film entwickeln?**
*kur'-nen zee deezen film ent**vi**-keln*

When will the photos be ready?
**Wann werden die Bilder fertig sein?**
*van **vayr**-den dee bilder **fer**tikh zine*

Can I take photos in here?
**Darf ich hier fotografieren?**
*darf ikh heer foto-gra-**fee**ren*

Would you take a photo of us?
**Würden Sie ein Bild von uns machen?**
*voorden zee ine **bilt** fon oons **ma**khen*

# POLICE

*Streetwise*

*If you have an accident, you should always call the police. Police stations are indicated by a blue sign bearing the word* Polizei. *German policemen wear green uniforms. Traffic wardens* (Politessen) *wear blue uniforms.*

We should call the police
**Wir sollten die Polizei holen**
*veer zolten dee poli-tsy hoh-len*

Where is the police station?
**Wo ist das Polizeirevier?**
*voh ist das poli-tsy-rayveer*

My car has been broken into
**Mein Auto ist aufgebrochen worden**
*mine owto ist owf-gebro-khen vorden*

I've been robbed
**Ich bin bestohlen worden**
*ikh bin beshtoh-len vorden*

I have had an accident
**Ich habe einen Unfall gehabt**
*ikh hah-be ine-en oonfal gehapt*

How much is the fine?
**Wie hoch ist das Bußgeld?**
*vee hohkh ist das boosgelt*

How do I pay it?
**Wie soll ich es zahlen?**
*vee zol ikh es tsah-len*

I don't have my driving licence on me
**Ich habe meinen Führerschein nicht bei mir**
*ikh hah-be mine-en foorer-shine nikht by meer*

I'm very sorry, officer
**Es tut mir wirklich sehr leid**
*es toot meer veerk-likh zayr lite*

I didn't know the regulations
**Ich kannte die Vorschrift nicht**
*ikh kan-te dee forshrift nikht*

# POST OFFICE

*Streetwise*

*Post offices are indicated by a yellow sign bearing a black post horn. They are open 0800-1800 on weekdays and 0800-1200 on Saturdays. Letter boxes and phone boxes are yellow too. Stamps can also be obtained at newspaper kiosks.*

| | |
|---|---|
| How much is a letter to England? | **Wieviel kostet ein Brief nach England?** *veefeel kostet ine breef nakh eng-lant* |
| I'd like six stamps for postcards to America, please | **Ich hätte gern sechs Briefmarken für Ansichtskarten nach Amerika bitte** *ikh het-te gern zeks breef-marken foor an-zikhts-karten nakh amay-reeka bi-te* |
| Twelve 80 Pfennig stamps, please | **Zwölf Briefmarken zu achtzig Pfennig bitte!** *tsvur'lf breef-marken tsoo akh-tsikh pfe-nikh bi-te* |
| I want to send a telegram | **Ich möchte gern ein Telegramm schicken** *ikh mur'kh-te gern ine taylay-gram shicken* |
| When will it arrive? | **Wann wird es ankommen?** *van veert es an-kommen* |
| I want to send this parcel | **Ich möchte gern dieses Paket aufgeben** *ikh mur'kh-te gern deezez pakayt owf-gayben* |
| I'd like to make a telephone call | **Ich möchte gern telefonieren** *ikh mur'kh-te gern taylay-fo-neeren* |
| I want to draw some money out of my Giro account | **Ich möchte gern Geld von meinem Postscheckkonto abheben** *ikh mur'kh-te gern gelt fon mine-em postshek-konto ap-hayben* |

| | |
|---|---|
| Can you help me, please? | **Können Sie mir bitte helfen?**<br>*kur'-nen zee meer **bi**-te helfen* |
| What is the matter? | **Was ist los?**<br>*vas ist lohs* |
| I am in trouble | **Ich habe Probleme**<br>*ikh **hah**-be problay-me* |
| I don't understand | **Ich verstehe das nicht**<br>*ikh fer-**shtay**-e das nikht* |
| Do you speak English? | **Sprechen Sie Englisch?**<br>*shpre khen zee **eng**-lish* |
| Please repeat that | **Bitte wiederholen Sie das**<br>***bi**-te veeder-**hoh**-len zee das* |
| I have run out of money | **Ich habe kein Geld mehr**<br>*ikh **hah**-be kine gelt mayr* |
| My son is lost | **Mein Sohn ist verschwunden**<br>*mine zohn ist fer-**shvoon**den* |
| I have lost my way | **Ich habe mich verlaufen**<br>*ikh **hah**-be mikh fer-**low**fen* |
| I have forgotten my passport | **Ich habe meinen Paß vergessen**<br>*ikh **hah**-be mine-en pahs fer-**ge**ssen* |
| Please give me my passport back | **Geben Sie mir bitte meinen Paß zurück**<br>*gayben zee meer **bi**-te mine-en pahs tsoo**rook*** |
| Where is the British Consulate? | **Wo ist das britische Konsulat?**<br>*voh ist das british-e konsoo-**laht*** |

See also **ACCIDENTS, COMPLAINTS, EMERGENCIES, POLICE**

# PRONUNCIATION

In the pronunciation system used in this book, German sounds are represented by spellings of the nearest possible sounds in English. Hence, when you read out the pronunciation – the line in italics after each phrase or word – sound the letters as if you were reading an English word. Whenever we think it is not sufficiently clear where to stress a word or phrase, we have used heavy italics to highlight the syllable to be stressed. The following notes should help you:

|     | REMARKS | EXAMPLE | PRONUNCIATION |
|-----|---------|---------|---------------|
| ow  | Always as in *brown*, NOT as in *low* | **erlauben** | *erlow-ben* |
| e   | When this is the last vowel in a word, it is pronounced as a weak *uh* sound as in *travel*. | **hatte Beutel** | *hat-te boytel* |
|     | Otherwise as in *met* | **etwas** | *etvas* |
| y   | At the end of syllable, as in *fry* | **reisen** | *ry-zen* |
|     | At the beginning of a syllable, as in *yet* | **Jahr** | *yahr* |
| oh  | As in *go, low* | **wo** | *voh* |
| o   | As in *dot* | **Wolke** | *vol-ke* |
| kh  | As in Scottish *loch* | **Woche** | *vo-khe* |
| ah  | As in *far* (without the '*r*') | **Vater** | *fahter* |
| ur' | As in *hurt*, without the '*r*' pronounced | **Möbel** | *mur'-bel* |

Spelling in German is very regular and, with a little practice, you will soon be able to pronounce German words from their spelling alone. The only letters which are unlike English are:

|    |                        |           |           |
|----|------------------------|-----------|-----------|
| ä  | as in *bed*            | **hätte** | *het-te*  |
| äu | as in *boy*            | **läutet**| *loy-tet* |
| ö  | as in *ur'* (see above)| **öl**    | *ur'l*    |
| ü  | as in *food*           | **grün**  | *groon*   |
| ß  | as *s*                 | **Fuß**   | *foos*    |

*Streetwise*

*Some holidays such as Corpus Christi (Fronleichnam) or Assumption (Mariä Himmelfahrt) are official holidays in some of the predominantly Catholic German states.* Rosenmontag *(42 days before Easter) and the following Tuesday* (Karnevalsdienstag *or* Faschingsdienstag) *are unofficial holidays in the centres of the* Karneval *or* Fasching *(carnival), i.e. Cologne, Dusseldorf, Mainz and Munich. In these areas there are street parades four or five miles long involving huge floats, horses, bands, groups of masked jesters and 'regiments' of the Fools' Guilds in their traditional costumes.*

| | |
|---|---|
| **New Year's Day** | January 1st |
| **Epiphany** | January 6th |
| **Good Friday** | (not Austria) |
| **Easter Monday** | |
| **Labour Day** | May 1st |
| **Ascension Day** | |
| **Whit Monday** | |
| **Day of Unity** | June 17th (Germany only) |
| **Corpus Christi** | |
| **Assumption** | August 15th (Austria only) |
| **National Day** | October 26th (Austria only) |
| **All Saints' Day** | November 1st |
| **Repentance Day** | November 21st (not Austria or Bavaria) |
| **Immaculate Conception** | December 8th (Austria only) |
| **Christmas Day** | December 25th |
| **St Stephen's Day** | December 26th |

# RAILWAY STATION

*Streetwise*

*The inter-city network is first class only and you will need a reservation. You may also have to pay a supplement. Children under 12 pay half fare while those under 4 travel free. Enquire about special rates at the Reiseauskunft (travel information office).*

| | |
|---|---|
| When is the next train to ...? | **Wann fährt der nächste Zug nach ...?**<br>*van fayrt der **nekh**-ste tsook nakh ...* |
| What time does it get there? | **Wann kommt er an?**<br>*van komt er an* |
| Do I have to change? | **Muß ich umsteigen?**<br>*moos ikh **oom**-shty-gen* |
| A return to ..., first class | **Eine Rückfahrkarte nach ..., erster Klasse**<br>*ine-e **rook**far-kar-te nakh ... **er**-ster **kla**-se* |
| A single to ..., second class | **Einmal einfach nach ..., zweiter Klasse**<br>*ine-mal **ine**-fakh nakh ... **tsvy**-ter **kla**-se* |
| Is there a supplement to pay? | **Muß man einen Zuschlag zahlen?**<br>*moos man ine-en **tsoo**shlak **tsah**-len* |
| I would like a seat in a non-smoking compartment | **Ich möchte gern eine Platzkarte in einem Nichtraucherabteil**<br>*ikh mur'kh-te gern ine-e **plats**kar-te in ine-em **nikht**-rowkher-**ap**-tile* |
| I want to reserve a couchette | **Ich möchte gern einen Liegewagenplatz reservieren**<br>*ikh mur'kh-te gern ine-en **lee**-ge-vahgen-plats ray-zer-**vee**ren* |
| Which platform for the train to ...? | **Von welchem Gleis fährt der Zug nach ... ab?**<br>*fon **vel**-khem glice fayrt der tsook nakh ... ap* |

See also **LUGGAGE, TRAIN TRAVEL**

*Streetwise*

*Most department stores have counters where you can have your shoes repaired while you wait.*

| | |
|---|---|
| I have broken the window | **Mir ist die Fensterscheibe kaputt gegangen**<br>*meer ist dee **fen**ster-shy-be ka**poot** ge**gang**-en* |
| There is a hole in my shoe/these trousers | **In meinem Schuh/dieser Hose ist ein Loch**<br>*in mine-em **shoo**/deezer **hoh**-ze ist ine lokh* |
| This is broken/torn | **Das ist kaputt/zerrissen**<br>*das ist ka**poot**/tser-**ri**ssen* |
| Can you repair this? | **Können Sie das reparieren?**<br>***kur'**-nen zee das raypa-**ree**ren* |
| When can you get it done by? | **Bis wann können Sie es machen?**<br>*bis van **kur'**-nen zee es **makh**-en* |
| I need some adhesive tape/a safety pin | **Ich brauche etwas Klebstreifen/eine Sicherheitsnadel**<br>*ikh **brow**-khe **et**vas **klayp**-shtry-fen/ine-e **zi**-kher-hites-nah-del* |
| Can you reheel these shoes? | **Können Sie neue Absätze auf diese Schuhe machen?**<br>***kur'**-nen zee noy-e **ap**-zet-se owf dee-ze shoo-e **makh**-en* |
| The screw has come loose | **Die Schraube hat sich gelöst**<br>*dee **shrow**-be hat zikh ge**lur'st*** |
| The handle has come off | **Der Griff ist abgegangen**<br>*der grif ist **ap**-gegang-en* |

# ROAD CONDITIONS

*Streetwise*

*Roads in Germany are very good and there are no tolls except on some mountain roads in Austria. In winter, studded snow-tyres or chains may be compulsory.*

Is there a route that avoids the traffic?
**Gibt es hier eine Umgehungsstraße?**
*gipt es heer ine-e **oom**-gay-oongs-shtrah-se*

Is the traffic heavy on the motorway?
**Gibt es viel Verkehr auf der Autobahn?**
*gipt es feel fer-**kayr** owf der **ow**to-bahn*

What is causing this hold-up?
**Warum kommen wir hier nicht weiter?**
*va**room** kommen veer heer nikht **vy**-ter*

When will the road be clear?
**Wann wird die Straße frei sein?**
*van veert dee **shtrah**-se fry zine*

Is there a diversion?
**Gibt es eine Umleitung?**
*gipt es ine-e **oom**ly-toong*

Is the road to … snowed up?
**Ist die Straße nach … eingeschneit?**
*ist dee **shtrah**-se nakh … **ine**-geshnite*

Is the pass/tunnel open?
**Ist der Paß/Tunnel frei?**
*ist der pahs/toonel fry*

Do I need chains/ studded tyres?
**Brauche ich Schneeketten/Spikereifen?**
*brow-khe ikh **shnay**-ketten/**shpyk**-ry-fen*

See also **DRIVING, WEATHER**

# ROOM SERVICE

| | |
|---|---|
| Come in! | **Herein!**<br>*he-rine* |
| We'd like breakfast/<br>a bottle of wine in<br>our room | **Wir hätten gern das Frühstück/eine<br>Flasche Wein auf unserem Zimmer**<br>*veer hetten gern das froo-shtook/ine-e fla-she<br>vine owf oon-ze-rem tsimmer* |
| Put it on my bill | **Schreiben Sie es auf die Rechnung**<br>*shry-ben zee es owf dee rekh-noong* |
| I'd like an outside<br>line, please | **Geben Sie mir bitte ein Amt**<br>*gayben zee meer bi-te ine amt* |
| I have lost my key | **Ich habe meinen Schlüssel verloren**<br>*ikh hah-be mine-en shloo-sel ferloh-ren* |
| I have locked myself<br>out of my room | **Ich habe mich aus meinem Zimmer<br>ausgesperrt**<br>*ikh hah-be mikh ows mine-em tsimmer<br>ows-ge-shpayrt* |
| Where is the socket<br>for my electric razor? | **Wo gibt es eine Steckdose für meinen<br>Rasierapparat?**<br>*voh gipt es ine-e shtek-doh-ze foor mine-en<br>razeer-apa-raht* |
| What's the voltage? | **Wie hoch ist die Spannung hier?**<br>*vee hohkh ist dee shpanoong heer* |
| I need a hairdryer/<br>an iron | **Ich brauche einen Fön/ein Bügeleisen**<br>*ikh brow-khe ine-en fur'n/ine<br>boogel-ize-en* |
| Please send someone<br>to collect my luggage | **Schicken Sie bitte jemanden für mein<br>Gepäck**<br>*shicken zee bi-te yay-manden foor mine ge-pek* |

See also **CLEANING, COMPLAINTS, HOTEL DESK, TELEPHONE**

# SELF-CATERING

*Streetwise*

*You won't find kettles in hotel rooms or self-catering apartments, so be prepared to boil water in a saucepan.*

| | |
|---|---|
| We've booked an apartment in the name of … | **Wir haben ein Apartment auf den Namen … gebucht** <br> *veer **hah**-ben ine apartment owf dayn **nah**-men … ge-**bookht*** |
| Which is the key for the front door? | **Welcher Schlüssel ist für die Haustür?** <br> *vel-kher **shloo**-sel ist foor dee **how**stoor* |
| Where is the electricity meter/ the water heater? | **Wo ist der Stromzähler/der Heißwasserbereiter?** <br> *voh ist der **shtrohm**-tsayler/der hice-vasser-be-**ry**-ter* |
| How does the heating/ the shower work? | **Wie funktioniert die Heizung/die Dusche?** <br> *vee foonk-tsyoh-**neert** dee **hy**-tsoong/dee **doo**-she* |
| Which day does the cleaner come? | **An welchem Tag kommt die Reinemachefrau?** <br> *an **vel**-khem tahk komt dee **rine**-e-makh-e-**frow*** |
| Is the cost of electricity included in the rental? | **Sind die Stromkosten in der Miete enthalten?** <br> *zint dee **shtrohm**-kosten in der mee-te ent-**hal**ten* |
| Is there any spare bedding? | **Gibt es hier noch weiteres Bettzeug?** <br> *gipt es heer nokh **vite**-e-res **bet**-tsoyk* |
| Where can I contact you? | **Wo kann ich Sie erreichen?** <br> *voh kan ikh zee er-**ry**-khen* |

*Streetwise*

In Germany all shops are obliged by law to close from 1830 until
0700 and at 1400 on Saturdays. On every first Saturday in the month
and on the four Saturdays before Christmas shops can be kept open
until 1800. In tourist centres, however, shops are permitted to remain
open all day on Saturdays and Sundays.

| | |
|---|---|
| Where is the main shopping area? | **Wo ist hier das Geschäftsviertel?**<br>*voh ist heer das ge**shefts**-feertel* |
| Where are the big stores? | **Wo sind die großen Kaufhäuser?**<br>*voh zint dee **groh**-sen **kowf**-hoyzer* |
| What time do the shops close? | **Um wieviel Uhr schließen die Geschäfte?**<br>*oom vee**feel** oor **shlee**-sen dee ge**shef**-te* |
| How much does that cost? | **Wieviel kostet das?**<br>*vee**feel** kostet das* |
| How much is it per kilo/per metre? | **Wieviel kostet das Kilo/der Meter?**<br>*vee**feel** kostet das keelo/der mayter* |
| Can I try it on? | **Kann ich es anprobieren?**<br>*kan ikh es **an**pro-beeren* |
| Where is the food department? | **Wo ist die Lebensmittelabteilung?**<br>*voh ist dee **lay**benz-mittel-**ap**-ty-loong* |
| I'm looking for a gift for my wife | **Ich suche ein Geschenk für meine Frau**<br>*ikh **zoo**-khe ine ge**shenk** foor mine-e frow* |
| I'm just looking | **Ich schaue mich nur um**<br>*ikh **show**-e mikh noor oom* |
| Can I have a carrier bag, please? | **Kann ich bitte eine Tragetüte haben?**<br>*kan ikh **bi**-te ine-e **trah**-ge-**too**-te **hah**-ben* |

See also **BUYING, PAYING**

# SIGHTSEEING

*Streetwise*

*Details of sightseeing tours can be obtained from the local tourist office (das Fremdenverkehrsbüro – **frem**den-vayr**kayrs**-boor**oh**).*

| | |
|---|---|
| What is there to see here? | **Was ist hier sehenswert?**<br>*vas ist heer **zay**-enz-vert* |
| Excuse me, how do I get to the cathedral? | **Entschuldigen Sie bitte, wie komme ich zum Dom?**<br>*ent-**shool**-di-gen zee **bi**-te vee **ko**-me ikh tsoom **dohm*** |
| Where is the museum/ the … square? | **Wo ist das Museum/der ...-Platz?**<br>*voh ist das moo-**zay**-oom/der …plats* |
| What time does the guided tour begin? | **Um wieviel Uhr beginnt die Führung?**<br>*oom vee**feel** oor be**gint** dee **foo**roong* |
| What time does the museum open? | **Um wieviel Uhr macht das Museum auf?**<br>*oom vee**feel** oor makht das moo-**zay**-oom owf* |
| Is the castle open to the public? | **Ist das Schloß der Öffentlichkeit zugänglich?**<br>*ist das shlos der **ur'**-fent-likh-kite **tsoo**-geng-likh* |
| How much does it cost to get in? | **Wieviel kostet der Eintritt?**<br>*vee**feel** kostet der **in**etrit* |
| Is there a reduction for senior citizens? | **Gibt es eine Ermäßigung für Rentner?**<br>*gipt es ine-e er-**may**-sigoong foor rentner* |
| Where can I buy some postcards? | **Wo kann ich Ansichtskarten kaufen?**<br>*voh kan ikh **an**-zikhts-karten kowfen* |

See also **MAPS & GUIDES, TRIPS & EXCURSIONS**

*Streetwise*

*Tobacconists'* (Tabakwarengeschäft) *sell tobacco, cigars and cigarettes. The no-smoking sign is* Rauchen verboten, *though there are very few places where smoking is forbidden. Cigarettes can be bought at any kiosk. You will find cigarette machines in most restaurants and also in the streets.*

| | |
|---|---|
| Do you mind if I smoke? | **Macht es Ihnen etwas aus, wenn ich rauche?** |
| | *makht es ee-nen etvas ows ven ikh row-khe* |
| May I have an ashtray? | **Kann ich bitte einen Aschenbecher haben?** |
| | *kan ıkh bi-te ine-en ashen-bekher hah-ben* |
| Is this a no-smoking area? | **Ist rauchen hier verboten?** |
| | *ist row-khen heer terboh-ten* |
| A packet of ..., please | **Eine Schachtel ... bitte!** |
| | *ine-e shakh-tel ... bi-te* |
| Have you got any American/English brands? | **Haben Sie amerikanische/englische Marken?** |
| | *hah-ben zee amay-reekah-nish-e/eng-lish-e* |
| Do you have any matches/pipe cleaners? | **Haben Sie Streichhölzer/Pfeifenreiniger?** |
| | *hah-ben zee shtrykh-hur'l-tser/pfy-fen-ryni-ger* |
| Have you a refill for my gas lighter? | **Haben Sie eine Nachfüllpatrone für mein Gasfeuerzeug?** |
| | *hah-ben zee ine-e nakh-fool-patroh-ne foor mine gas-foy-er-tsoyk* |
| Have you got a light? | **Haben Sie Feuer?** |
| | *hah-ben zee foy-er* |

# SPORTS

| | |
|---|---|
| Which sports activities are available here? | **Welche Sportmöglichkeiten gibt es hier?** *vel-khe **shport**-mur'-glikh-kite-en gipt es heer* |
| Is it possible to go fishing/riding? | **Kann man hier angeln gehen/reiten?** *kan man heer **ang**-eln gay-en/**ry**-ten* |
| Where can we play tennis/golf? | **Wo können wir Tennis/Golf spielen?** *voh **kur'**-nen veer tennis/golf shpeelen* |
| Is there a swimming pool? | **Gibt es hier ein Schwimmbad?** *gipt es heer ine **shvimm**baht* |
| Are there any interesting walks nearby? | **Gibt es hier in der Nähe interessante Wanderwege?** *gipt es heer in der **nay**-e intay-re**san**-te **van**der-vay-ge* |
| Can we rent the equipment? | **Können wir die Ausrüstung leihen?** ***kur'**-nen veer dee **ows**-roostoong **ly**-en* |
| How much does it cost per hour? | **Wieviel kostet es pro Stunde?** *vee**feel** kostet es pro **shtoon**-de* |
| Do we need to be members? | **Müssen wir Mitglieder sein?** *moossen veer **mit**-gleeder zine* |
| Where do we buy our tickets? | **Wo können wir die Karten kaufen?** *voh **kur'**-nen veer dee **kar**ten kowfen* |
| Can we take lessons? | **Können wir Unterricht nehmen?** ***kur'**-nen veer **oon**ter-rikht naymen* |

See also **BEACH, ENTERTAINMENT, WATERSPORTS, WINTER SPORTS**

*Streetwise*

*Taxis cannot be hailed in the street. You must go to a taxi rank or order one by telephone. Rates vary from town to town; they depend on the time of day, the number of passengers and the amount of luggage transported. A tip of 10% should be given. Taxis are normally white Mercedes.*

| | |
|---|---|
| Can you order me a taxi, please? | **Können Sie mir bitte ein Taxi bestellen?** *kur'-nen zee meer bi-te ine taxi be-shtellen* |
| To the main station/airport, please | **Zum Hauptbahnhof/Flughafen bitte!** *tsoom howpt-bahn-hohf/flook-hahfen bi-te* |
| Take me to this address | **Fahren Sie mich bitte zu dieser Adresse!** *fah-ren zee mikh bi-te tsoo deezer a-dres-e* |
| How much will it cost? | **Wieviel wird es kosten?** *veefeel veert es kosten* |
| I'm in a hurry | **Ich habe es eilig** *ikh hah-be es ile-ikh* |
| Can you wait here for a few minutes? | **Können Sie hier bitte ein paar Minuten warten?** *kur'-nen zee heer bi-te ine pahr minoo-ten varten* |
| Stop here/at the corner | **Halten Sie hier/an der Ecke!** *halten zee heer/an der e-ke* |
| How much is it? | **Wieviel kostet es?** *veefeel kostet es* |
| Keep the change | **Stimmt so!** *shtimt zoh* |

*For international calls, first dial 00, then the country code (for Britain: 44) and then the number you want, but leave out the 0 from the town code; e.g. to dial London: 00 44 1 ... . Telephone boxes are yellow – there are both coin-operated and card-operated phone boxes. Cards can be obtained at the post office.*

| | |
|---|---|
| I want to make a phone call | **Ich möchte gern telefonieren**<br>*ikh mur-kh'te gern taylay-fo-**nee**ren* |
| Can I have a line? | **Kann ich bitte ein Amt haben?**<br>*kan ikh **bi**-te ine amt **hah**-ben* |
| I would like 345 56/extension 89 | **Ich hätte gern 345 56/Apparat 89**<br>*ikh het-te gern .../apa-**raht** ...* |
| I want to reverse the charges | **Ich hätte gern ein R-Gespräch**<br>*ikh het-te gern ine **er**-ge-shprekh* |
| Have you got change for the phone? | **Haben Sie Kleingeld für das Telefon?**<br>***hah**-ben zee **kline**-gelt foor das taylay-**fohn*** |
| What coins do I need? | **Welche Münzen brauche ich?**<br>***vel**-khe **moon**-tsen **brow**-khe ikh* |
| How much is it to phone Britain/the USA? | **Wieviel kostet es, nach Großbritannien/in die USA zu telefonieren?**<br>*vee**feel** kostet es nakh grohs-bri**tah**-nee-en/in dee oo-es-**ah** tsoo taylay-fo-**nee**ren* |
| I can't get through | **Ich komme nicht durch**<br>*ikh **ko**-me nikht doorkh* |
| The line's engaged | **Es ist besetzt**<br>*es ist be**zetst*** |

Hello, this is …
**Guten Tag, hier ist …**
*goo*ten tahk, heer ist …

Can I speak to …?
**Kann ich bitte … sprechen?**
kan ikh **bi**-te … **shpre**-khen

I've been cut off
**Ich bin unterbrochen worden**
ikh bin oonter-**bro**-khen vorden

It's a bad line
**Die Verbindung ist schlecht**
dee fer**bin**-doong ist shlekht

## YOU MAY HEAR:

**Ich verbinde (Sie)**
*ikh for**bin** de (zee)*

I'm putting you
through

**Einen Augenblick bitte!**
*ine-en **ow**gen-blik **bi**-te*

Hold the line

**Es ist besetzt**
*es ist be**zetst***

I'm sorry, it's
engaged

**Versuchen Sie es bitte später noch
einmal!**
*fer**zoo**-khen zee es **bi**-te shpayter nokh
**ine**-mal*

Please try again
later

**Wer ist am Apparat?**
*vayr ist am apa-**raht***

Who's calling?

**Sie haben sich verwählt**
*zee **hah**-ben zikh fer**vaylt***

Sorry, wrong
number

The 24-hour clock is widely used. Thus you may hear:

| 9.00 pm | 2100 | einundzwanzig Uhr |
| | | *ine-oont-**tsvan**-tsikh oor* |
| 4.45 pm | 1645 | sechzehn Uhr fünfundvierzig |
| | | ***zekh**-tsayn oor foonf-oont-**feer**-tsikh* |

| | |
|---|---|
| What's the time? | **Wie spät ist es?/Wieviel Uhr ist es?** |
| | *vee **shpayt** ist es/vee**feel** oor ist es* |
| It's: | **Es ist:** |
| | *es ist* |
| **8.00** | **acht Uhr** |
| | *akht oor* |
| **8.05** | **acht Uhr fünf** |
| | *akht oor foonf* |
| **8.10** | **acht Uhr zehn** |
| | *akht oor tsayn* |
| **8.15** | **acht Uhr fünfzehn** |
| | *akht oor foonf-tsayn* |
| **8.20** | **acht Uhr zwanzig** |
| | *akht oor **tsvan**-tsikh* |
| **8.25** | **acht Uhr fünfundzwanzig** |
| | *akht oor foonf-oont-**tsvan**-tsikh* |
| **8.30** | **halb neun/acht Uhr dreißig** |
| | *halp noyn/akht oor **dry**-sikh* |
| **8.35** | **acht Uhr fünfunddreißig** |
| | *akht oor foonf-oont-**dry**-sikh* |
| **8.40** | **acht Uhr vierzig/zwanzig Minuten vor neun** |
| | *akht oor **feer**-tsikh/**tsvan**-tsikh mi**noo**-ten vor noyn* |
| **8.45** | **Viertel vor neun** |
| | *feertel for noyn* |
| **8.50** | **acht Uhr fünfzig** |
| | *akht oor **foonf**-tsikh* |
| **8.55** | **acht Uhr fünfundfünfzig** |
| | *akht oor foonf-oont-**foonf**-tsikh* |
| **12.00** | **zwölf Uhr** (12 o'clock); **Mitternacht** (midnight) |
| | *tsvur'lf oor           **mit**-ter-nakht* |

See also **NUMBERS**

| | |
|---|---|
| What time do you open/close? | **Wann öffnen/schließen Sie?** <br> *van **ur'f**-nen/**shlee**-sen zee* |
| Do we have time to visit the town? | **Haben wir Zeit, um die Stadt zu besichtigen?** <br> *hah-ben veer tsite oom dee shtat tsoo be-**zikh**-ti-gen* |
| How long will it take to get to ...? | **Wie lange braucht man, bis zu ...?** <br> *vee lang-e **browkht** man bis tsoo ...* |
| We arrived early/ late | **Wir kamen bald/spät an** <br> *veer **kah**-men balt/shpayt an* |
| We must be back at the hotel before ... o'clock | **Wir müssen vor ... Uhr** (see TIME) **im Hotel zurück sein** <br> *veer moossen for ... oor im hotel tsoorook zine* |
| When does the coach leave in the morning? | **Wann fährt der Bus am Vormittag ab?** <br> *van fayrt der boos am **for**-mitak ap* |
| The tour starts at about ... | **Die Tour beginnt gegen ...** (see TIME) <br> *dee tour be**gint gay**gen ...* |
| The museum is open in the morning/ afternoon | **Der Museum ist vormittags/nachmittags geöffnet** <br> *der moo-**zay**-oom ist **for**-mitaks/**nakh**-mitaks ge-**ur'f**-net* |
| The table is booked for ... o'clock this evening | **Der Tisch ist für heute abend um ...** (see TIME) **bestellt** <br> *der tish ist foor **hoy**-te **ah**bent oom ... be-**shtelt*** |

# TIPPING

*Streetwise*

*A service charge is usually added to hotel and restaurant bills. However, if you were happy with the service you should give the waiter a tip of approximately 10%. It is also customary to tip taxi drivers, hairdressers and lavatory attendants.*

| | |
|---|---|
| Sorry, I don't have any change | **Ich kann leider nicht rausgeben**<br>*ikh kan **lye**-der nikht **rows**-gayben* |
| Could you give me change of 10 Marks? | **Könnten Sie mir auf zehn Mark rausgeben?**<br>*kur'n-ten zee meer owf tsayn mark **rows**-gayben* |
| Is it usual to tip? | **Gibt man normalerweise ein Trinkgeld?**<br>*gipt man nor-**mal**er-vy-ze ine **trink**-gelt* |
| How much should I tip? | **Wieviel Trinkgeld soll ich geben?**<br>*vee**feel trink**-gelt zol ikh gayben* |
| Is the tip included? | **Ist Trinkgeld inbegriffen?**<br>*ist **trink**-gelt **in**-be-griffen* |
| Keep the change | **Stimmt so**<br>*shtimt zoh* |
| Make it ... Marks | **Machen Sie ... Mark!** (*see* NUMBERS)<br>***ma**-khen zee ... mark* |

There are not many public toilets so use those in bars or restaurants.
Look for the sign Toiletten or WC. The sign for men's toilets is H for
Herren and for women's it is either F for Frauen or D for Damen. Most
department stores have toilets for the use of customers.

| | |
|---|---|
| Where are the toilets, please? | **Wo sind die Toiletten bitte?**<br>*voh zint dee twa-**le**-ten **bi**-te* |
| Where is the Gents'/ the Ladies'? | **Wo ist die Herrentoilette/Damentoilette?**<br>*voh ist dee **he**rren-twa-**le**-te/**dah**-men-twa-**le**-te* |
| This toilet does not flush | **Die Spülung geht nicht**<br>*dee **shpool**oong gayt nikht* |
| There is no toilet paper/soap | **Es gibt hier kein Toilettenpapier/keine Seife**<br>*es gipt heer kine twa-**le**-ten-pa**peer**/kine-e **zy**-fe* |
| Do I have to pay extra to use the washbasin? | **Muß man fürs Händewaschen extra zahlen?**<br>*moos man foors **hen**-de-vashen extra **tsah**-len* |
| Is there a toilet for the disabled? | **Gibt es hier eine Toilette für Behinderte?**<br>*gipt es heer ine-e twa-**le**-te foor be-**hin**-der-te* |
| Are there facilities for mothers with babies? | **Gibt es hier einen Raum für Mütter mit Babys?**<br>*gipt es heer ine-en rowm foor **moo**ter mit babies* |
| The towels have run out | **Es gibt hier kein Handtuch**<br>*es gipt heer kine **hant**-tookh* |
| The door will not close | **Die Tür schließt nicht**<br>*dee toor shleest nikht* |

# TRAIN TRAVEL

*Streetwise*

The railway network is excellent in Germany. European city and inter-city trains (EC- and IC-Züge) connect the main cities while Personenzüge serve smaller towns. For the inter-city train you have to pay a supplement (Zuschlag) – this costs less if you pay for it when you buy your ticket rather than on the train. In the summer time it is advisable to make a seat reservation (Platzkarte) in advance of your trip. A sleeper (Schlafwagen) should always be booked in advance.

| | |
|---|---|
| Is this the train for ...? | **Ist das der Zug nach ...?**<br>*ist das der tsook nakh ...* |
| Is this seat free? | **Ist dieser Platz noch frei?**<br>*ist deezer plats nokh fry* |
| I have a seat reservation | **Ich habe eine Platzreservierung**<br>*ikh **hah**-be ine-e **plats**-ray-zer-**vee**roong* |
| May I open the window? | **Darf ich das Fenster aufmachen?**<br>*darf ikh das fenster **owf**-makhen* |
| What time do we get to ...? | **Wann kommen wir in ... an?**<br>*van kommen veer in ... an* |
| Do we stop at ...? | **Halten wir in ...?**<br>*halten veer in ...* |
| Where do I change for ...? | **Wo muß ich nach ... umsteigen?**<br>*voh moos ikh nakh ... **oom**-shty-gen* |
| Is there a restaurant car? | **Gibt es einen Speisewagen?**<br>*gipt es ine-en **shpy**-ze-vahgen* |
| Please tell me when we get to ... | **Würden Sie mir bitte Bescheid sagen, wenn wir nach ... kommen**<br>*voorden zee meer **bi**-te be**shite** zagen ven veer nakh ... kommen* |

See also **LUGGAGE, RAILWAY STATION**

| | |
|---|---|
| What's the best way to get to ...? | **Wie komme ich am besten nach ...?** <br> *vee ko-me ikh am besten nakh …* |
| How much is it to fly to ...? | **Wieviel kostet ein Flug nach ...?** <br> *veefeel kostet ine flook nakh …* |
| Are there any cheap flights/train fares? | **Gibt es billige Flüge/Zugfahrten?** <br> *gipt es bili-ge floo-ge/tsook-fahrten* |
| What times are the trains? | **Zu welchen Zeiten fahren die Züge?** <br> *tsoo vel-khen tsy-ten fah-ren dee tsoo-ge* |
| Can I buy the tickets here? | **Kann ich hier die Tickets kaufen?** <br> *kan ikh heer dee tickets kowfen* |
| Can I change my booking? | **Kann ich umbuchen?** <br> *kan ikh oom-boo-khen* |
| Can you book me on the London flight? | **Können Sie mir bitte einen Platz für den Flug nach London buchen?** <br> *kur'-nen zee meer bi-te ine-en plats foor dayn flook nakh London boo-khen* |
| Can I get back to Manchester tonight? | **Kann ich heute abend nach Manchester zurückfliegen?** <br> *kan ikh hoy-te ahbent nakh Manchester tsoorook-fleegen* |
| Two second class returns to ..., please | **Zwei Rückfahrkarten zweiter Klasse nach ... bitte!** <br> *tsvy rookfar-kar-ten tsvy-ter kla-se nakh … bi-te* |
| Can you book me into a hotel? | **Können Sie mir bitte ein Hotelzimmer reservieren?** <br> *kur'-nen zee meer bi-te ine hotel-tsimmer ray-zer-veeren* |

# TRIPS & EXCURSIONS

Are there any sightseeing tours?

**Gibt es hier irgendwelche Rundfahrten?**
*gipt es heer **eer**gent-vel-khe **roont**farten*

When is the bus tour of the town?

**Wann ist die Stadtrundfahrt?**
*van ist dee **shtat**-roontfart*

How long does the tour take?

**Wie lange dauert die Rundfahrt?**
*vee lang-e **dow**-ert dee **roont**fart*

Are there any boat trips on the river/lake?

**Gibt es hier Schiffsrundfahrten auf dem Fluß/See?**
*gipt es heer **shifs**-roont-farten owf daym floos/zay*

Is there a reduction for a group?

**Gibt es eine Gruppenermäßigung?**
*gipt es ine-e **groop**en-er-may-sigoong*

Is there a reduction for children?

**Gibt es eine Ermäßigung für Kinder?**
*gipt es ine-e ayr-**may**-sigoong foor kinder*

Is there a commentary in English?

**Gibt es eine Beschreibung auf englisch?**
*gipt es ine-e be**shry**-boong owf **eng**-lish*

Where do we stop for lunch?

**Wo machen wir Mittagspause?**
*voh **makh**-en veer **mi**taks-pow-ze*

Please stop the bus, my child is feeling sick!

**Halten Sie bitte an, meinem Kind ist übel!**
***hal**ten zee **bi**-te an mine-em kint ist oobel*

See also **SIGHTSEEING**

| | |
|---|---|
| Is it possible to go water-skiing/ windsurfing | **Kann man hier Wasserski fahren/ windsurfen?** <br> *kan man heer va sser-shee fah-ren/vint-zoorfen* |
| Can we rent a motor boat/rowing boat? | **Können wir ein Motorboot/Ruderboot mieten?** <br> *kur'-nen veer ine mohtor-boht/rooder-boht meeten* |
| Can I rent a surfboard? | **Kann ich ein Surfbrett leihen?** <br> *kan ikh ine zoorf-brett ly-en* |
| Can one swim in the river? | **Kann man in dem Fluß schwimmen?** <br> *kan man in daym floos shvimmen* |
| Can we fish here? | **Können wir hier angeln?** <br> *kur'-nen veer heer ang-eln* |
| Is there a paddling pool for the children? | **Gibt es hier ein Planschbecken für die Kinder?** <br> *gipt es heer ine plansh-becken foor dee kinder* |
| Do you give lessons? | **Geben Sie Unterricht?** <br> *gayben zee oonter-rikht* |
| Where is the municipal swimming pool? | **Wo ist das städtische Schwimmbad?** <br> *voh ist das shtaytish-e shvimbaht* |
| Is the pool heated? | **Ist das Becken beheizt?** <br> *ist das becken behytst* |
| Is it an outdoor pool? | **Ist es ein Freibad?** <br> *ist es ine fry-baht* |

See also **BEACH**

# WEATHER

Streetwise

*Germany's warmest area is the Upper Rhine Valley, in the southwest, while the coldest weather occurs in the Alps. Summer temperatures can get into the 90s while in winter the temperatures often fall below freezing point.*

| | |
|---|---|
| It's a lovely day | **Es ist ein herrlicher Tag**<br>*es ist ine **her**-likh-er tahk* |
| What dreadful weather! | **Was für ein furchtbares Wetter!**<br>*vas foor ine **foorkht**-bar-es vetter* |
| It is raining/snowing | **Es regnet/schneit**<br>*es **rayg**net/shnite* |
| It's windy | **Es ist windig**<br>*es ist **vin**-dikh* |
| Will it be cold tonight? | **Wird es heute abend kalt sein?**<br>*veert es **hoy**-te **ah**bent kalt zine* |
| Is it going to rain/ to snow? | **Wird es wohl regnen/schneien?**<br>*veert es vohl **rayg**-nen/**shny**-en* |
| Will there be a thunderstorm? | **Wird es ein Gewitter geben?**<br>*veert es ine ge**vi**-ter gayben* |
| Is it going to be fine? | **Wird das Wetter schön werden?**<br>*veert das vetter **shur'n vayr**-den* |
| Is the weather going to change? | **Wird sich das Wetter ändern?**<br>*veert zikh das vetter **en**dern* |
| What is the temperature? | **Wieviel Grad sind es?**<br>*vee**feel** graht zint es* |

Germany is the most northerly of the major wine-growing countries and produces a huge variety of wines, the bulk of which are white.

The best-known wine-producing regions are the sheltered valleys of the Rhine, Mosel, Saar, Ahr, and Nahe, as well as Baden, Württemberg, Franken and Rheinhessen. Among the best types of grape are: Gewürztraminer (full-bodied white), Müller-Thurgau (light, fruity white), Riesling (medium-dry to semi-sweet), Ruländer (full-bodied sweet), Silvaner (medium-dry white), and Spätburgunder (full-bodied red).

Strict government controls apply to wine production in Germany and the wine labels will always indicate three different aspects of the wine: the quality, the wine-growing area, and the type of grape. There are three levels of quality:

**Deutscher Tafelwein – DTW** – light table wine;
**Qualitätswein bestimmter Anbaugebiete – QbA** – wine with more body; must originate in one of the 11 approved wine-growing areas;
**Qualitätswein mit Prädikat – QmP** – top-quality wine. Within this category there are six sub-categories divided according to the level of sweetness of the wine. These are, in ascending order: *Kabinett*; *Spätlese* (made from late-harvest grapes); *Auslese* (made from the ripest grapes); *Beerenauslese* (made from specially selected over-ripe grapes); *Trockenbeerenauslese* (made from selected grapes which have been allowed to dry on the vine); *Eiswein* (made from grapes picked after the first frost; rare and very expensive).

Some basic wine terms:

| | |
|---|---|
| *trocken* | dry |
| *herb* | very dry |
| *halbtrocken* | medium dry |
| *Weißwein/Rotwein* | white/red wine |
| *Weißherbst* | type of rosé wine |
| *Hauswein* | house wine |
| *Sekt* | good-quality sparkling wine or champagne |

Most well-known brands of spirits are served in German bars. Fruit brandies (apple, cherry, plum, etc) are particularly popular. Schnapps is a type of strong spirit, and it too is often made with fruit.

# WINES & SPIRITS 2

We'd like an aperitif

**Wir hätten gern ein Aperitif**
*veer hetten gern ine a-peri-**teef***

May I have the wine
list, please?

**Kann ich bitte die Weinkarte haben?**
*kan ikh **bi**-te dee **vine**kar-te **hah**-ben*

Can you recommend
a good red/white/
rosé wine?

**Können Sie mir einen guten
Rotwein/Weißwein/Rosé empfehlen?**
***kur'**-nen zee meer ine-en **goo**-ten **roht**vine/
**vice**vine/ro**zay** emp-**faylen***

A bottle/carafe of
house wine

**Eine Flasche/Karaffe offener Wein**
*ine-e **fla**-she/ka**ra**-fe offen-er vine*

A half bottle of …

**Eine halbe Flasche …**
*ine-e **hal**-be **fla**-she …*

Would you bring
another glass, please?

**Würden Sie bitte noch ein Glas bringen?**
*voorden zee **bi**-te nokh ine glahs bringen*

This wine is not
chilled

**Dieser Wein ist nicht kalt genug**
*deezer vine ist nikht kalt ge**nook***

What liqueurs do
you have?

**Was für Liköre haben Sie?**
*vas foor lee**kur'**-re **hah**-ben zee*

I'll have a brandy/
scotch

**Ich hätte gern einen Cognak/Whisky**
*ikh het-te gern ine-en **kon**yak/**vis**kee*

A gin and tonic

**Einen Gin Tonic**
*ine-en gin tonic*

A Campari and soda

**Einen Campari mit Soda**
*ine-en campari mit soda*

A Martini and
lemonade

**Einen Martini mit Limonade**
*ine-en martini mit leemo-**nah**-de*

See also **DRINKS, EATING OUT, MENUS, ORDERING**

# WINTER SPORTS

| | |
|---|---|
| Can we hire skis here? | **Können wir hier Skier leihen?** <br> *kur'-nen veer heer **shee**-er **ly**-en* |
| Could you adjust my bindings? | **Könnten Sie bitte meine Bindungen einstellen?** <br> *kur'n-ten zee **bi**-te mine-e **bin**-doongen **ine**-shtellen* |
| What are the snow conditions? | **Wie sind die Schneebedingungen?** <br> *vee zint dee **shnay**-be**ding**-oongen* |
| Is there a restaurant at the top station? | **Gibt es bei der Bergstation ein Restaurant?** <br> *gipt es by der **berk**-sta-tsy-**ohn** ine restoh-**rong*** |
| Which are the easiest runs? | **Welche sind die leichtesten Abfahrten?** <br> ***vel**-khe zint dee **lykh**-tes-ten **ap**-farten* |
| We'll take the gondola | **Wir fahren mit der Gondelbahn** <br> *veer **fah**-ren mit der **gon**del-bahn* |
| When is the last ascent? | **Wann ist die letzte Bergfahrt?** <br> *van ist dee **let**-ste **berk**fart* |
| Is there a danger of avalanches? | **Besteht hier Lawinengefahr?** <br> *be**shtayt** heer la**vee**-nen-ge**fahr*** |
| The snow is very icy/ heavy | **Der Schnee ist sehr vereist/pappig** <br> *der shnay ist zayr fer-**iced**/**pa**-pikh* |
| Where can we go skating? | **Wo können wir hier eislaufen?** <br> *voh **kur'**-nen veer heer **ice**-lowfen* |
| Is there a toboggan run? | **Gibt es hier eine Schlittenbahn?** <br> *gipt es heer ine-e **shlit**ten-bahn* |

**a** *(with 'der' words)* ein *ine*; *(with 'die' words)* eine *ine-e*; *(with 'das' words)* ein *ine*

**abbey** die Abtei *ap-ty*

**about** *(concerning)* über *oober*; *(place)* umher *oom-her*, herum *heroom*; *(approximately)* ungefähr *oongefayr*; **about 4 o'clock** ungefähr 4 Uhr *oongefayr feer oor*

**above** *(overhead)* oben *ohben*; *(higher than)* über *oober*

**accident** der Unfall *oonfal*

**accommodation** die Unterkunft *oonter-koonft*

**ache** weh tun *vay toon*; **my head aches** mir tut der Kopf weh *meer toot der kopf vay*

**adaptor** *(electrical)* der Zwischenstecker *tsvishen-shtecker*

**address** die Adresse *a-dre-se*

**adhesive tape** das Klebeband *klaybe-bant*

**admission charge** der Eintrittspreis *inetrits-price*

**adult** der/die Erwachsene *ervakse-ne*

**advance: in advance** im voraus *im for-ows*

**after** *(afterwards)* danach *danakh*; *(place, order)* hinter *hinter*

**afternoon** der Nachmittag *nakh-mitak*

**aftershave** das Rasierwasser *razeer-vasser*

**again** wieder *veeder*

**agent** der Vertreter *fer-trayter*; *(organization)* die Vertretung *fer-traytoong*

**ago: long ago** vor langer Zeit *for langer tsite*; **a week ago** vor einer Woche *for ine-er vo-khe*

**air-conditioning** die Klimaanlage *kleema-anlah-ge*

**air line** die Fluggesellschaft *floog-gezellshaft*

**air mail: by air mail** per Luftpost *per looftpost*

**air-mattress** die Luftmatratze *looft-matra-tse*

**airport** der Flughafen *flook-hahfen*

**aisle** *(in theatre)* der Gang *gang*; *(in church)* das Seitenschiff *zyten-shif*

**alarm call** der Weckruf *wek-roof*

**alarm clock** der Wecker *vecker*

**alcohol** der Alkohol *al-kohol*

**alcoholic** alkoholisch *alko-hohlish*

**all** alle *a-le*

**allergic to** allergisch gegen *a-ler-gish gaygen*

**allowance** *(customs)* die zollfreie Menge *dee tsol-fry-e meng-e*

**all right** *(agreed)* in Ordnung *in ortnoong*; **are you all right?** geht es Ihnen gut? *gayt es eenen goot*

**almost** fast *fast*

**also** auch *owkh*

**always** immer *immer*

**am** see GRAMMAR

**ambulance** der Krankenwagen *kranken-vahgen*

**America** Amerika *amay-reeka*

**American** amerikanisch *amay-reekah-nish*

**anaesthetic** die Narkose *narkoh-ze*

**and** und *oont*

**another** *(additional)* noch ein(e,s) *nokh ine(-e, s)*; *(different)* ein

**anderer** ine **an**-de-rer; eine andere ine-e **an**-de-re; (different) ein anderes ine **an**-de-res

**antibiotic** das Antibiotikum anti-bee-**oh**-tikoom

**antifreeze** der Frostschutz **frost**-shootz

**antiseptic** das Antiseptikum anti-**zepti**-koom

**any** (with singular) irgendein(e) **irgent**-ine(-e); **I haven't any** ich habe keines ikh **hah**-be **kine**-es

**apartment** das Appartement apar-**temong**

**aperitif** der Aperitif a-peri-**teef**

**apple** der Apfel **apfel**

**appointment** (engagement) der Termin **termeen**, (job) die Stelle **shte**-le

**apricot** die Aprikose apri-**koh**-ze

**are** see GRAMMAR

**arm** der Arm arm

**armbands** (for swimming) die Schwimmflügel **shvim**-floogel

**arrival** die Ankunft **an**-koonft

**arrive** ankommen **an**-kommen

**art gallery** die Kunstgalerie **koonst**-ga-leree

**artichoke** die Artischocke arti-**sho**-ke

**ashtray** der Aschenbecher **ashen**-bekher

**asparagus** der Spargel **shpargel**

**aspirin** das Aspirin aspi-**reen**

**asthma** das Asthma **ast**ma

**at** bei by; **at home** zu Hause tsoo **how**-ze

**aubergine** die Aubergine ober-**jee**-ne

**Australia** Australien ow**strah**-li-en

**Australian** australisch ow**strah**-lish

**Austria** Österreich **ur's**-te-rykh

**Austrian** österreichisch **ur's**-te-rykhish

**automatic** automatisch owto-**mah**tish

**autumn** der Herbst herpst

**avalanche** die Lawine la-**vee**-ne

**avocado** die Avocado avocado

**baby** das Baby baby

**baby food** die Babynahrung baby-nahroong

**babysitter** der Babysitter baby-zitter

**back** (of body, hand) der Rücken rooken

**bacon** der Frühstücksschinken **froosh**tooks-shinken

**bad** schlecht shlekht

**bag** die Tasche **ta**-she; (suitcase) der Koffer **koffer**

**baggage: baggage reclaim** die Gepäckausgabe ge**pek**-owsgah-be

**baker's** die Bäckerei be-ke-**ry**

**balcony** der Balkon bal**kohn**

**ball** (dance, sphere) der Ball bal

**banana** die Banana bana-ne

**band** (musical) die Band bant; (group) die Schar shar

**bandage** der Verband fer-**bant**

**bank** die Bank bank

**bar** (place) die Bar bar

**barber** der (Herren)friseur (**herr**en)fri**zur**

**basket** der Korb korp

**Basle** Basel **bah**zel

**bath** das Bad baht; **to take a bath**

baden *bahden*
**bathing cap** die Badekappe *bahde-kap-e*
**bathroom** das Badezimmer *bahde-tsimmer*
**battery** die Batterie *ba-teree*
**be** sein *zine*
**beach** der Strand *shtrant*
**bean** die Bohne *boh-ne*
**beautiful** schön *shur'n*
**bed** das Bett *bet*
**bedding** das Bettzeug *bet-tsoyk*
**bedroom** das Schlafzimmer *shlaf-tsimmer*
**beef** das Rindfleisch *rint-flysh*
**beer** das Bier *beer*
**beetroot** die Rote-Bete *roh-te bay-te*
**before** vor *for*
**begin** beginnen *be-ginen*
**behind** hinter *hinter*
**below** unterhalb *oonter-halp*
**belt** der Gürtel *goor-tel*
**beside** (at the side of, compared with) neben *nayben*; (near) an *an*
**best** (do something) am besten *am besten*; **the best** der/die/das beste *der/dee/das bes-te*
**better** besser *besser*
**between** zwischen *tsvishen*
**bicycle** das Fahrrad *far-raht*
**big** groß *grohs*
**bigger** größer *grur'ser*
**bikini** der Bikini *bi-keenee*
**bill** (account) die Rechnung *rekh-noong*
**bin** der Mülleimer *mool-ime-er*
**binoculars** das Fernglas *fern-glahs*

**bird** der Vogel *fohgel*
**birthday** der Geburtstag *geboortstahk*; **happy birthday!** alles Gute zum Geburtstag! *a-les goo-te tsoom geboortstahk*
**birthday card** die Geburtstagskarte *geboorts-tahks-kar-te*
**bit** (piece) das Stück *shtook*; **a bit** (a little) ein bißchen *bis-khen*
**bite** beißen *by-sen*; (insect) stechen *shte-khen*
**bitten** (by insect) gestochen *gesto-khen*
**bitter** bitter *bitter*
**black** schwarz *shvarts*
**blackcurrants** die schwarzen Johannisbeeren *shvar-tsen yoh-hannis-bay-ren*
**blanket** die Decke *de-ke*
**bleach** das Bleichmittel *blykh-mittel*
**blocked** verstopft *fer-shtopft*
**blood group** die Blutgruppe *blootgroo-pe*
**blouse** die Bluse *bloo-ze*
**blow-dry** fönen *fur'-nen*
**blue** blau *blow*
**boarding card** die Bordkarte *bort-kar-te*
**boarding house** die Pension *pen-zyohn*
**boat** das Boot *boht*; (ship) das Schiff *shif*
**boat trip** die Bootsfahrt *bohtsfart*
**boil** kochen *ko-khen*
**book**[1] n das Buch *bookh*; **book of tickets** das Fahrscheinheft *farshine-heft*
**book**[2] vb buchen *boo-khen*

**booking** *(in hotel)* die Reservierung ray-zer-**vee**roong

**booking office** die Vorverkaufsstelle **for**-ferkowfs-shte-le

**bookshop** die Buchhandlung **bookh**-hantloong

**boot** der Stiefel **shtee**fel; *(of car)* der Kofferraum **kof**er-rowm

**border** *(frontier)* die Grenze **gren**-tse

**both** beide **by**-de

**bottle** die Flasche **fla** she

**bottle opener** der Flaschenöffner **fla**-shen-ur'f-ner

**box** *(container)* die Kiste **kis**-te

**box office** die Kasse **ka**-se

**boy** der Junge **yoong**-e

**boyfriend** der Freund **froynt**

**bra** der Büstenhalter **boos**-ten-halter

**bracelet** das Armband **arm**bant

**brake fluid** die Bremsflüssigkeit **brems**-floo-sikh-kite

**brakes** die Bremsen **brem**zen

**brandy** der Kognak **kon**yak

**bread** das Brot **broht**

**breakable** zerbrechlich tser-**brekh**likh

**breakdown** die Panne **pa**-ne

**breakdown van** der Abschleppwagen **ap**shlep-vahgen

**breakfast** das Frühstück **froo**shtook

**breast** die Brust **broost**

**briefcase** die Aktentasche **akten**-ta-she

**bring** bringen **bring**en

**Britain** Großbritannien grohs-**britah**-nee-en

**British** britisch **british**

**brochure** die Broschüre bro-**shoo**-re

**broken** *(object, bone)* kaputt ka**poot**

**broken down** *(machine, car)* kaputt ka**poot**

**brooch** die Brosche **brosh**-e

**brother** der Bruder **broo**der

**brown** braun **brown**

**brush** die Bürste **boor**-ste; *(for floor)* der Handfeger **hant**-fayger

**bucket** der Eimer **ime**-er

**buffet** das Büffet **boo**fay

**buffet car** *(on train)* der Speisewagen **shpy**-ze-vahgen

**bulb** *(electric)* die Glühbirne **gloo**bir-ne

**bun** *(cake)* das süße Brötchen **zoo**-se **bru**'t-khen

**bureau de change** die Wechselstube **vek**sel-shtoo-be

**burst** platzen **plat**sen

**bus** der Bus **boos**

**business** das Geschäft ge**sheft**

**bus station** der Busbahnhof **boos**-bahnhohf

**bus stop** die Bushaltestelle **boos**-hal-te-shte-le

**bus tour** die Busfahrt **boos**fart

**busy** beschäftigt be-**shef**-tikht

**but** aber **ah**ber

**butcher** der Metzger **mets**-ger

**butter** die Butter **boo**ter

**button** der Knopf **knopf**

**buy** kaufen **kow**fen

**by** *(close to)* bei **by**; *(via)* über **oo**ber

**bypass** die Umgehungsstraße oom-**gay**oongs-shtrah-se

# WORDS

**cabaret** das Kabarett *kaba-ret*
**cabbage** der Kohl *kohl*
**cable car** die Seilbahn *zile-bahn*
**café** das Café *kafay*
**cake** der Kuchen *kookhen*
**call¹** *vb (shout)* rufen *roofen; (on telephone)* anrufen *an-roofen*
**call²** *n (on telephone)* der Anruf *anroof;* **long-distance call** das Ferngespräch *fern-geshprekh*
**calm** *(person)* ruhig *roo-ikh; (weather)* windstill *vintshtil*
**camera** die Kamera *kamera*
**camp** campen *kempen*
**camp site** der Campingplatz *kemping-plats*
**can¹** *n* die Dose *doh-ze*
**can²** *vb* : **I/he/she can** ich/er/sie kann *ikh/er/zee kan;* **we/you/they can** wir/Sie/sie können *veer/zee/zee kur'nen*
**Canada** Kanada *kanada*
**Canadian** kanadisch *kanah-dish*
**cancel** rückgängig machen *rook-gengikh makhen*
**canoe** das Kanu *kanoo*
**canoeing** der Kanusport *kanoo-shport*
**can opener** der Dosenöffner *dohzen-ur'f-ner*
**car** das Auto *owto*
**carafe** die Karaffe *kara-fe*
**caravan** der Wohnwagen *vohn-vahgen*
**carburettor** der Vergaser *fer-gahzer*
**card** *(greetings)* die (Glückwunsch-)karte *(glookvoonsh-)kar-te; (playing)* die Spielkarte *shpeelkar-te*

**cardigan** die Strickjacke *shtrik-ya-ke*
**careful** vorsichtig *for-zikhtikh*
**car ferry** die Autofähre *owto-fay-re*
**car park** der Parkplatz *park-plats*
**carpet** der Teppich *teppikh*
**carriage** *(railway)* der Wagen *vahgen*
**carrot** die Karotte *ka-rot-e*
**carry** *(bring)* tragen *trahgen*
**car wash** die Autowäsche *owto-ve-she*
**case** *(suitcase)* der Koffer *koffer*
**cash¹** *vb (cheque)* einlösen *ine-lur'zen*
**cash²** *n* das Bargeld *bargelt*
**cash desk** die Kasse *ka-se*
**cashier** *(male)* der Kassierer *ka-seerer; (female)* die Kassiererin *ka-see-rerin*
**casino** das Kasino *ka-zeeno*
**cassette** die Kassette *kase-te*
**castle** das Schloß *shlos*
**catch** *(ball)* fangen *fangen; (bus, train)* nehmen *nay-men*
**cathedral** der Dom *dohm*
**Catholic** katolisch *katoh-lish*
**cauliflower** der Blumenkohl *bloomen-kohl*
**cave** die Höhle *hur'-le*
**celery** der Stangensellerie *shtangen-ze-leree*
**cemetery** der Friedhof *freet-hohf*
**centimetre** der Zentimeter *tsenti-mayter*
**central** zentral *tsentrahl*
**centre** das Zentrum *tsentroom*

**cereal** *(for breakfast)* die Getreideflocken *(pl)* ge**try**-de-flocken

**certain** *(sure)* sicher *zikher*

**certificate** die Bescheinigung be**shine**-igoong

**chain** die Kette *ke-te*

**chair** der Stuhl *shtool*

**chairlift** der Sessellift *zessel-lift*

**chalet** das Chalet *shalay*

**champagne** der Champagner sham**pan**-yer

**change**[1] *n (money)* das Wechselgeld *veksel-gelt*

**change**[2] *vb (exchange)* wechseln *vekseln; (alter)* ändern *endern*

**changing room** *(in shop)* der Umkleideraum **oom**-kly-derowm; *(at swimming pool)* die Umkleidekabine **oom**-kly-de-ka**bee**-ne

**chapel** die Kapelle *ka-pe-le*

**charge** *(fee)* die Gebühr *geboor*

**cheap** billig *bilikh*

**cheaper** billiger *bili-ger*

**check** *(examine)* überprüfen **oober**-proofen; *(passports, tickets)* kontrollieren *kontro-leeren*

**check in** *(at airport)* zum Checkin gehen *tsoom* **check**in *gayen; (at hotel)* sich an der Rezeption anmelden *zikh an der raytsep-tsyohn an-melden*

**check-in desk** der Abfertigungsschalter **ap**-ferti-goongs-**shal**ter

**cheerio** tschüs! *choos*

**cheers** *(toast)* Prost! *prohst*

**cheese** der Käse *kay-ze*

**chemist's** *(for cosmetics etc)* die Drogerie *droh-ge**ree**; (for medicines)* die Apotheke *apoh-**tay**-ke*

**cheque** der Scheck *shek*

**cheque book** das Scheckheft **shek**-heft

**cheque card** die Scheckkarte **shek**-kar-te

**cherries** die Kirschen *kirshen*

**chestnut** *(tree)* der Kastanienbaum *kas-**tanyen**-bowm; (nut)* die Kastanie *kas-**tanye***

**chewing gum** der Kaugummi **kow**-goomi

**chicken** das Hähnchen

**chicken pox** die Windpocken **vint**-pocken

**child** das Kind *kint*

**children** die Kinder *kinder*

**chips** *(French fries)* die Pommes frites *pomfreet*

**chocolate** die Schokolade *shoko-**lah**-de*

**chocolates** die Pralinen *prahlee-nen*

**Christmas** Weihnachten *vy-nakh-ten;* **merry Christmas!** frohe Weihnachten! **froh**-e *vy-nakh-ten*

**church** die Kirche **kir**-khe

**cider** der Apfelwein **apfel**-vine

**cigar** die Zigarre *tsiga-re*

**cigarette** die Zigarette *tsiga-**re**-te*

**cigarette papers** die Zigarettenpapiere *tsiga-**re**ten-pa**pee**-re*

**cinema** das Kino *keeno*

**circus** der Zirkus *tsirkoos*

**city** die Stadt *shtat*

**clean**[1] *adj* sauber *zowber*

**clean**[2] *vb* säubern *zoybern*

**cleansing cream** die Reinigungscreme **ry**-nigoongs-kray-me

**client** *(male)* der Kunde *koon-de*; *(female)* die Kundin *koon-din*

**climbing** das Bergsteigen **berk**-shty-gen

**climbing boots** die Bergschuhe **berk**-shoo-e

**cloakroom** die Garderobe *gar-de-roh-be*

**clock** die Uhr *oor*

**close**[1] *adj (near)* nahe *nah-e*

**close**[2] *vb* schließen **shlee**-sen

**closed** geschlossen *geshlos-en*

**cloth** der Lappen *lappen*

**clothes** die Kleider **kly**-der

**clothes peg** die Wäscheklammer **vesh**-e-klammer

**cloves** die Gewürznelken *gevoorts-nelken*

**club** der Club *kloop*

**coach** *(bus)* der Bus *boos*; *(of train)* der Wagen **vah**gen

**coach trip** die Busreise **boos**-ry-ze

**coast** die Küste *koos-te*

**coastguard** die Küstenwache **koos**ten-vakh-e

**coat** der Mantel *mantel*

**coat hanger** der Kleiderbügel **kly**der-boogel

**cocktail** der Cocktail *cocktail*

**cocoa** der Kakao *ka-kow*

**coconut** die Kokosnuß **kohk**os-noos

**coffee** der Kaffee *kafay*; **white coffee** Kaffee mit Milch **ka**fay mit milkh; **black coffee** der schwarze Kaffee **shvar**-tse kafay

**coin** die Münze *moon-tse*

**Coke ®** das Cola *kola*

**colander** das Sieb *zeep*

**cold**[1] *n (illness)* die Erkältung *er-kel*toong

**cold**[2] *adj* kalt *kalt*; **I'm cold** mir ist kalt *meer ist kalt*

**Cologne** Köln *kur'ln*

**colour** die Farbe *far-be*

**comb** der Kamm *kam*

**come** kommen *kommen*; *(arrive)* ankommen **an**-kommen; **to come back** zurückkommen *tsoorook-kommen*; **to come in** hereinkommen *herine-kommen*; **come in!** herein! *he-rine*

**comfortable** bequem *bekvaym*

**company** die Gesellschaft *ge-zelshaft*

**compartment** das Abteil *aptile*

**complain** sich beschweren *zikh be-shvayren*

**compulsory** obligatorisch *obli-ga-tohrish*

**computer** der Computer *computer*

**concert** das Konzert *kon-tsert*

**condensed milk** die Kondensmilch *kon-densmilkh*

**conditioner** *(for hair)* die Haarschnellkur *har-shnelkoor*

**conference** die Konferenz *konfay-rents*

**confession** die Konfession *kon-fesyohn*

**confirm** bestätigen *be-shtay-tigen*

**congratulations!** herzliche Glückwünsche! **herts**-likh-e **glook**-voon-she

**connect** verbinden *fer-binden*

**connection** die Verbindung *ferbin-doong*

**constipated** verstopft *fer-shtopft*

**consulate** das Konsulat *konzoo-laht*

**contact** sich in Verbindung setzen mit *zikh in fer-bindoong zetsen mit*

**contact lens cleaner** die Kontaktlinsenreiniger *kontakt-linzen-ry-niger*

**contact lenses** die Kontaktlinsen *kontakt-linzen*

**Continental breakfast** das kleine Frühstück *kline-e frooshtook*

**contraceptive** das Verhütungsmittel *ferhoo-toongz-mittel*

**cook** kochen *kokhen*

**cooker** der Herd *hayrt*

**cool** kühl *kool*

**copy**[1] *n* die Kopie *kopee*

**copy**[2] *vb* kopieren *ko-peeren*

**corkscrew** der Korkenzieher *korken-tsee-er*

**corner** die Ecke *e-ke*

**cornflakes** die Cornflakes *cornflakes*

**cosmetics** die Schönheitspflegemittel *shur'nhites-pflay-ge-mittel*

**cost** kosten *kosten*

**cotton** die Baumwolle *bowm-vo-le*

**cotton wool** die Watte *va-te*

**couchette** der Liegewagen *lee-ge-vahgen*

**cough** der Husten *hoosten*

**country** das Land *lant*

**couple** *(pair)* das Paar *pahr*

**courgettes** die Zucchini *tsoo-keenee*

**courier** der Kurier *koo-reer*

**course** *(of meal)* der Gang *gang*

**cover charge** der Preis für ein Gedeck *price foor ine gedeck*

**crab** die Krabbe *kra-be*

**crash** *(noise)* das Krachen *krakh-en*; *(collision)* der Zusammenstoß *tsoo-za-menshtohs*

**crash helmet** der Sturzhelm *shtoorts-helm*

**cream** *(lotion)* die Creme *kray-me*; *(on milk)* die Sahne *zah-ne*

**credit card** die Kreditkarte *kredeet-kar-te*

**crisps** die Chips *chips*

**croquette** die Krokette *kro-ke-te*

**cross** *(road)* überqueren *oober-kvayren*

**crossed line** gestörte Leitung *ge-shtur-te ly-toong*

**crossroads** die Kreuzung *kroytsoong*

**crowded** *(full)* überfüllt *oober-foolt*

**cruise** die Kreuzfahrt *kroyts-fart*

**cucumber** die Gurke *goor-ke*

**cup** die Tasse *ta-se*

**cupboard** der Schrank *shrank*

**currant** die Korinthe *korin-te*

**current** *(electric)* der Strom *shtrohm*

**cushion** das Kissen *kissen*

**custard** die Vanillesoße *vani-le-zoh-se*

**customs** der Zoll *tsol*

**cut**[1] *n* die Schnittwunde *shnitvoon-de*

**cut**[2] *vb* schneiden *shny-den*

**cutlery** das Besteck *beshtek*

**cycle** radfahren *rat-fahren*

**cycling** das Radfahren *rat-fahren*

**daily** *(each day)* täglich *teklikh*

**damage** der Schaden *shah-den*

**damp** feucht *foykht*

**dance**[1] *n* der Tanz *tants*

**dance**[2] *vb* tanzen *tantsen*

**dangerous** gefährlich *ge-fayrlikh*

**dark** dunkel *doonkel*

**date** das Datum *dahtoom*

**date of birth** das Geburtsdatum *geboorts-dahtoom*

**daughter** die Tochter *tokhter*

**day** der Tag *tahk*

**dear** lieb *leep*; *(expensive)* teuer *toyer*

**decaffeinated** koffeinfrei *kofay-eenfry*

**deck chair** der Liegestuhl *lee-ge-shtool*

**declare** erklären *er-klayren*

**deep** tief *teef*

**deep freeze** die Tiefkühltruhe *teef-kool-troo-e*

**defrost** entfrosten *ent-frosten*

**de-ice** enteisen *ent-ise-en*

**delay** die Verspätung *fer-shpay-toong*

**delicious** köstlich *kur'st-likh*

**dentist** der Zahnarzt *tsahnartst*

**dentures** das Gebiß *gebiss*

**deodorant** das Deodorant *day-o-dorant*

**department store** das Kaufhaus *kowfhows*

**departure** die Abfahrt *apfart*

**departure lounge** die Abflughalle *apflook-ha-le*

**deposit** die Anzahlung *an-tsahloong*

**dessert** der Nachtisch *nakh-tish*

**details** die Details *day-tys*

**detergent** das Reinigungsmittel *ry-nigoongs-mittel*

**detour** der Umweg *oom-vayk*

**develop** entwickeln *entvi-keln*

**diabetic** der Diabetiker *dee-a-bay-tiker*

**dialling code** die Vorwahl *forvahl*

**diamond** der Diamant *dee-a-mant*

**diarrhoea** der Durchfall *doorkh-fal*

**diary** das Tagebuch *tah-ge-bookh*

**dictionary** das Wörterbuch *vurter-bookh*

**diesel** das Dieselöl *deezel-ur'l*

**diet** *(slimming)* die Abmagerungskur *apmah-geroongs-koor*; *(special)* die Diät *dee-ayt*

**different** verschieden *fer-sheeden*

**difficult** schwierig *shveerikh*

**dinghy** das Dingi *dingee*

**dining room** das Eßzimmer *ess-tsimmer*

**dinner** *(lunch)* das Mittagessen *mitakh-essen*; *(evening meal)* das Abendessen *ahbent-essen*

**direct** *(route, train)* direkt *deerekt*

**dirty** dreckig *dre-kikh*

**disabled** behindert *be-hindert*

**disco** die Disko *disko*

**discount** der Rabatt *rabat*

**dish** die Schale *shah-le*; *(food)* das Gericht *ge-rikht*

**dishtowel** das Abtrockentuch *ap-troken-tookh*

**dishwasher** die Geschirrspül-maschine *geshir-shpool-mashee-ne*

**disinfectant** das Desinfektions-mittel *dayzin-fek-tsyohns-mittel*

**distilled water** das destillierte Wasser *desti-leer-te vasser*

**divorced** geschieden *ge-sheeden*

**dizzy** schwindelig *shvin-delik*

**do: I do** ich mache *ikh ma-khe*

**doctor** der Arzt *artst*

**dollar** der Dollar *dollar*

**door** die Tür *toor*

**double** Doppel- *dopel*

**double bed** das Doppelbett *dopel-bet*

**double room** das Doppelzimmer *dopel-tsimmer*

**down: to go down** *(downstairs)* heruntergehen *her-oonter-gayen*

**downstairs** unten *oonten*

**draught** *(in room)* der Durchzug *doorkh-tsook*

**dress¹** n das Kleid *klite*

**dress²** vb : **to get dressed** sich anziehen *zikh an-tsee-en*

**dressing** *(for food)* die Soße *zoh-se*

**drink¹** n das Getränk *ge-trenk*

**drink²** vb trinken *trinken*

**drinking chocolate** die heiße Schokolade *hy-se shoko-lah-de*

**drinking water** das Trinkwasser *trink-vasser*

**drive** fahren *fahren*

**driver** *(of car)* der Fahrer *fahrer*

**driving licence** der Führerschein *foorer-shine*

**drunk** betrunken *be-troonken*

**dry¹** adj trocken *trocken*

**dry²** vb trocknen *troknen*

**dry cleaner's** die Reinigung *ry-nigoong*

**duck** die Ente *en-te*

**due: when is it due?** *(train etc)* wann soll es ankommen? *van zol es an-kommen*

**dummy** *(for baby)* der Schnuller *shnooler*

**during** während *vayrent*

**duty-free** duty-free *duty-free*

**duty-free shop** der Duty-free-Shop *duty-free-shop*

**duvet** die Bettdecke *bet-de-ke*

**each** jede(r/s) *yay-de(r/s)*

**ear** das Ohr *ohr*

**earache: I have earache** ich habe Ohrenschmerzen *ikh hah-be oh-ren-shmertsen*

**earlier** früher *froo-er*

**early** früh *froo*

**earrings** die Ohrringe *ohrring-e*

**east** der Osten *osten*

**Easter** Ostern *oh-stern*

**easy** leicht *lykht*

**eat** essen *essen*

**egg** das Ei *eye*; **eggs** die Eier *eye-er*; **fried egg** das Spiegelei *shpeegel-eye*; **hard-boiled egg** das hart gekochte Ei *hart gekokh-te eye*; **scrambled egg** das Rührei *roor-eye*

**either** eine(r/s) *(von beiden)* *ine-e(r/s) (fon by-den)*

**elastic** elastisch *e-las-tish*

**elastic band** das Gummiband *goomee-bant*

**electric** elektrisch *e-lektrish*

**electrician** der Elektriker *aylek-triker*

**electricity** die Elektrizität *aylek-tritsee-tayt*

**electricity meter** der Stromzähler *shtrohm-tsayler*

**electric razor** der Electrorasierer *e-lektro-razeer-er*

**embassy** die Botschaft *bohtshaft*

**emergency** der Notfall *nohtfal*

**empty** leer *layr*

**end** das Ende *en-de*

**engaged** *(to be married)* verlobt *fer-lohpt*; *(toilet, telephone)* besetzt *bezetst*

**engine** der Motor *mohtor*

**England** England *eng-lant*

**English** englisch *eng-lish*

**enjoy: I enjoyed the tour** die Reise hat mir gefallen *dee ry-ze hat meer gefal-en*; **I enjoy swimming** ich schwimme gern *ikh shvim-e gern*

**enough** genug *genook*

**enquiry desk** die Auskunft *owskoonft*

**entrance** der Eingang *ine-gang*

**entrance fee** das Eintrittsgeld *ine-tritsgelt*

**envelope** der Umschlag *oomshlahk*

**equipment** die Ausrüstung *ows-roostoong*

**escalator** die Rolltreppe *rol-tre-pe*

**especially** besonders *bezon-ders*

**essential** wesentlich *vay-zentlikh*

**Eurocheque** der Euroscheck *oyro-shek*

**Europe** Europa *oy-rohpa*

**evening** der Abend *ahbent*; **in the evening** am Abend *am ahbent*

**every** *(each)* jede(r/s) *yay-de(r/s)*

**everyone** jeder *yay-der*

**everything** alles *a-les*

**excellent** ausgezeichnet *ows-ge-tsykh-net*

**except** außer *ow-ser*

**excess luggage** das Übergewicht *oober-gevikht*

**exchange**[1] *n* der Austausch *ows-towsh*

**exchange**[2] *vb* tauschen *towshen*; *(money)* wechseln *vekseln*

**exchange rate** der Wechselkurs *veksel-koors*

**excursion** der Ausflug *owsflook*

**excuse** entschuldigen *entshool-di-gen*; **excuse me!** *(sorry)* Entschuldigung *entshool-digoong*; *(when passing)* entschuldigen Sie, bitte *entshool-di-gen zee bi-te*

**exhaust pipe** das Auspuffrohr *owspoof-rohr*

**exhibition** die Ausstellung *ows-shteloong*

**exit** der Ausgang *owsgang*

**expensive** teuer *toy-er*

**expert** der Experte *ex-per-te*

**expire** *(ticket, passport)* ungültig werden *oon-gooltikh vayrden*

**express**[1] *n* *(train)* der Schnellzug *shneltsook*

**express**[2] *adj* *(parcel etc)* per Expreß *per express*

**extra** *(spare)* übrig *oobrikh*; *(more)* noch ein(e) *nokh ine(-e)*

**eye** das Auge *ow-ge*

**eye liner** der Eyeliner *eyeliner*

**eye shadow** der Lidschatten *leet-shatten*

**face** das Gesicht *gezikht*

**facilities** die Einrichtungen *ine-rikh-toongen*

**faint: she has fainted** sie ist in

ohnmacht gefallen *zee ist in ohnmakht ge-fal-en*

**fair** *(funfair)* die Kirmes *kir-mes*

**fall** fallen *fallen*

**family** die Familie *fa-mee-lee-e*

**famous** berühmt *be-roomt*

**fan** *(electric)* der Ventilator *venti-lahtor*

**fan belt** der Keilriemen *kile-reemen*

**far** weit *vite*

**fare** der Fahrpreis *farprice*

**farm** der Bauernhof *bow-ern-hohf*

**farmhouse** das Bauernhaus *bow-ern-hows*

**fast** schnell *shnel*

**fat** dick *dik*

**father** der Vater *fahter*

**fault** *(defect)* der Fehler *fayler; it wasn't my fault* das war nicht meine Schuld *das var nikht mine-e shoolt*

**favourite** Lieblings- *leeplings*

**feed** füttern *footern*

**feel** fühlen *foolen; I don't feel well* ich fühle mich nicht wohl *ikh foole mikh nikht vohl; I feel sick* mir ist schlecht *meer ist shlekht*

**ferry** die Fähre *fay-re*

**festival** das Fest *fest*

**fetch** *(bring)* holen *hoh-len*

**fever** das Fieber *feeber*

**few: a few** ein paar *ine par*

**fiancé(e)** der/die Verlobte *fer-lohp-te*

**field** das Feld *felt*

**fill** füllen *foolen; to fill up (petrol tank)* volltanken *fol-tanken*

**fillet** das Filet *fee-lay*

**film** der Film *film*

**filter** der Filter *filter*

**filter-tipped** Filter- *filter*

**finish** beenden *be-enden*

**fire** das Feuer *foy-er*

**fire brigade** die Feuerwehr *foy-er-vayr*

**fire extinguisher** der Feuerlöscher *foy-er-lur'sher*

**first** erste(r/s) *er-ste(r/s)*

**first aid** die Erste Hilfe *er-ste hil-fe*

**first class** *(travel)* erster Klasse *er-ster kla-se*

**first floor** die erste Etage *er-ste aytah-je*

**first name** der Vorname *for-nah-me*

**fish**[1] *n* der Fisch *fish*

**fish**[2] *vb* fischen *fishen*

**fit**[1] *vb* passen *passen*

**fit**[2] *n (seizure)* der Anfall *anfal*

**fix** reparieren *raypa-reeren*

**fizzy** sprudelnd *shproo-delnt*

**flash** das Blitzlicht *blits-likht*

**flask** die Thermosflasche *termohs-fla-she*

**flat** *(apartment)* die Wohnung *voh-noong*

**flat tyre** die Reifenpanne *ryfen-pa-ne*

**flight** der Flug *flook*

**flippers** die Flossen *flossen*

**floor** *(of building)* die Etage *aytah-je; (of room)* der Boden *boh-den*

**flour** das Mehl *mayl*

**flowers** die Blumen *bloomen*

**flu** die Grippe *gri-pe*

**fly sheet** das Überzelt *oober-tselt*

**foggy** neblig *nay*blikh
**follow** folgen *folgen*
**food** das Essen *essen*
**food poisoning** die Lebensmittelvergiftung *laybens-mittel-fer-gift*oong
**foot** *see* CONVERSION CHARTS
**football** der Fußball *foos*-bal
**for** für *foor*
**foreign** ausländisch *ows*-lendish
**forest** der Wald *valt*
**forget** vergessen *fer*gesen
**fork** *(at table)* die Gabel *gahb*el; *(in road)* die Gabelung *gah*-beloong
**fortnight** zwei Wochen *tsvy vokhen*
**France** Frankreich *frank*-rykh
**free** *(not occupied)* frei *fry*; *(costing nothing)* umsonst *oomzonst*
**freezer** die Tiefkühltruhe *teef*kool-troo-e
**French** französisch fran-*tsur'*zish
**French beans** die grünen Bohnen *groonen bohnen*
**frequent** häufig *hoy*fikh
**fresh** frisch *frish*
**fridge** der Kühlschrank *kool*-shrank
**fried** gebraten ge-*brah*ten
**friend** *(male)* der Freund *froynt*; *(female)* die Freundin *froyn*-din
**from** von *fon*
**front** die Vorderseite *forder*-zy-te
**frozen** gefroren ge-*froh*ren
**fruit** das Obst *ohpst*
**fruit juice** der Fruchtsaft *frookht*-zaft
**fruit salad** der Obstsalat *ohpst*-zalaht

**frying-pan** die Bratpfanne *brat*-pfa-ne
**fuel** der Brennstoff *bren*-shtof
**fuel pump** die Benzinpumpe ben*tseen*-poom-pe
**full** voll *fol*
**full board** die Vollpension *fol*pen-zyohn
**funny** *(amusing)* lustig *loos*tikh; *(odd)* komisch *koh*mish
**fur** der Pelz *pelts*
**fuse** die Sicherung *zikh*-eroong

**gallery** *(art gallery)* die Galerie ga-le*ree*
**gallon** *see* CONVERSION CHARTS
**game** das Spiel *shpeel*
**garage** die Werkstatt *verk*-shtat
**garden** der Garten *garten*
**garlic** der Knoblauch *knohp*-lowkh
**gas** das Gas *gahs*
**gas cylinder** die Gasflasche *gahs*fla-she
**gears** das Getriebe ge*tree*-be
**gentleman** der Herr *hayr*
**gents'** Herrentoilette *herr*en-twa-le-te
**genuine** echt *ekht*
**German** deutsch *doytch*
**German measles** die Röteln *rur'*-teln
**Germany** Deutschland *doytch*-lant
**get** *(receive, obtain)* bekommen be-*kommen*; *(fetch)* holen *hoh*-len; **to get into** *(vehicle)* einsteigen *ine*-shtygen; **to get off** *(from vehicle)* aussteigen *ows*-shtygen
**gift** das Geschenk ge-*shenk*

**gift shop** der Souvenirladen *zoo-veneerladen*

**gin** der Gin *gin*

**girl** das Mädchen *mayt-khen*

**girlfriend** die Freundin *froyn-din*

**give** geben *gayben*

**glass** das Glas *glahs*

**glasses** die Brille *bri-le*

**gloves** die Handschuhe *hant-shoo-e*

**glucose** der Traubenzucker *trowben-tsooker*

**glue** der Klebstoff *klaypshtof*

**go** gehen *gayen*; **to go back** zurückgehen *tsoorook-gayen*; **to go down** (sun) untergehen *oonter-gayen*; **to go in** hineingehen *hinine-gayen*; **to go out** hinausgehen *hinows-gayen*

**goggles** (for swimming) die Taucherbrille *towkher-bri-le*; (for skiing) die Schneebrille *shnaybri-le*

**gold** golden *gol-den*

**golf** das Golf *golf*

**golf course** der Golfplatz *golfplats*

**good** gut *goot*; (pleasant) schön *shu'rn*

**good afternoon** guten Tag *gooten tahk*

**goodbye** auf Wiedersehen *owf veeder-zayn*

**good evening** guten Abend *gooten ahbent*

**good morning** guten Morgen *gooten morgen*

**good night** gute Nacht *goo-te nakht*

**gramme** das Gramm *gram*

**grandfather** der Großvater *grohs-fahter*

**grandmother** die Großmutter *grohs-mooter*

**grapefruit** die Grapefruit *grapefruit*

**grapefruit juice** der Grapefruitsaft *grapefruit-zaft*

**grapes** die Trauben *trowben*

**greasy** fettig *fettikh*

**green** grün *groon*

**green card** die grüne Karte *groo-ne kar-te*

**grey** grau *grow*

**grilled** gegrillt *ge-grilt*

**grocer's** (shop) der Lebensmittelladen *laybens-mittel-lahden*

**ground** der Boden *bohden*

**ground floor** das Erdgeschoß *ert-geshoss*

**groundsheet** der Zeltboden *tselt-bohden*

**group** die Gruppe *groo-pe*

**group passport** der Gruppen-reisepaß *groopen-ry-zepass*

**guarantee** die Garantie *garan-tee*

**guard** der Schaffner *shaf-ner*

**guest** der Gast *gast*; (in hotel) der Hausgast *howsgast*

**guesthouse** die Pension *pen-zyohn*

**guide**[1] n der Führer *foorer*

**guide**[2] vb führen *foo-ren*

**guidebook** der Führer *foorer*

**guided tour** die Fremdenführung *fremden-fooroong*

**gym shoes** die Turnschuhe *toorn-shoo-e*

**haemorrhoids** die Hämorrhoiden *hemo-roh-eeden*

**hair** die Haare *(pl) hah*-re
**hairbrush** die Haarbürste *hahr-boor*-ste
**haircut** der Haarschnitt *hahrshnit*
**hairdresser** der Friseur *free-zur*
**hairdryer** der Fön *fur'n*
**hairgrip** die Haarklemme *hahr-kle-me*
**hair spray** das Haarspray *hahr-shpray*
**half** halb *halp*; **a half bottle** eine kleine Flasche *ine-e kline-e fla-she*
**half board** die Halbpension *halp-pen-zyohn*
**half fare** der halbe Fahrpreis *hal-be far-price*
**ham** der Schinken *shinken*
**hand** die Hand *hant*
**handbag** die Handtasche *hant-ta-she*
**handicapped** behindert *be-hindert*
**handkerchief** das Taschentuch *tashen-tookh*
**hand luggage** das Handgepäck *hant-gepek*
**hand-made** handgearbeitet *hant-ge-ar-bytet*
**hangover** der Kater *kah-ter*
**Hanover** Hannover *hanoh-fer*
**happen** geschehen *ge-shay-en*; **what happened?** was ist passiert? *vas ist paseert*
**happy** glücklich *glooklikh*
**harbour** der Hafen *hahfen*
**hard** hart *hart*
**hat** der Hut *hoot*
**have** haben *hah-ben; see* GRAMMAR
**hay fever** der Heuschnupfen *hoy-shnoopfen*

**he** er *er; see* GRAMMAR
**head** der Kopf *kopf*
**headache** die Kopfschmerzen *kopf-shmertsen*
**head waiter** der Oberkellner *ohber-kelner*
**hear** hören *huren*
**heart** das Herz *herts*
**heart attack** der Herzanfall *herts-anfal*
**heater** das Heizgerät *hyts-gerayt*
**heating** die Heizung *hy-tsoong*
**heavy** schwer *shvayr*
**hello** hallo *ha-loh*
**help¹** *n* die Hilfe *hil-fe*; **help!** Hilfe! *hil-fe*
**help²** *vb* helfen *helfen*; **can you help me?** können Sie mir helfen? *kur'nen zee meer helfen*
**herb** das Kraut *krowt*
**here** hier *heer*
**high** hoch *hohkh*; *(number, speed)* groß *grohs*
**high blood pressure** der hohe Blutdruck *hoh-e blootdrook*
**high chair** der Kinderstuhl *kinder-shtool*
**high tide** die Flut *floot*
**hill** der Hügel *hoogel*
**hill-walking** das Bergwandern *berk-vandern*
**hire** mieten *meeten*
**hit** schlagen *shlahgen*
**hitchhike** trampen *trampen*
**hold** halten *halten; (contain)* enthalten *ent-halten*
**hold-up** *(traffic jam)* die Stockung

*shtok*ung

**hole** das Loch *lokh*

**holiday** der Feiertag *fy-er-tahk*; **on holiday** in den Ferien *in den fay-ree-en*

**home** das Zuhause *tsoo-how-ze*

**homesick: to be homesick** Heimweh haben *hime-vay hah-ben*

**honey** der Honig *hoh*nikh

**honeymoon** die Flitterwochen *(pl) flitter-vokhen*

**hope** hoffen *hoffen*; **I hope so/not** hoffentlich/hoffentlich nicht *hoffent-likh/hoffent-likh nikht*

**hors d'oeuvre** die Vorspeise *for-shpy-ze*

**horse** das Pferd *pfayrt*

**hose** der Schlauch *shlowkh*

**hospital** das Krankenhaus *kranken-hows*

**hot** heiß *hice*; **I'm hot** mir ist heiß *meer ist hice*; **it's hot** *(weather)* es ist heiß *es ist hice*

**hotel** das Hotel *ho-tel*

**hour** die Stunde *shtoon-de*

**house** das Haus *hows*

**house wine** der Hauswein *hows-vine*

**hovercraft** das Luftkissenboot *looft-kissen-boht*

**how** wie *vee*; **how much?** wieviel *veefeel*; **how many?** wieviele *veefee-le*; **how are you?** wie geht es Ihnen? *vee gayt es ee-nen*

**hungry: I am hungry** ich habe Hunger *ikh hah-be hoong-er*

**hurry: I'm in a hurry** ich habe es eilig *ikh hah-be es eye-likh*

**hurt** *(feel pain)* schmerzen *shmert-*

*sen*; **my back hurts** mir tut der Rücken weh *meer toot der roo-ken vay*

**husband** der Ehemann *ay-e-man*

**hydrofoil** das Tragflügelboot *trak-floogelboht*

**I** ich *ikh*; see GRAMMAR

**ice** das Eis *ice*

**ice cream** das Eis *ice*

**iced** eisgekühlt *ice-gekoolt*

**ice rink** die Schlittschuhbahn *shlit*shoo-bahn

**if** wenn *ven*

**ignition** die Zündung *tsoon-doong*

**ill** krank *krank*

**immediately** sofort *zo-fort*

**important** wichtig *vikh-tikh*

**impossible** unmöglich *oon-mur'klikh*

**in** *(place, position)* in *in*

**inch** see CONVERSION CHARTS

**included** eingeschlossen *ine-ge-shlossen*

**indigestion** die Magenverstimmung *mah*gen-fer-shtimmoong

**indoors** drinnen *drinnen*; *(at home)* zu Hause *tsoo how-ze*

**infectious** ansteckend *an-shteckend*

**information** die Auskunft *ows-koonft*

**information office** das Informationsbüro *infor-matsyohns-booroh*

**injection** die Spritze *shprit-se*

**injured** *(person)* verletzt *fer-letst*

**ink** die Tinte *tin-te*

**insect** das Insekt *in*zekt

# WORDS

**insect bite** der (Insekten)stich (*inzek-ten-)shtikh*)

**insect repellent** das Insektenschutzmittel *inzek-ten-shoots-mittel*

**inside** in *in*

**instant coffee** der Pulverkaffee *poolfer-kafay*

**instead** statt dessen *shtat dessen*

**instructor** (for skiing, male) der Skilehrer **shee**-layrer; (female) die Skilehrerin **shee**lay-rerin

**insulin** das Insulin *inzoo-leen*

**insurance** die Versicherung *ferzikh-eroong*

**insurance certificate** die Versicherungsbescheinigung *ferzikh-eroongs-beshy-nigoong*

**interesting** interessant *intay-ressant*

**international** international *inter-natsyoh-nahl*

**interpreter** der Dolmetscher *dol-metcher*

**into** in *in*

**invitation** die Einladung *ine-lahdoong*

**invite** einladen *ine-lahden*

**invoice** die Rechnung *rekhnoong*

**Ireland** Irland *eerlant*

**Irish** irisch *eerish*

**iron** (for clothes) das Bügeleisen *boogel-ize-en*

**ironmonger's** die Eisenwarenhandlung *ize-en-vahren-hantloong*

**is** see GRAMMAR

**island** die Insel *inzel*

**it** er/sie/es *er/zee/es*; see GRAMMAR

**Italian** italienisch *ital-ee-aynish*

**Italy** Italien *ital-yen*

**itch** das Jucken *yooken*

**jack** (for car) der Wagenheber *vah*gen-hayber

**jacket** die Jacke *ya-ke*

**jam** die Marmelade *mar-melah-de*

**jammed** (camera, lock) blockiert *blokeert*

**jar** (container) das Gefäß *gefess*

**jazz** der Jazz *jazz*

**jeans** die Jeans *jeans*

**jelly** (dessert) die (rote) Grütze (*rohte*) *groot-se*

**jellyfish** die Qualle *kva-le*

**jersey** der Pullover *poo-lohver*

**jeweller's** der Juwelier *yoovay-leer*

**jewellery** der Schmuck *shmook*

**Jewish** jüdisch *yoodish*

**job** (employment) die Stelle *shte-le*

**joke** der Witz *vits*

**journey** die Reise *ry-ze*

**jug** der Krug *krook*

**juice** der Saft *zaft*

**jump leads** die Starthilfekabel *shtarthil-fe-kahbel*

**junction** (roads) die Kreuzung *kroytsoong*

**just: just two** nur zwei *noor tsvy*; **I've just arrived** ich bin gerade angekommen *ikh bin gerah-de an-ge-kommen*

**keep** behalten *be-halten*

**kettle** der Wasserkocher *vasser-kokher*

**key** der Schlüssel *shloo-sel*
**kidneys** *(as food)* die Nieren *nee-ren*
**kilo** das Kilo *keelo*
**kilometre** der Kilometer *keelo-mayter*
**kind**[1] *n (sort, type)* die Art *art*
**kind**[2] *adj (person)* nett *nett*
**kiss** küssen *koosen*
**kitchen** die Küche *koo-khe*
**knife** das Messer *messer*
**know** *(facts)* wissen *vissen*; *(be acquainted with)* kennen *kennen*

**lace** *(of shoe)* der Schnürsenkel *shnoor-zenkel*
**ladder** die Leiter *lyter*
**ladies'** Damentoilette *dahmen-twa-le-te*
**lady** die Dame *dah-me*
**lager** das helle Bier *he-le beer*
**lake** der See *zay*
**lamb** das Lammfleisch *lam-flysh*
**lamp** *(for table)* die Lampe *lam-pe*
**lane** *(of road)* das Sträßchen *shtrays-khen*; *(of motorway)* die Spur *shpoor*
**large** groß *grohs*
**last** *(final)* letzte(r/s) *let-ste(r/s)*; **last week** letzte Woche *let-ste vo-khe*
**late** spät *shpayt*; **the train is late** der Zug hat Verspätung *der tsook hat fer-shpay-toong*; **sorry we are late** es tut uns leid daß wir zu spät gekommen sind *es toot oons lite dass weer tsoo shpayt ge-kom-en zint*
**later** später *shpayter*
**launderette** der Waschsalon *vash-zalong*
**laundry service** der Wäscherei

Service *ve-she-ry zervis*
**lavatory** die Toilette *twa-le-te*
**lawyer** der Rechtsanwalt *rekhts-anvalt*
**laxative** das Abführmittel *apfoor-mittel*
**layby** die Parkbucht *parkbookht*
**lead** *(electric)* das Kabel *kahbel*
**leader** der Führer *foorer*
**learn** lernen *lernen*
**least: at least** mindestens *min-destens*
**leather** das Leder *layder*
**leave** *(leave behind)* zurücklassen *tsoo-rook-lassen*; **when does the train leave?** wann fährt der Zug ab? *van fayrt der tsook ap*
**left: on/to the left** links/nach links *links/nakh links*
**left-luggage (office)** die Gepäckaufbewahrung *gepek-owf-bevah-roong*
**leg** das Bein *bine*
**lemon** die Zitrone *tsitroh-ne*
**lemonade** die Limonade *leemo-nah-de*
**lemon tea** der Zitronentee *tsi-trohnen-tay*
**lend** leihen *ly-en*
**lens** die Linse *lin-ze*
**less** weniger *vay-niger*
**lesson** die Unterrichtsstunde *oonter-rikhts-shtoon-de*
**let** *(allow)* erlauben *er-lowben*; *(hire out)* vermieten *fer-meeten*
**letter** *(written)* der Brief *breef*
**lettuce** der Kopfsalat *kopf-zalaht*
**library** die Bibliothek *bibli-o-tek*

**licence** *(driving licence)* der Führerschein *foorer-shine*; *(for gun)* der Waffenschein *va-fen-shine*

**lie down** sich hinlegen *zikh hin-laygen*

**lifeboat** das Rettungsschiff *retoongs-shif*

**lifeguard** der Rettungsschwimmer *retoongs-shvimmer*

**life jacket** die Schwimmweste *shvim-ves-te*

**lift** der Aufzug *owftsook*

**lift pass** *(on ski slopes)* der Liftpaß *liftpahs*

**light** das Licht *likht*; **have you got a light?** können Sie mir Feuer geben? *kur'nen zee meer foyer gayben*

**light bulb** die Glühbirne *gloo-bir-ne*

**lighter** das Feuerzeug *foyer-tsoyk*

**like**[1] *prep* wie *vee*; **like you** wie Sie *vee zee*; **like this** so *zoh*

**like**[2] *vb* mögen *mur'gen*; **I like coffee** ich trinke gern Kaffee *ikh trin-ke gern kafay*; **I would like a newspaper** ich möchte eine Zeitung *ikh mur'kh-te ine-e tsite-oong*

**lime** *(fruit)* die Limone *leemoh-ne*

**line** *(row, of railway)* die Linie *lee-nee-e*; *(queue)* die Schlange *shlang-e*; *(telephone)* die Leitung *lite-oong*

**lip salve** die Lippenpomade *lippen-pomah-de*

**lipstick** der Lippenstift *lippen-shtift*

**liqueur** der Likör *leekur*

**listen: to listen to** horchen *hor-khen*

**litre** der Liter *leeter*

**little: a little milk** ein bißchen Milch

ine **bis**-khen milkh

**live** *(exist)* leben *layben*; *(reside)* wohnen *vohnen*; **I live in London** ich wohne in London *ikh voh-ne in london*

**liver** die Leber *layber*

**living room** das Wohnzimmer *vohn-tsimmer*

**loaf** das Brot *broht*

**lobster** der Hummer *hoomer*

**local** *(wine, speciality)* hiesig *heezikh*

**lock**[1] *vb* zuschließen *tsoo-shleesen*

**lock**[2] *n* *(on door, box)* das Schloß *shlos*

**lollipop** der Lutscher *lootcher*

**London** London *london*

**long** lang *lang*; **for a long time** lange Zeit *lang-e tsite*

**look** schauen *showen*; **to look after** sich kümmern um *zikh koomern oom*; **to look for** suchen *zookhen*

**lorry** der Lastwagen *last-vahgen*

**lose** verlieren *fer-leeren*

**lost** *(object)* verloren *fer-lohren*; **I have lost my wallet** ich habe meine Brieftasche verloren *ikh hah-be mine-e breef-ta-she fer-lohren*; **I am lost** *(on foot)* ich habe mich verlaufen *ikh hah-be mikh fer-lowfen*; *(by car)* ich habe mich verfahren *ikh hah-be mikh fer-fahren*

**lost property office** das Fundbüro *foont-booroh*

**lot: a lot** viel *feel*

**lotion** die Lotion *loh-tsyohn*

**loud** laut *lowt*

**lounge** *(in hotel)* der Aufenthaltsraum *owf-enthalts-rowm*

**love** lieben *leeben*; **I love swimming** ich schwimme sehr gern *ikh shvi-me zayr gern*

**lovely** hübsch *hoopsh*

**low** niedrig *needrikh*; *(standard, quality)* minderwertig *minder-vertikh*

**low tide** die Ebbe *e-be*

**lucky** glücklich *glooklikh*

**luggage** das Gepäck *gepek*

**luggage allowance** das Höchstgewicht *hur'khst-gevikht*

**luggage rack** die Gepäckablage *gepek-aplah-ge*

**luggage tag** der Kofferanhänger *koffer-an-henger*

**luggage trolley** der Gepäckwagen *gepek-vahgen*

**lunch** das Mittagessen *mitak-essen*

**luxury** Luxus- *looksoos*

**macaroni** die Makkaroni *(pl)* maka-*rohnee*

**machine** die Maschine *mashee-ne*

**madam** gnädige Frau *gnaydi-ge frow*

**magazine** die Zeitschrift *tsiteshrift*

**maid** *(in hotel)* das Zimmermädchen *tsimmer-maytkhen*

**main** Haupt- *howpt*

**main course** das Hauptgericht *howpt-gerikht*

**mains** *(switch)* der Hauptschalter *howpt-shalter*

**make** machen *makhen*; *(meal)* zubereiten *tsoo-be-ryten*

**make-up** *(cosmetics)* das Make-up *make-up*

**mallet** der Holzhammer *holts-hammer*

**man** der Mann *man*

**manager** der Geschäftsführer *geshefts-foorer*

**many** viele *fee-le*

**map** die Karte *kar-te*

**margarine** die Margarine *marga-ree-ne*

**mark** *(stain)* der Fleck *fleck*

**market** der Markt *markt*

**marmalade** die Marmelade aus Zitrusfrüchten *mar-melah-de ows tsi-troos-frookh-ten*

**married** verheiratet *fer-hyrah-tet*

**mascara** die Wimperntusche *vimpern-too-she*

**mass** *(in church)* die Messe *me-se*

**matches** die Streichhölzer *shtrykh-hur'l tser*

**material** der Stoff *shtoff*

**matter: it doesn't matter** es macht nichts *es makht nikhts*; **what's the matter?** was ist los? *vas ist lohs*

**mayonnaise** die Mayonnaise *mayo-ne-ze*

**meal** das Essen *essen*

**mean** bedeuten *be-doyten*; **what does this mean?** was bedeutet das? *vas be-doy-tet das*

**measles** die Masern *mahzern*

**meat** das Fleisch *flysh*

**mechanic** der Mechaniker *mekha-niker*

**medicine** die Medizin *maydi-tseen*

**medium** mittlere(r/s) *mit-le-re(r/s)*

**medium rare** halbdurch *halpdoorkh*

**meet** *(by accident)* treffen *treffen*; *(by arrangement)* sich treffen *zikh treffen*

# WORDS                    MEL – MOV

**melon** die Melone *meloh*-ne
**member** das Mitglied *mit*gleet
**men** die Männer *men*-er
**menu** die Speisekarte *shpy*-ze-kar-te
**message** die Nachricht *nakh*-rikht
**metal** das Metall *may*tal
**meter** der Zähler *tsay*ler
**metre** der Meter *may*ter
**migraine** die Migräne mee-*gre*-ne
**milk** die Milch *milkh*
**milkshake** das Milchmixgetränk *milkh*-mix-getrenk
**millimetre** der Millimeter *mili-may*ter
**million** die Million *mil*yohn
**mince** das Hackfleisch *hak*-flysh
**mind: do you mind if I...?** haben Sie etwas dagegen, wenn ich ...? *hah*-ben zee *et*vas da*gay*-gen, ven ikh ...
**mineral water** das Mineralwasser mi-ne*rahl*-vasser
**minimum** das Minimum *mee*-nimoom
**minister** (in church) der Pfarrer *pfa*rer
**minor road** die Nebenstraße *nay*ben-shtrah-se
**mint** (herb) die Minze *mint*-se; (sweet) die Pfefferminz *pfef*-ermints
**minute** die Minute mi*noo*-te
**mirror** der Spiegel *shpee*gel
**miss** (train, etc) verpassen fer-*pass*en
**Miss** Fräulein *froy*line
**missing: my son is missing** mein Sohn ist vermißt mine zohn ist fer-*mist*
**mistake** der Fehler *fay*ler
**misty** dunstig *doon*stikh

**misunderstanding: there's been a misunderstanding** wir haben uns mißverstanden veer *hah*-ben oons misfer-*shtan*den
**modern** modern mo-*dern*
**moisturizer** die Feuchtigkeitscreme *foykh*-tikh-kites-kray-me
**monastery** das Kloster *kloh*ster
**money** das Geld *gelt*
**money order** die Postanweisung *post*-an-vyzoong
**month** der Monat *moh*nat
**monument** das Monument monoo-*ment*
**mop** (for floor) der Mop *mop*
**more** mehr *mayr*; **more wine, please** noch etwas Wein, bitte nokh *et*vas vine *bi*-te
**morning** der Morgen *mor*gen
**mosquito** die Stechmücke *shtekh*-moo-ke
**most: the most popular discotheque** die populärste Disko dee popoo*layr*-ste disko
**mother** die Mutter *moo*ter
**motor** der Motor *moh*-tor
**motor boat** das Motorboot *moh*-tor-boht
**motor cycle** das Motorrad
**motorway** die Autobahn *owto*-bahn
**mountain** der Berg *berk*
**mousse** die Creme(speise) *kray*-me (-shpy-ze)
**mouth** der Mund *moont*
**move** bewegen be-*vay*gen; **he can't move his leg** er kann sein Bein nicht bewegen er kan zine bine nikht be-*vay*gen

110

**Mr** Herr *hayr*
**Mrs** Frau *frow*
**much** viel *feel*; **it costs too much** es kostet zuviel *es kos-tet tsoofeel*
**muesli** das Müsli *moozli*
**mumps** der Mumps *moomps*
**Munich** München *moon-khen*
**museum** das Museum *moo-zay-oom*
**mushrooms** die Pilze *pilt-se*
**music** die Musik *moozeek*
**mussel** die Muschel *mooshel*
**must** müssen *moosen*
**mustard** der Senf *zenf*
**mutton** das Hammelfleisch *hamel-flysh*

**nail** der Nagel *nahgel*
**nail polish** der Nagellack *nahgel-lak*
**nail polish remover** der Nagellackentferner *nahgel-lak-entfer-ner*
**naked** nackt *nakt*
**name** der Name *nah-me*
**napkin** die Serviette *zervi-e-te*
**nappy** die Windel *vindel*
**narrow** eng *eng*
**nationality** die Nationalität *natsyoh-nalee-tayt*
**navy blue** marineblau *maree-ne-blow*
**near** *(place, time)* nahe *nah-e*
**necessary** notwendig *noht-vendikh*
**neck** der Hals *hals*
**necklace** die Halskette *halsket-te*
**need: I need an aspirin** ich brauche ein Aspirin *ikh brow-khe ine aspi-reen*

**needle** die Nadel *nahdel*
**negative** *(photography)* das Negativ *nayga-teef*
**neighbour** der Nachbar *nakhbar*
**never** nie *nee*; **I never drink wine** Wein trinke ich nie *vine trin-ke ikh nee*
**new** neu *noy*
**news** die Nachrichten *(pl) nakh-rikhten*
**newsagent** der Zeitungshändler *tsytoongs-hentler*
**newspaper** die Zeitung *tsy-toong*
**New Year** das neue Jahr *noy-e yahr*; **happy New Year!** ein gutes Neues Jahr *ine goo-tes noy-es yahr*
**New Zealand** Neuseeland *noy zaylant*
**next** nächste(r/s) *nekh-ste(r/s)*; **the next stop** die nächste Haltestelle *dee nekh-ste hal-te-shte-le*; **next week** nächste Woche *nekh-ste vo-khe*
**nice** *(person)* nett *net*; *(pleasant)* angenehm *an-genaym*
**night** die Nacht *nakht*; **at night** nachts *nakhts*
**night club** der Nachtklub *nakht-kloop*
**nightdress** das Nachthemd *nakht-hemt*
**no** nein *nine*; **no thank you** nein danke *nine dan-ke*
**nobody** niemand *neemant*
**noisy** laut *lowt*
**non-alcoholic** nichtalkoholisch *nikht-alko-hohlish*
**none** keine(r/s) *kine-e(r/s)*; **there's none left** es ist nichts ubrig *es ist*

*nikhts* **oo**brikh

**non-smoking** nichtraucher *nikht-rowkher*

**north** der Norden *norden*

**Northern Ireland** Nordirland *nort-irlant*

**not** nicht *nikht;* **I don't know** ich weiß nicht *ikh vice nikht*

**note** *(banknote)* der Geldschein *geltshine; (letter)* das Briefchen *breef-khen*

**note pad** der Notizblock *noteets-blok*

**nothing** nichts *nikhts*

**now** jetzt *yetst*

**number** die Zahl *tsahl*

**Nuremberg** Nürnberg *noorn-berk*

**nurse** die Krankenschwester *kranken-shvester*

**nursery slope** der Anfängerhügel *an-fenger-hoogel*

**nut** *(to eat)* die Nuß *noos; (for bolt)* die Schraubenmutter *shrowben-mutter*

**occasionally** gelegentlich *gelay-gentlikh*

**of** von *fon*

**off** *(not on)* aus *ows; (rotten)* schlecht *shlekht*

**offer** anbieten *an-beeten*

**office** das Büro *booroh*

**often** oft *oft*

**oil** das Öl *ur'l*

**oil filter** der Ölfilter *ur'l-filter*

**ointment** die Salbe *zal-be*

**O.K.** okay *okay*

**old** alt *alt;* **how old are you?** wie alt

sind Sie? *vee alt zint zee*

**olive oil** das Olivenöl *olee-venur'l*

**olives** die Oliven *olee-ven*

**omelette** das Omelett(e) *omlet(-e)*

**on**[1] *adj (light, engine)* an *an*

**on**[2] *prep* auf *owf;* **on the table** auf dem Tisch *owf daym tish*

**once** einmal *ine-mal*

**one** ein *ine*

**one-way street** die Einbahnstraße *inebahn-shtrah-se*

**onions** die Zwiebeln *tsveebeln*

**only** nur *noor*

**open**[1] *adj* geöffnet *ge-ur'f-net*

**open**[2] *vb* öffnen *ur'f-nen*

**opera** die Oper *oh-per*

**operator** die Vermittlung *fer-mitloong*

**opposite: opposite the hotel** dem Hotel gegenüber *daym ho-tel gay-gen-oober*

**or** oder *oh-der*

**orange**[1] *adj* orange *oron-je*

**orange**[2] *n* die Orange *oron-je*

**orange juice** der Orangensaft *oron-jen-zaft*

**order** bestellen *be-shtelen*

**oregano** der Origano *oree-gano*

**original** das Original *oree-geenahl*

**other: the other one** der/die/das andere *an-de-re;* **do you have any others?** haben Sie noch andere da? *hah-ben zee nokh an-de-re da*

**ounce** *see* **CONVERSION CHARTS**

**out** *(light etc)* aus *ows;* **she's out** sie ist nicht da *zee ist nikht da*

**outdoor** *(pool etc)* im Freien *im fry-en*

**outside** draußen *drow-sen*

**oven** der Herd *hert*

**over** *(on top of, above)* über *oober*

**overcharge** zuviel berechnen *tsoofeel be-rekhnen*

**overnight** über Nacht *oober nakht*

**owe** schulden *shool-den*; **I owe you ...** ich schulde Ihnen ... *ikh shool-de ee-nen*

**owner** der Besitzer *be-zitser*

**pack** *(luggage)* packen *pa-ken*

**package** das Paket *pakayt*

**package tour** die Pauschalreise *powshal-ry-ze*

**packed lunch** das Lunchpaket *lunch-pakayt*

**packet** das Paket *pakayt*

**paddling pool** das Planschbecken *plansh-beken*

**paid** bezahlt *betsahlt*

**painful** schmerzhaft *shmerts-haft*

**painkiller** das schmerzstillende Mittel *shmerts-shtillen-de mittel*

**painting** das Bild *bilt*

**pair** das Paar *pahr*

**palace** der Palast *palast*

**pan** *(pot)* der Topf *topf*

**pancake** der Pfannkuchen *pfan-kookhen*

**pants** *(underwear)* der Slip *slip*

**paper** das Papier *papeer*

**paraffin** das Paraffin *para-feen*

**parcel** das Paket *pakayt*

**pardon** *(please repeat that)* wie bitte? *vee bi-te*; **I beg your pardon!** *(excuse me)* Entschuldigung *entshool-digoong*

**parents** die Eltern *eltern*

**park**[1] *n* der Park *park*

**park**[2] *vb* parken *parken*

**parking disc** die Parkscheibe *park-shy-be*

**parsley** die Petersilie *payter-zeelee-e*

**part** der Teil *tile*

**party** *(of tourists)* die Reisegruppe *ry-ze-groo-pe*; *(celebration)* die Party *party*

**passenger** der Fahrgast *fargast*

**passport** der Reisepaß *ry-ze-pass*

**passport control** die Paßkontrolle *pass-kontro-le*

**pasta** die Teigwaren *(pl)* *tike-vahren*

**pastry** der Teig *tike*; *(cake)* das Gebäck *gebek*

**pâté** die Pastete *pastay-te*

**path** der Weg *vayk*

**pay** zahlen *tsah-len*

**payment** die Bezahlung *be-tsahloong*

**peach** der Pfirsich *pfirzikh*

**peanuts** die Erdnüsse *ert-noo-se*

**pear** die Birne *bir-ne*

**peas** die Erbsen *erpsen*

**peg** *(for clothes)* die Wäscheklammer *ve-she-klammer*

**pen** der Füller *fooler*

**pencil** der Bleistift *blyshtift*

**penicillin** das Penizillin *peni-tsileen*

**penknife** das Taschenmesser *tashen-messer*

**pensioner** *(male)* der Pensionär *penzyo-nayr*; *(female)* die Pensionärin *penzyo-nayrin*

**pepper** *(spice)* der Pfeffer *pfeffer*; *(red/green pepper)* die

Paprikaschote *pa*preeka-shoh-te

**per: per hour** pro Stunde *pro **shtoon**-de*; **per week** pro Woche *pro **vo**-khe*

**perfect** perfekt *per**fekt***

**performance** die Vorstellung *for-shteloong*

**perfume** das Parfüm *par**foom***

**perhaps** vielleicht *fee-**lykht***

**period** *(menstruation)* die Periode *payree-**oh**-de*

**perm** die Dauerwelle *dower-ve-le*

**permit** die Genehmigung *ge-**nay**-migoong*

**person** die Person *per-**zohn***

**petrol** das Benzin *bentseen*

**petrol station** die Tankstelle *tank-shte-le*

**phone** *see* **telephone**

**photocopy** fotokopieren *foto-kopee-ren*

**photograph** das Foto *foto*

**picnic** das Picknick *picnic*

**picture** *(painting)* das Bild *bilt*; *(photo)* das Foto *foto*

**pie** die Pastete *pa**stay**-te*

**piece** das Stück *shtook*

**pill** die Pille *pi-le*

**pillow** das (Kopf)kissen *(**kopf**-)kissen*

**pillowcase** der (Kopf)kissenbezug *(**kopf**-)kissen-betsook*

**pin** die Stecknadel *shteck-nahdel*

**pineapple** die Ananas *a-nanas*

**pink** rosa *rohza*

**pint** *see* **CONVERSION CHARTS; a pint of beer** eine Halbe *ine-e **hal**-be*

**pipe** die Pfeife *pfy-fe*

**plane** das Flugzeug *flook-tsoyk*

**plaster** *(sticking plaster)* das Pflaster *pflaster*

**plastic** das Plastik *plastik*

**plate** der Teller *teller*

**platform** die Plattform *platform*

**play** spielen *shpeelen*

**playroom** das Spielzimmer *shpeel-tsimmer*

**please** *(in polite request)* bitte *bi-te*

**pleased** erfreut *er**froyt***

**pliers** die Zange *tsang-e*

**plug** *(electrical)* der Stecker *shtecker*; *(in bath)* der Stöpsel *shtur'p-sel*

**plum** die Pflaume *pflow-me*

**plumber** der Installateur *insta-latur*

**points** *(in car)* die Unterbrecherkontakte *oonter-brekher-kontak-te*

**police** die Polizei *poli-tsy*; **police!** Polizei! *poli-tsy*

**policeman** der Polizist *poli-tsist*

**police station** das Polizeirevier *poli-**tsy**-rayveer*

**polish** *(for shoes)* die Schuhcreme *shoo*kray-me

**polluted** verschmutzt *fer-**shmootst***

**pony trekking** das Ponyreiten *poni-ryten*

**popular** beliebt *beleept*

**pork** das Schweinefleisch *shvine-e-flysh*

**port** *(seaport)* der Hafen *hahfen*; *(wine)* der Portwein *port-vine*

**porter** der Portier *portyay*; *(in station)* der Gepäckträger *ge**pek**-trayger*

**possible** möglich *mur'k-likh*

**post** aufgeben *owf-gayben*

**postbox** der Briefkasten *breef-kasten*
**postcard** die Ansichtskarte *anzikhts-kar-te*
**postcode** die Postleitzahl *post-lite-tsahl*
**post office** das Postamt *postamt*
**pot** *(for cooking)* der Topf *topf*
**potatoes** die Kartoffeln *kar-tofeln*
**pottery** die Tonwaren *tohn-vahren*
**pound** das Pfund *pfoont*
**powdered milk** das Milchpulver *milkh-poolfer*
**pram** der Kinderwagen *kinder-vahgen*
**prawn** die Garnele *garnay-le*
**prefer** vorziehen *for-tsee-en*
**pregnant** schwanger *shvanger*
**prepare** vorbereiten *for-bery-ten*
**prescription** das Rezept *raytsept*
**present** das Geschenk *geshenk*
**pretty** hübsch *hoopsh*
**price** der Preis *price*
**price list** die Preisliste *price-lis-te*
**priest** der Priester *preester*
**private** privat *preevaht*
**probably** wahrscheinlich *vahr-shine-likh*
**problem** das Problem *problem*
**programme** das Programm *program*
**pronounce** aussprechen *ows-shprekhen*; **how do you pronounce it?** wie spricht man das aus? *vee shprikht man das ows*
**Protestant** protestantisch *protes-tantish*
**public** öffentlich *ur'fent-likh*
**public holiday** der gesetzliche

Feiertag *gezets-li-khe fyer-tahk*
**pudding** der Pudding *pudding*
**pull** *(drag, draw)* ziehen *tsee-en*
**pullover** der Pullover *poo-lohver*
**puncture** die Reifenpanne *ryfen-pa-ne*
**purple** violett *vee-o-let*
**purse** der Geldbeutel *gelt-boytel*
**push** stoßen *shtoh-sen*
**put** *(insert)* einsetzen *ine-zetsen; (put down)* stellen *shtellen*
**pyjamas** der Pyjama *poo-jah-ma*

**queue** die Schlange *shlang-e*
**quick** schnell *shnel*
**quickly** schnell *shnel*
**quiet** ruhig *roo-ikh*
**quilt** die Bettdecke *bet-de-ke*
**quite** *(rather)* ziemlich *tseemlikh; (completely)* ganz *gants*

**rabbit** das Kaninchen *ka-neenkhen*
**racket** der Schläger *shlayger*
**radio** das Radio *rah-dyo*
**railway station** der Bahnhof *bahn-hohf*
**rain** der Regen *raygen*
**raincoat** der Regenmantel *raygen-mantel*
**raining: it's raining** es regnet *es raygnet*
**raisins** die Rosinen *rozee-nen*
**rare** *(unique)* selten *zelten; (steak)* blutig *blootikh*
**raspberries** die Himbeeren *him-bayren*
**rate** *(ratio)* die Rate *rah-te; (price)* der

Preis *price*; **rate of exchange** der Wechselkurs *veksel-koors*

**raw** roh *roh*

**razor** der Rasierapparat *razeer-apa-raht*

**razor blades** die Rasierklingen *razeer-klingen*

**ready** fertig *fertikh*

**real** echt *ekht*

**receipt** die Quittung *kvi-toong*

**recently** kürzlich *koorts-likh*

**reception** der Empfang *empfang*

**recipe** das Rezept *raytsept*

**recommend** empfehlen *emp-faylen*

**record** *(music)* die Schallplatte *shal-pla-te*

**red** rot *roht*

**reduction** die Ermäßigung *er-may-sigoong*

**refill** *(for pen)* die Ersatzmine *erzats-mee-ne*; *(for lighter)* die Nachfüllpatrone *nakh-fool-patrohne*

**refund** die Rückerstattung *rooker-shtattoong*

**registered** *(mail)* Einschreib-*ineshripe*

**regulation** die Regelung *ray-geloong*

**reimburse** entschädigen *ent-shay-digen*

**relation** *(family)* der/die Verwandte *fer-vant-te*

**reliable** *(person)* zuverläßig *tsoofer-lessikh*; *(secure, sound)* verläßlich *fer-leslikh*

**remain** bleiben *blyben*

**remember** sich erinnern *zikh er-innern*

**rent** mieten *meeten*

**rental** *(house)* die Miete *mee-te*

**repair** reparieren *raypa-reeren*

**repeat** wiederholen *veeder-hohlen*

**reservation** die Reservierung *ray-zer-veeroong*

**reserve** reservieren *ray-zer-veeren*

**reserved** reserviert *ray-zer-veert*

**rest**[1] *n* die Ruhe *roo-e*; **the rest of the wine** der Rest des Weins *der rest des vines*

**rest**[2] *vb* ruhen *roo-en*

**restaurant** das Restaurant *restoh-rong*

**restaurant car** der Speisewagen *shpy-ze-vahgen*

**return** *(go back)* zurückgehen *tsoorook-gayen*; *(give back)* zurückgeben *tsoorook-gayben*

**return ticket** die Rückfahrkarte *rookfar-kar-te*

**reverse charge call** das R-Gespräch *er-geshprekh*

**rheumatism** der Rheumatismus *royma-tismoos*

**rice** der Reis *rice*

**ride** *(horse)* reiten *ry-ten*; *(in car)* fahren *fah-ren*; **to go for a ride** *(on horse)* reiten gehen *ry-ten gayen*; *(in car)* eine Fahrt machen *ine-e fahrt makh-en*

**right**[1] *adj* richtig *rikhtikh*

**right**[2] *n* : **on the right** rechts *rekhts*; **to the right** nach rechts *nakh rekhts*

**ring** der Ring *ring*

**ripe** reif *rife*

**river** der Fluß *floos*

**road** *(route)* der Weg *vayk*; *(street)* die Straße *shtrah-se*

**road map** die Straßenkarte
*shtrahsen-kar-te*
**roast** Rost- *rost*
**roll** *(bread)* das Brötchen ***brur't**-khen*
**roof** das Dach *dakh*
**roof-rack** der Dachträger ***dakh**-trayger*
**room** *(in house, hotel)* das Zimmer
*tsimmer; (space)* der Platz *plats*
**room service** der Zimmerservice
*tsimmer-**zur**vis*
**rope** das Seil *zile*
**rosé** rosé *rozay*
**rough** rauh *row*
**round** rund *roont;* **round the corner**
um die Ecke *oom dee e ke*
**route** die Route *roo-te*
**rowing boat** das Ruderboot ***rooder**-boht*
**rubber** *(eraser)* der Radiergummi
*ra**deer**-goomee; (material)* das
Gummi ***goo**mee*
**rubber band** das Gummiband
***goo**mee-bant*
**rubbish** der Abfall *apfal*
**rucksack** der Rucksack ***rook**zak*
**ruin** der Ruin *roo-**een***
**rum** der Rum *room*
**run** *(skiing)* die Abfahrt *apfahrt*
**rush hour** die Hauptverkehrszeit
***howpt**-verkayrs-tsite*

**safe¹** *n* der Safe *sayf*
**safe²** *adj (not dangerous)*
ungefährlich ***oon**-gefayr-likh*
**safety pin** die Sicherheitsnadel *zikher-hites-nah-del*
**sailboard** das Segelbrett *zaygel-bret*

**sailing** *(sport)* das Segeln *zaygeln*
**salad** der Salat *zalaht*
**salad dressing** die Salatsoße
*zalaht-zoh-se*
**salmon** der Lachs *laks*
**salt** das Salz *zalts*
**same** gleich *glykh*
**sand** der Sand *zant*
**sandals** die Sandalen *zan-**dah**-len*
**sandwich** das Sandwich ***zant**-vich*
**sanitary towels** die Damenbinden
***dah**men-binden*
**sardine** die Sardine *zardee-ne*
**sauce** die Soße *zoh-se*
**saucepan** der Kochtopf ***kokh**topf*
**saucer** die Untertasse *oonter-ta-se*
**sauna** die Sauna *zowna*
**sausage** die Wurst *voorst*
**savoury** schmackhaft *shmakhaft*
**say** sagen *zahgen*
**scallop** die Jakobsmuschel *yahkops-mooshel*
**scampi** die Scampi *skampi*
**scarf** das Kopftuch ***kopf**-tookh; (for
neck)* das Halstuch ***hals**-tookh*
**school** die Schule *shoo-le*
**scissors** die Schere *shay-re*
**Scotland** Schottland ***shot**lant*
**Scottish** schottisch ***sho**-tish*
**screw** die Schraube *shrow-be*
**screwdriver** der Schraubenzieher
***shrow**ben-tsee-er*
**sculpture** die Skulptur *skoolp-**toor***
**sea** die See *zay*
**seafood** die Meeresfrüchte ***mayres**-frookh-te*
**seasickness** die Seekrankheit *zay-*

*krank-hite*

**season ticket** die Zeitkarte *tsite-kar-te*

**seat** *(chair)* der Sitz *zits; (in bus, train, theatre)* der Platz *plats*

**second** zweite(r/s) *tsvy-te(r/s)*

**second class** *(seat)* zweiter Klasse *tsvy-ter kla-se*

**see** sehen *zay-en*

**self-service** die Selbstbedienung *zelpst-bedee-noong*

**sell** verkaufen *fer-kowfen*

**Sellotape ®** der Tesafilm *teza-film*

**send** schicken *shicken*

**senior citizen** der Rentner *rentner*

**separate** *(apart)* getrennt *ge-trent; (different)* verschieden *fer-sheeden*

**serious** schlimm *shlim*

**serve** *(in shop etc)* bedienen *bedee-nen*

**service** die Bedienung *bedee-noong*

**service charge** die Bedienung *bedee-noong*

**set menu** die Tageskarte *tah-ges-kar-te*

**shade** *(of colour)* der Ton *tohn*

**shallow** seicht *zykht*

**shampoo** das Shampoo *shampoo*

**shandy** das Bier mit Limonade *beer mit leemo-nah-de*

**share** teilen *ty-len*

**shave** rasieren *razee-ren*

**shaving cream** die Rasiercreme *razeer-kray-me*

**she** sie *zee; see* GRAMMAR

**sheet** *(on bed)* das Bettuch *bet-tookh*

**shellfish** die Schaltiere *shal-tee-re*

**sherry** der Sherry *sherry*

**ship** das Schiff *shif*

**shirt** das Hemd *hemt*

**shock absorber** der Stoßdämpfer *shtohs-dempfer*

**shoe** der Schuh *shoo*

**shop** der Laden *lah-den*

**shopping: to go shopping** einkaufen gehen *ine-kowfen gayen*

**short** kurz *koorts*

**short cut** die Abkürzung *ap-koortsoong*

**shorts** die Shorts *shorts*

**show¹** *n* die Aufführung *owf-fooroong*

**show²** *vb* zeigen *tsy-gen*

**shower** *(bath)* die Dusche *doo-she*

**shrimp** die Garnele *garnay-le*

**sick** *(ill)* krank *krank*

**sightseeing** die Besichtigungen *bezikh-ti-goongen*

**sign** das Schild *shilt*

**signature** die Unterschrift *oonter-shrift*

**silk** die Seide *zy-de*

**silver** silber *zilber*

**similar** ähnlich *ayn-likh*

**simple** einfach *ine-fakh*

**single** *(unmarried)* ledig *laydikh; (not double)* Einzel- *ine-tsel; (ticket)* einfach *ine-fakh*

**single bed** das Einzelbett *ine-tsel-bett*

**single room** das Einzelzimer *ine-tsel-tsimmer*

**sir** mein Herr *mine hayr*

**sister** die Schwester *shvester*

**sit** sitzen *zitsen*

**size** die Größe *grur'-se*

**skates** die Schlittschuhe *shlitt*shoo-e
**skating** der Eislauf *ice*-lowf
**ski**[1] *vb* skifahren *shee-fahren*
**ski**[2] *n* der Ski *shee*
**ski boot** der Skistiefel *shee-shteefel*
**skiing** das Skilaufen *shee-lowfen*
**ski jacket** die Skijacke *shee-ya-ke*
**skimmed milk** die Magermilch *mahger-mılkh*
**skin** die Haut *howt*
**skin diving** das Tauchen *tow-khen*
**ski pants** dle Skihose *shee-hoh-ze*
**ski pole** der Skistock *shee*shtock
**skirt** der Rock *rock*
**ski run** die Abfahrt *ap-fahrt*
**ski suit** der Skianzug *shee*an-tsook
**sledge** der Schlitten *shlitten*
**sleep** schlafen *shlahfen*
**sleeper** (*berth*) der Schlafwagenplatz *shlahf-vahgen-plats*
**sleeping bag** der Schlafsack *shlahf-zak*
**sleeping car** der Schlafwagen *shlahf-vahgen*
**sleeping pills** die Schlaftabletten *shlahf-ta-ble-ten*
**slice** die Scheibe *shy-be*
**slide** (*photograph*) das Dia *dee-a*
**slow** langsam *langzam*
**small** klein *kline*
**smaller** kleiner *kline-er*
**smell** der Geruch *gerookh*; (*unpleasant*) der Gestank *ge-shtank*
**smoke**[1] *n* der Rauch *rowkh*
**smoke**[2] *vb* rauchen *row-khen*
**smoked** geräuchert *ge-roy-khert*
**snack bar** die Snack Bar *snack bar*

**snorkel** der Schnorchel *shnor-khel*
**snow** die Schnee *shnay*
**snowed up** eingeschneit *ine-geshnite*
**snowing: it's snowing** es schneit *es shnite*
**snowplough** der Schneepflug *shnay-pflook*
**so: so much** soviel *zoh-feel*
**soap** die Seife *zy-fe*
**soap powder** das Seifenpulver *zy-fen-poolfer*
**sober** nüchtern *nookh-tern*
**socket** (*electrical*) die Steckdose *shtek-doh-ze*
**socks** die Socken *zocken*
**soda** das Soda *zoh-da*
**soft** weich *vykh*
**soft drink** das alkoholfreie Getränk *al-kohol-fry-e getrenk*
**some** einige *eye-ni-ge*
**someone** irgendjemand *irgent-yaymant*
**something** etwas *etvas*
**sometimes** manchmal *mankh-mal*
**son** der Sohn *zohn*
**song** das Lied *leet*
**soon** bald *balt*
**sore** weh *vay*; **I have a sore throat** ich habe Halsschmerzen *ikh hah-be hals-shmertsen*
**sorry: I'm sorry!** tut mir leid! *toot meer lite*
**sort** die Art *art*; **what sort of cheese?** was für ein Käse? *vas foor ine kay-ze*
**soup** die Suppe *zoo-pe*
**south** der Süden *zooden*

**souvenir** das Souvenir *zoo-ve**neer***

**space: parking space** der Parkplatz *park-plats*

**spade** der Spaten *shpah-ten*

**spanner** der Schraubenschlüssel *shrowben-shloo-sel*

**spare wheel** der Ersatzreifen *erzats-ry-fen*

**sparkling** perlend *perlent*

**spark plugs** die Zündkerzen *tsoont-kertsen*

**speak** sprechen *shpre-khen*

**special** besondere *bezon-de-re*

**speciality** die Spezialität *shpe-tsee-ali-tayt*

**speed** die Geschwindigkeit *geshvin-dikh-kite*

**speed limit** die Geschwindigkeitsbegrenzung *geshvin-dikh-kites-be-gren-tsoong*

**spell: how do you spell it?** wie buchstabiert man das? *vee bookh-shtabeert man das*

**spicy** würzig *voort-sikh*

**spirits** die Spirituosen *shpee-ree-too-ohzen*

**sponge** der Schwamm *shvam*

**spoon** der Löffel *lur'-fel*

**sport** der Sport *shport*

**spring** *(season)* der Frühling *frooling*

**square** *(in town)* der Platz *plats*

**squash** *(game, drink)* das Squash *squash*

**stairs** die Treppe *tre-pe*

**stalls** *(in theatre)* das Parkett *parket*

**stamp** die Briefmarke *breef-mar-ke*

**start** *(begin)* anfangen *an-fangen*

**starter** die Vorspeise *for-shpy-ze*; *(in car)* der Anlasser *an-lasser*

**station** der Bahnhof *bahn-hohf*

**stationer's** die Schreibwaren-handlung *shripe-vahren-hantloong*

**stay** bleiben *bly-ben*; **I'm staying at a hotel** ich wohne in ein Hotel *ikh voh-ne in ine ho-tel*

**steak** das Steak *stayk*

**steep** steil *shtile*

**sterling: pounds sterling** Pfund Sterling *pfoont shterling*

**stew** das Eintopfgericht *ine-topf-gerikht*

**steward** *(on plane)* der Steward *styoo-art*

**stewardess** die Stewardeß *styoo-ardess*

**sticking plaster** das Heftpflaster *heft-pflaster*

**still** *(motionless)* still *shtil*

**sting** der Stachel *shtakh-el*

**stockings** die Strümpfe *shtroomp-fe*

**stomach** der Magen *mahgen*

**stomach upset** der verdorbene Magen *fer-dor-be-ne mahgen*

**stop** halten *halten*

**stopover** die Zwischenlandung *tsvishen-landoong*

**storm** der Sturm *shtoorm*

**straight on** geradeaus *gerah-de-ows*

**straw** *(for drinking)* der Strohhalm *shtroh-halm*

**strawberries** die Erdbeeren *ert-bayren*

**street** die Straße *shtrah-se*

**street map** der Stadtplan *shtat-plan*

**string** die Schnur *shnoor*

**strong** stark *shtark*

**stuck: it's stuck** *(jammed)* es klemmt es klemt

**student** *(male)* der Student *shtoo-dent; (female)* die Studentin *shtoo-dentin*

**stung** gestochen *ge-shto-khen*

**stupid** dumm *doom*

**suddenly** plotzlich *plur'ts-likh*

**suede** das Wildleder *vilt-layder*

**sugar** der Zucker *tsooker*

**suit** *(man's)* der Anzug *an-tsook; (woman's)* das Kostüm *kos-toom*

**suitcase** der Koffer *koffer*

**summer** der Sommer *zommer*

**sun** die Sonne *zon-ne*

**sunbathe** sonnenbaden *zonnen-bahden*

**sunburn** der Sonnenbrand *zonnen-brant*

**sunglasses** die Sonnenbrille *zonnen-bri-le*

**sunny** sonnig *zonnikh*

**sunshade** der Sonnenschirm *zonnen-shirm*

**sunstroke** der Sonnenstich *zonnen-shtikh*

**suntan lotion** das Sonnenöl *zonnen-ur'l*

**supermarket** der Supermarkt *zooper-markt*

**supper** das Abendessen *ahbent-essen*

**supplement** die Ergänzung *er-gentsoong*

**sure** *(definite)* bestimmt *beshtimt*

**surface mail** die Post auf dem Land-/Seeweg *post owf daym lant-/zayvayk*

**surfboard** das Surfboard *zoorf-bohrt*

**surfing** das Surfen *zoor-fen*

**surname** der Nachname *nakh-nah-me*

**suspension** *(in car)* die Federung *fay-deroong*

**sweater** der Pullover *poo-lohver*

**sweet** süß *zoos*

**sweetener** der Süßstoff *zoos-shtoff*

**sweets** die Süßigkeiten *zoosikh-kite-en*

**swim** schwimmen *shvimmen*

**swimming pool** das Schwimmbad *shvimbaht*

**swimsuit** der Badeanzug *bah-de-antsook*

**Swiss** schweizerisch *shvites-erish*

**switch** der Schalter *shalter*

**switch off** *(light)* ausschalten *ows-shalten; (machine)* abschalten *ap-shalten; (gas, water)* abstellen *ap-shtellen*

**switch on** *(light, machine)* einschalten *ine-shalten; (gas, water)* anstellen *an-shtellen*

**Switzerland** die Schweiz *shvites*

**synagogue** die Synagoge *zoona-goh-ge*

**table** der Tisch *tish*

**tablecloth** die Tischdecke *tish-de-ke*

**tablespoon** der Eßlöffel *ess-lur'fel*

**tablet** die Tablette *ta-ble-te*

**table tennis** das Tischtennis *tish-tennis*

**take** nehmen *naymen*; **how long**

**does the journey take?** wie lange dauert die Reise? *vee lang-e dow-ert dee ry-ze*

**talc** der Körperpuder *kurper-pooder*

**talk** sprechen *shprekhen*

**tall** groß *grohs*

**tampons** die Tampons *tampons*

**tape-recorder** das Tonbandgerät *tohnbant-gerayt*

**tartar sauce** die Remouladensauce *remoo-lahden-zoh-se*

**taste**[1] *vb* probieren *probeer-en*

**taste**[2] *n* der Geschmack *geshmak*

**tax** die Steuer *shtoy-er*

**taxi** das Taxi *taxi*

**taxi rank** der Taxistand *taxi-shtant*

**tea** der Tee *tay*

**tea bag** der Teebeutel *tay-boytel*

**teach** unterrichten *oonter-rikhten*

**teacher** *(male)* der Lehrer *layrer*; *(female)* die Lehrerin *lay-rerin*

**teapot** die Teekanne *tayka-ne*

**teaspoon** der Teelöffel *tay-lur'fel*

**teat** die Brustwarze *broost-vart-se*; *(on bottle)* der Sauger *zowger*

**teeshirt** das T-shirt *tee-shirt*

**teeth** die Zähne *tsay-ne*

**telegram** das Telegramm *taylay-gram*

**telephone** das Telefon *taylay-fohn*

**telephone box** die Telefonzelle *taylay-fohn-tse-le*

**telephone call** der Anruf *anroof*

**telephone directory** das Telefonbuch *taylay-fohn-bookh*

**television** das Fernsehen *fern-zayen*

**television set** der Fernsehapparat *fern-zay-aparaht*

**telex** das Telex *taylex*

**tell** erzählen *er-tsaylen*

**temperature** die Temperatur *tempe-ratoor*; **to have a temperature** Fieber haben *feeber hah-ben*

**temporary** provisorisch *provi-zorish*

**tennis** das Tennis *tennis*

**tennis court** der Tennisplatz *tennis-plats*

**tennis racket** der Tennisschläger *tennis-shlayger*

**tent** das Zelt *tselt*

**tent peg** der Hering *hayring*

**terminus** die Endstation *ent-shtatsyohn*

**terrace** die Terrasse *tay-ra-se*

**than: better than this** besser als das *besser als das*

**thank you** danke *dang-ke*; **thank you very much** vielen Dank *fee-len dank*

**that** das *das*; **that one** das dort *das dort*

**theatre** das Theater *tay-ahter*

**then** dann *dan*

**there** dort *dort*; **there is/there are** es gibt *es gipt*

**thermometer** das Thermometer *termo-mayter*

**these** diese *dee-ze*

**they** sie *zee*; *see* GRAMMAR

**thief** der Dieb *deep*

**thing: my things** meine Sachen *mine-e zakh-en*

**think** denken *denken*

**third** dritte(r/s) *dri-te(r/s)*

**thirsty: I'm thirsty** ich habe Durst *ikh hah-be doorst*

**this** dies *dees*; **this one** das hier *das heer*

**those** jene *yay-ne*

**thread** der Faden *fahden*

**throat** die Kehle *kay-le*

**throat lozenges** die Halspastillen *hals-pas-tillen*

**through** durch *doorkh*

**thunderstorm** das Gewitter *gevll-ter*

**ticket** die Karte *kar-te*

**ticket collector** der Schaffner *shaf-ner*

**ticket office** der Fahrkartenschalter *far-karten-shalter*

**tide** die Gezeiten *getsite-ten*

**tie** die Krawatte *krava-te*

**tights** die Strumpfhose *shtroompf-hoh-ze*

**till**[1] *n* die Kasse *ka-se*

**till**[2] *prep* bis *bis*

**time** die Zeit *tsite*; **this time** diesmal *deesmal*

**timetable board** der Fahrplan *farplan*

**tin** die Dose *doh-ze*

**tinfoil** die Alufolie *ahloo-foh-lee-e*

**tin-opener** der Dosenöffner *dohzen-ur'fner*

**tip** *(to waiter etc)* das Trinkgeld *trink-gelt*

**tipped** *(cigarettes)* Filter- *filter*

**tired** müde *moo-de*

**tissues** die Papiertaschentücher *papeer-tashen-too-kher*

**to** zu *tsoo*; *(with names of places)* nach *nakh*

**toast** der Toast *toast*

**tobacco** der Tabak *tabak*

**tobacconist** die Tabakwarenhandlung *tabak-vahren-hantloong*

**today** heute *hoy-te*

**together** zusammen *tsoo-zamen*

**toilet** die Toilette *twa-le-te*

**toilet paper** das Toilettenpapier *twa-le-ten-papeer*

**toll** die Maut *mowt*

**tomato** die Tomate *tomah-te*

**tomato juice** der Tomatensaft *tomah-ten-zaft*

**tomorrow** morgen *morgen*

**tongue** die Zunge *tsoong-e*

**tonic water** das Tonic *tonic*

**tonight** heute abend *hoy-te ahbent*

**too** *(also)* auch *owkh*; **it's too big** es ist zu groß *es ist tsoo grohs*

**tooth** der Zahn *tsahn*

**toothache: I have toothache** ich habe Zahnschmerzen *ikh hah-be tsahn-shmertsen*

**toothbrush** die Zahnbürste *tsahn-boor-ste*

**toothpaste** die Zahnpasta *tsahn-pasta*

**top**[1] *adj* : **the top floor** das oberste Stockwerk *das ohber-ste shtokverk*

**top**[2] *n* *(of mountain)* der Gipfel *gipfel*; *(lid)* der Deckel *dekel*; *(surface)* die Oberfläche *ohber-fle-khe*; **on top of...** oben auf *oh-ben owf*

**torch** die Taschenlampe *tashen-lam-pe*

**torn** zerrissen *tser-rissen*

**total** die Endsumme *ent-zoom-e*

**tough** *(meat)* zäh *tsay*

**tour** die Fahrt *fart*

# WORDS

**tourist** der Tourist *toorist*

**tourist office** das Fremdenverkehrsbüro *fremden-ver kayrs-booroh*

**tourist ticket** die Touristenkarte *tooris-ten-kar-te*

**tow** *(car, boot)* abschleppen *ap-shleppen*

**towel** das Handtuch *hant-tookh*

**town** die Stadt *shtat*

**town centre** das Stadtzentrum *shtat-tsentroom*

**town plan** der Stadtplan *shtat-plan*

**tow rope** das Abschleppseil *apshlep-zile*

**toy** das Spielzeug *shpeel-tsoyk*

**traditional** traditionell *tradeet-syonel*

**traffic** der Verkehr *ferkayr*

**trailer** der Anhänger *anheng-er*

**train** der Zug *tsook*

**training shoes** die Trainingsschuhe *training sshoo-e*

**tram** die Straßenbahn *shtrah-sen-bahn*

**translate** übersetzen *oober-zetsen*

**translation** die Übersetzung *oober-zetsoong*

**travel** reisen *ry-zen*

**travel agent** das Reisebüro *ry-ze-booroh*

**traveller's cheques** die Reisechecks *ry-ze-sheks*

**tray** das Tablett *tablet*

**trim** nachschneiden *nakh-shnyden*

**trip** der Ausflug *owsflook*

**trouble** die Schwierigkeiten *shveerikh-kiten*

**trousers** die Hose *hoh-ze*

**true** wahr *vahr*

**trunk** der Überseekoffer *oober-zay-koffer*

**trunks** die Badehose *bah-de-hoh-ze*

**try** versuchen *fer-zookhen*

**try on** anprobieren *anpro-beeren*

**T-shirt** das T-shirt *tee-shirt*

**tuna** der Thunfisch *toonfish*

**tunnel** der Tunnel *toonel*

**turkey** der Truthahn *troothahn*

**turn** *(rotate)* drehen *drayen*

**turnip** die Rübe *roo-be*

**turn off** *(light)* ausmachen *ows-makhen*; *(tap)* zudrehen *tsoo-drayen*

**turn on** *(light)* anmachen *an-makhen*; *(tap)* aufdrehen *owf-drayen*

**tweezers** die Pinzette *pin-tse-te*

**twice** zweimal *tsvy-mal*

**twin-bedded room** das Zweibettzimmer *tsvy-bet-tsimmer*

**typical** typisch *toopish*

**tyre** der Reifen *ry-fen*

**tyre pressure** der Reifendruck *ry-fen-drook*

**umbrella** der Regenschirm *raygen-shirm*

**uncomfortable** unbequem *oon-bekvaym*

**unconscious** bewußtlos *bevoost-lohs*

**under** unter *oonter*

**underground** die U-Bahn *oo-bahn*

**underpass** die Unterführung *oonter-fooroong*

**understand** verstehen *fer-shtay-en*; **I don't understand** ich verstehe nicht

*ikh fer-**shtay**-e nikht*
**underwear** die Unterwäsche *oonter-ve-she*
**United States** die Vereinigten Staaten *fer-ine-ikh-ten shtahten*
**university** die Universität *oonee-verzee-tayt*
**up** auf *owf;* **up there** dort oben *dort ohben*
**upstairs** oben *ohben*
**urgent** dringend *dringent*
**USA** die USA *oo-es ah*
**use** benützen *benoot-sen*
**useful** nützlich *noots-likh*
**usual** gewöhnlich *gevur'n-likh*
**usually** gewöhnlich *gevur'n-likh*

**vacancies** Zimmer frei *tsimmer fry*
**vacuum cleaner** der Staubsauger *shtowp-zowger*
**valid** gültig *gooltikh*
**valley** das Tal *tahl*
**valuable** wertvoll *vertfol*
**valuables** die Wertsachen *vert-zakhen*
**van** der Lieferwagen *leefer-vahgen*
**vase** die Vase *vah-ze*
**VAT** die Mehrwertsteuer *mayrvert-shtoyer*
**veal** das Kalbfleisch *kalp-flysh*
**vegetables** das Gemüse *gemoo-ze*
**vegetarian** vegetarisch *vaygay-tarish*
**ventilator** der Ventilator *ventee-lahtor*
**vermouth** der Wermut *vermoot*
**very** sehr *zayr*
**vest** das Unterhemd *oonter-hemt*

**via** über *oober*
**video** das Video *veeday-o*
**view** die Aussicht *owszikht*
**villa** die Villa *villa*
**village** das Dorf *dorf*
**vinegar** der Essig *essikh*
**vineyard** der Weinberg *vineberk*
**visa** das Visum *veezoom*
**visit** besuchen *bezoo-khen*
**vitamin** das Vitamin *veetameen*
**vodka** der Wodka *vodka*
**voltage** das Volt *volt*

**waist** die Taille *tal-ye*
**wait (for)** warten (auf) *var-ten owf*
**waiter** der Ober *ohber*
**waiting room** der Warteraum *var-te-rowm*
**waitress** die Kellnerin *kel-nerin*
**wake up** aufwachen *owf-vakhen*
**Wales** Wales *wayls*
**walk¹** *vb* spazierengehen *shpat-seeren-gayen*
**walk²** *n* : **to go for a walk** einen Spaziergang machen *ine-en shpat-seergang makhen*
**wallet** die Brieftasche *breef-ta-she*
**walnut** die Walnuß *valnoos*
**want** wollen *vollen*
**warm** warm *varm*
**warning triangle** das Warndreieck *varndry-ek*
**wash** waschen *vashen;* **to wash oneself** sich waschen *zikh vashen*
**washbasin** das Waschbecken *vash-becken*
**washing machine** die

Waschmaschine **vash**-ma**shee**-ne

**washing powder** das Waschpulver **vash**-poolfer

**washing-up liquid** das Spülmittel **shpool**-mittel

**wasp** die Wespe **ves**-pe

**waste bin** der Abfalleimer **apfal**-ime-er

**watch**¹ n die Armbanduhr **armbant**-oor

**watch**² vb zuschauen **tsoo**-showen

**water** das Wasser **vasser**

**water heater** das Heißwassergerät **hice**-vasser-ge**rayt**

**water melon** die Wassermelone **vasser**-me**loh**-ne

**waterproof** wasserdicht **vasser**-dikht

**water-skiing** das Wasserskilaufen **vasser**-shee-**lowfen**

**wax** das Wachs **vaks**

**way** (means) die Weise **vy**-ze; (direction) der Weg **vayk**; **which is the way to ...?** wie kommt man zu ...? **vee komt man tsoo**

**we** wir **veer**; see GRAMMAR

**weak** schwach **shvakh**; (coffee) dünn **doon**

**wear** tragen **trahgen**

**weather** das Wetter **vetter**

**wedding** die Hochzeit **hokh**-tsite

**week** die Woche **vo**-khe

**weekday** der Werktag **verk**-tahk

**weekend** das Wochenende **vokhen**-en-de

**weekly rate** die Wochenrate **vokhen**-**rah**-te

**weight** das Gewicht ge**vikht**

**welcome** willkommen **vil**-kommen

**well** gut **goot**; **he's not well** ihm geht's nicht gut **eem gayts nikht goot**

**well done** (steak) durch **doorkh**

**Welsh** walisisch va-**leez**ish

**west** der Westen **vesten**

**wet** naß **nas**

**wetsuit** der Taucheranzug **towkher**-ant**sook**

**what** was **vas**; **what is it?** was ist das? **vas ist das**

**wheel** das Rad **rat**

**wheelchair** der Rollstuhl **rolshtool**

**when** wann **van**

**where** wo **voh**

**which: which man?** welcher Mann? **vel**-kher man; **which woman?** welche Frau? **vel**-khe **frow**; **which book?** welches Buch? **vel**-khes **bookh**

**while**¹ conj während **vay**rent

**while**² n : **in a while** bald **balt**

**whisky** der Whisky **viski**

**white** weiß **vice**

**who: who is it?** wer ist es? **vayr ist es**

**whole** vollständig **fol**-shtendikh

**wholemeal bread** das Vollkornbrot **folkorn**-broht

**whose: whose is it?** wem gehört es? **vaym gehurt es**

**why** warum va**hroom**

**wide** weit **vite**

**wife** die Frau **frow**

**window** das Fenster **fenster**; (of shop) das Schaufenster **show**-fenster

**windscreen** die Windschutz-scheibe **vint**shoots-shy-be

**windsurfing** das Surfen **zoorfen**

**wine** der Wein *vine*
**wine list** die Weinkarte *vinekar-te*
**winter** der Winter *vinter*
**with** mit *mit*
**without** ohne *oh-ne*
**woman** die Frau *frow*
**wood** *(material)* das Holz *holts*;
  *(forest)* der Wald *valt*
**wool** die Wolle *vo-le*
**word** das Wort *vort*
**work** *(person)* arbeiten *arby-ten*;
  *(machine)* funktionieren *toonk-
  tsyoh-nee-ren*
**worried** besorgt *bezorkt*
**worse** schlimmer *shlimmer*
**worth: it's worth £100** es ist £100
  wert *es ist hoondert ptoont vert*
**wrap (up)** einwickeln *ine-vikeln*
**wrapping paper** das Packpapier
  *pakpa-peer*
**write** schreiben *shry-ben*
**writing paper** das Briefpapier
  *breef-papeer*
**wrong** falsch *falsh*

**yacht** die Yacht *yakht*
**year** das Jahr *yahr*
**yellow** gelb *gelp*
**yes** ja *ya*; **yes please** (ja,) bitte *(ya,)
  bi-te*
**yesterday** gestern *gestern*
**yet: not yet** noch nicht *nokh nikht*
**yoghurt** der Joghurt *yoh-goort*
**you** Sie *zee*; *(with friends)* du *doo*;
  *(plural)* ihr *eer*; *see* GRAMMAR
**young** jung *yoong*
**youth hostel** die Jugendherberge
  *yoogent-herber-ge*

**zero** null *nool*
**zip** der Reißverschluß *rice-fer-shloos*
**zoo** der Zoo *tsoh*

**Aal** *m* eel; **Aal Grün mit Dillsauce** fresh eel with dill sauce

**Aalsuppe** *f* eel soup

**ab** off; from; **ab 8 Uhr** from 8 o'clock; **ab Mai** from May onward; **Jugendliche ab 16 Jahren** children from (the age of) 16 up

**abbestellen** to cancel

**Abbiegerspur** *f* filter lane

**Abbildung** *f* illustration

**abblenden** to dip *(headlights)*

**Abblendlicht** *nt* dipped headlights

**Abend** *m* evening

**Abendessen** *nt* dinner

**Abendkasse** *f* box office

**abends** in the evening(s)

**aber** but

**abfahren** to pull out; to leave

**Abfahrt** *f* departure

**Abfahrtszeit** *f* departure time

**Abfall** *m* rubbish

**Abfalleimer** *m* dustbin

**Abfertigung** *f* handling service

**Abfertigungsschalter** *m* check-in desk

**abfliegen** to take off *(plane)*

**Abflug** *m* takeoff; departure; **Abflug Inland** national departures; **Abflug Ausland** international departures

**Abflughalle** *f* departure lounge

**Abflugschalter** *m* check-in desk

**Abflugtafel** *m* departure board

**Abflugzeit** *f* departure time

**Abführmittel** *nt* laxative

**abgelaufen** out-of-date

**abheben** to withdraw *(money)*

**abholen** to fetch; to claim *(lost property, baggage)*; **abholen lassen** to

send for

**ablaufen** to expire

**abmelden: sich abmelden** to check out

**Abonnent** *m* subscriber

**Abreise** *f* departure

**abreisen** to depart; to set out

**absagen** to cancel

**abschalten** to switch off

**abschicken** to dispatch

**Abschleppdienst** *m* breakdown service

**abschleppen** to tow; **Fahrzeug wird abgeschleppt** on tow

**Abschleppöse** *f* towing fixture

**Abschleppseil** *nt* towrope

**Abschleppstange** *f* tow bar

**Abschleppwagen** *m* breakdown van

**abschließen** to lock

**Abschmierdienst** *m* lubrication service

**Abschnitt** *m* counterfoil

**Absender** *m* sender

**Abstand** *m* distance; interval *(time)*; **Abstand halten!** keep your distance

**abstellen** to turn off; to park *(car)*

**Abtei** *f* abbey

**Abteil** *nt* compartment *(on train)*

**Abwesenheit** *f* absence

**Abzug(-züge)** *m* print(s)

**abzüglich** minus, less

**Achse** *f* axle

**acht** eight

**achten: achten auf** to pay attention to

**Achtung** *f* attention; danger; **Achtung, Achtung eine Durchsage**

your attention, please!; **Achtung Lebensgefahr!** danger; **Achtung Stufe!** mind the step

**Ackersalat** *m* corn salad; lamb's lettuce

**Adreßbuch** *nt* directory

**Adresse** *f* address

**adressieren** to address *(letter)*

**Alarmanlage** *f* alarm

**Alkohol** *m* liquor; alcohol

**alkoholfrei** nonalcoholic

**alkoholisch** alcoholic *(drink)*

**alle** all *(plural)*; everybody; everyone; **alle zwei Tage** every other day

**Allee** *f* avenue

**allein** alone

**allergisch: allergisch gegen** allergic to

**Allerheiligen** *nt* All Saints' Day

**alle(r/s)** all *(with singular noun)*

**alles** everything; all *(singular)*

**allgemein** general; universal

**Allzweckreiniger** *m* all-purpose cleaner

**Alpen** *pl* Alps

**als** than; when *(with past tense)*

**Alsterwasser** *nt* shandy

**alt** old

**Altbier** *nt* top-fermented dark beer

**Alter** *nt* age *(of person)*

**ältere(r/s)** older; elder

**älteste(r/s)** oldest; eldest

**Alufolie** *f* foil *(for food)*

**am: am Bahnhof** at the station; **am Abend/Morgen** in the evening/ morning; **am Freitag** on Friday

**Ampel** *f* traffic light

**Amt** *nt* department; office; authority; operator *(telephone)*

**amtlich** official

**Amtszeichen** *nt* dialling tone

**Amüsierviertel** *nt* nightclub district

**an** at; on; near; **Frankfurt an 1300** arriving Frankfurt 13.00; **an/aus** on/off

**Ananas(se)** *f* pineapple(s)

**Anbau** *m* extension *(building)*

**anbieten** to offer

**Andenken** *nt* souvenir

**andere(r/s)** other; **andere Richtungen** other destinations

**ändern** to change *(alter)*

**anders** differently; else

**anderthalb** one and a half

**Änderung** *f* change

**Anfang** *m* start *(beginning)*

**anfangen** to begin

**Anfänger** *m* beginner

**Anflug** *m* approach *(of plane)*

**anfordern** to demand

**Anfrage** *f* enquiry

**Angaben** *pl* details; directions *(to a place)*; **technische Angaben** specifications; **Angaben machen** to make a statement; **nähere Angaben** particulars

**angeben** to give; **genau angeben** to specify

**Angebot** *nt* offer

**Angehörige(r)** *m/f* relative; **der nächste Angehörige** the next of kin

**Angelegenheit** *f* affair *(matter)*

**Angeln** *nt* fishing, angling

**Angelschein** *m* fishing permit

**angenehm** pleasant

**Angestellte(r)** m/f employee

**angezeigt: angezeigter Betrag** m amount indicated

**anhalten** to stop

**Anhalter** m hitchhiker; **per Anhalter fahren** to hitchhike

**Anhänger** m trailer; label; pendant

**Anis** m aniseed

**Anker** m anchor

**Ankleidekabine** f changing cubicle

**ankommen** to arrive

**ankreuzen** to mark with a cross

**ankündigen** to announce

**Ankunft(-künfte)** f arrival(s)

**Anlage** f park; grounds; facilities; **öffentliche Anlagen** public park

**Anlegeplatz** m dock; berth

**Anlegestelle** f landing stage; jetty

**Anlieferungsgebühr** f delivery charge

**Anlieger** m : **Anlieger frei** except for access

**anmachen** to toss (salad); **das Licht anmachen** to put on the light

**anmelden: sich anmelden** to check in (at hotel)

**Anmeldung** f registration; appointment; reception (place)

**Annahme** f acceptance; reception

**annehmen** to assume; to accept

**Annehmlichkeiten** pl amenities

**annulieren** to cancel

**anprobieren** to try on (clothes)

**Anruf** m phone call

**Anrufbeantworter** m telephone answering device

**anrufen** to telephone

**Anschluß** m connection (train etc);

**dieser Zug hat Anschluß an den 1645** this train connects with the 16.45; **kein Anschluß unter dieser Nummer** number unobtainable; **elektrischer Anschluß** electric outlet

**Anschlußflug** m connecting flight

**anschnallen: sich anschnallen** to fasten one's seat belt

**Anschrift** f address

**Ansicht** f view

**Ansichtskarte(n)** f picture postcard(s)

**anstatt** instead of

**ansteckend** infectious

**anstrengend** strenuous; tiring

**Anteil** m share (part)

**Antenne** f aerial

**Antibiotikum** nt antibiotic

**Antihistamin** nt antihistamine

**Antiquariat** nt second-hand bookshop

**Antiquität(en)** f antique(s)

**Antiquitätenhändler** m antique dealer

**Antritt** m : **vor Antritt der Reise/Fahrt** before starting the journey

**Antwort** f answer; reply

**An- und Verkauf** m 'we buy and sell'; ≈ second-hand shop

**Anweisungen** pl instructions

**anwenden** to use; to apply

**Anzahl** f number

**Anzahlung** f deposit

**Anzeige** f advertisement; notice (poster); report (to police)

**Anzug(-züge)** m suit(s)

**anzünden** to light (fire, cigarette)

**Anzünder** m lighter

**Apfel (Äpfel)** m apple(s)

**Apfelkorn** m (corn) schnapps made from apples

**Apfelkuchen** m apple cake

**Apfelmus** nt apple purée

**Apfelrösti** pl slices of apple and bread fried in butter

**Apfelsaft** m apple juice

**Apfelsine(n)** f orange(s)

**Apfelwein** m cider

**Apotheke** f chemist's shop

**apothekenpflichtig** available only from chemists

**Apparat** m appliance; camera; set

**Aprikose(n)** f apricot(s)

**April** m April

**Arbeit** f labour; employment; work

**arbeitslos** unemployed

**Armaturenbrett** nt dash(board)

**Armband(-bänder)** nt bracelet(s)

**Armbanduhr** f watch

**Ärmel** m sleeve

**Ärmelkanal** m Channel

**Art** f type; sort; manner

**Artikel** m article; item

**Artischocke** f globe artichoke

**Artischockenboden** m artichoke base

**Artischockenherz** nt artichoke heart

**Arznei** f medicine

**Arzt (Ärzte)** m doctor(s); **der Arzt für Allgemeinmedizin** general practitioner; G.P.

**Aschenbecher** m ashtray

**Aschermittwoch** m Ash Wednesday

**atmen** to breathe

**auch** also; too; as well

**auf** onto; on; upon; on top of; **auf deutsch** in German

**aufbewahren** to keep

**aufblasbar** inflatable

**Aufenthalt** m stay; visit

**Aufenthaltsgenehmigung** f residence permit

**Aufenthaltsraum** m day room; lounge

**Auffahrt** f slip-road

**Aufführung** f performance

**aufgeben** to quit; to register (baggage); to check in

**aufhalten** to delay; to hold up; **sich aufhalten** to stay

**Auflauf** m soufflé

**auflegen** to hang up (phone)

**aufmachen** to open (shop, bank); **sich aufmachen** to set off

**Aufnahme** f reception; photograph

**aufpassen** to pay attention

**aufpumpen** to pump up; to inflate

**Aufruf** m : **letzter Aufruf** last call (for flight)

**aufschließen** to unlock

**Aufschnitt** m cold meat; assorted cheese

**aufschreiben** to write down

**Aufschub** m delay

**Aufstieg** m ascent

**Aufzug** m lift

**Auge(n)** nt eye(s)

**Augenblick** m moment; instant; point (in time); **einen Augenblick!** hold on! (on phone)

**Augenbraue(n)** f eyebrow(s)

**Augentropfen** pl eye drops

**August** m August
**Auktion** f auction
**aus** off *(machine, light)*; from; out of
**Ausdruck** m expression; printout; term *(word)*
**auseinander** apart
**Ausfahrt** f exit; **Ausfahrt freihalten** keep clear
**Ausfall** m failure *(mechanical)*
**Ausflug(-flüge)** m trip(s)
**Ausfuhr** f export(s)
**ausführen** to export; to carry out *(job)*
**ausführlich** in detail; detailed
**ausfüllen** to fill in; **bitte nicht ausfüllen** please leave blank
**Ausgabe** f issue *(of magazine)*; issuing counter
**Ausgaben** pl expenditure; expenses
**Ausgang** m exit; gate *(at airport)*
**ausgeben** to spend *(money)*
**ausgeschaltet** off *(radio)*
**ausgeschlossen** impossible
**ausgestellt** issued *(passport)*
**ausgewiesen: ausgewiesen durch** means of identification
**Ausgrabungen** pl excavations
**Auskunft** f information; information desk
**Ausland** nt foreign countries; abroad; **aus dem Ausland** overseas
**Ausländer(in)** m(f) foreigner
**ausländisch** foreign
**Auslandsbrief(e)** m overseas letter(s)
**Auslandsgespräch(e)** nt international call(s)
**auslassen** to leave out; to miss out

**auslaufen** to sail *(ship)*
**Auslöser** m shutter (release)
**ausmachen** to put out *(light)*
**Ausnahme(n)** f exception(s)
**Auspuff** m exhaust pipe
**Ausreise** f: **bei der Ausreise** on leaving the country
**Ausreisegenehmigung** f exit permit
**ausrufen: ausrufen lassen** to page
**Ausrüstung** f kit; equipment
**ausschalten** to switch off
**Ausschank** m bar; serving of drinks
**Ausschlag** m rash
**ausschließlich** exclusive of
**außen** outside
**Außenbord-** outboard
**Außenraum** m outer zone
**Außenseite** f outside
**Außenspiegel** m outside mirror
**außer** except (for); **außer Betrieb** out of order
**außerdem** besides
**äußere(r/s)** exterior; external; **äußere Stadtbezirke** suburbs
**außerhalb** out of *(outside)*
**äußerlich** exterior; **nur zur äußerlichen Anwendung** for external use only
**äußerst** extremely
**Aussicht** f prospect; outlook; view
**Aussichtsterrasse** f observation deck
**Aussichtsturm** m observation tower
**Ausstattung** f equipment *(of car)*
**aussteigen** to get out
**Ausstelldatum** nt date of issue

**Ausstellung** f show; exhibition
**Ausstellungsdatum** nt date of issue
**ausstreichen** to cross out
**Auster(n)** f oyster(s)
**Ausverkauf** m sale
**ausverkauft** sold out
**Auswahl** f choice
**Ausweis** m identity card; pass *(permit)*; membership card
**ausweispflichtig** proof of identity required
**auswuchten** to balance *(wheel)*
**auszahlen** to pay
**Auto(s)** nt car(s); **Auto fahren** to drive
**Autobahn** f motorway
**Autobahngebühr** f toll
**Autofähre** f car-ferry
**Autofahrer** m motorist
**Autokarte** f road map
**Autokino** nt drive-in
**Automat** m vending machine; **Automat wechselt** change given
**Automatikwagen** m automatic *(car)*
**automatisch** automatic; **automatisches Getriebe** automatic gearbox
**Automobilausstellung** f motor show
**Automobilklub** m automobile association
**Autoreisezug** m motorail service/train
**Autoreparatur** f car repair(s)
**Autoverleih** m/**Autovermietung** f car hire
**Autowäsche** f car wash

**Babyflasche** f bottle
**Babynahrung** f baby food
**Babyraum** m mother and baby room
**Bachforelle** f river trout
**Backmischung** f cake mix
**Backofen** m oven
**Backpflaume(n)** f prune(s)
**Backpulver** nt baking powder
**Bad** nt bath
**Badeanstalt** f public swimming baths
**Badeanzug** m swimsuit
**Badehose** f swimming trunks
**Bademeister** m (pool) attendant
**Bademütze** f bathing cap
**baden** to bathe; to swim; **Baden verboten!** no swimming
**Baden** m district famous for white and rosé wines
**Bäder** pl public baths
**Badewanne** f bath
**Badezimmer** nt bathroom
**Badischer Wein** m wine from south-west Germany, usually white and sweetish
**Baggersee** m artificial lake
**Bahn** f railway; rink; **per Bahn** by rail; **mit der Bahn fahren** to go by train
**Bahnbus** m bus run by railway company
**Bahnhof** m station; depot
**Bahnhofsmission** f travellers' aid
**Bahnlinie** f line *(railway)*
**Bahnpolizei** f railway police
**Bahnsteig** m platform

**Bahnsteigkarte(n)** f platform ticket(s)

**Bahnübergang** m level crossing

**Bambussprossen** pl bamboo shoots

**Banane(n)** f banana(s)

**Band¹ (Bände)** m volume(s) (book)

**Band² (Bänder)** nt ribbon(s); tape(s)

**Band³** f band (musical)

**Bank** f bank (finance)

**Bankette** f : Bankette nicht befahrbar soft verges

**Bankkonto** nt bank account

**bar** cash

**Bar** f nightclub; bar

**Bargeld** nt cash

**Barscheck** m uncrossed cheque

**Batterie** f battery

**Bauarbeiten** pl roadworks

**Bauernfrühstück** nt bacon and potato omelette

**Bauernhof** m farm(yard)

**Bauernsuppe** f cabbage soup with frankfurters

**Baumwolle** f cotton (fabric)

**Baumwollgarn** nt cotton (thread)

**Baustelle** f roadworks

**bayerisches Kraut** nt shredded cabbage with apples, wine, sugar

**beachten** to observe; to obey

**Beamte(r)** m official; civil servant

**beantworten** to answer

**Becken** nt pool

**Bedarf** m : bei Bedarf when required

**Bedarfshaltestelle** f request stop

**bedauern** to regret

**bedeckt** cloudy (weather)

**Bedeutung** f meaning

**bedienen** to serve; to operate; **sich bedienen** to help oneself

**Bedienung** f service (in restaurant); service charge; **inklusive Bedienung/Bedienung inbegriffen** service included; **mit Bedienung** with attendant service

**Bedienungsgeld** nt : Bedienungsgeld enthalten service included

**Bedienungshinweise** pl instructions for use

**Bedingung** f condition (proviso)

**Beefsteak** nt steak; **deutsches Beefsteak** hamburger; beefburger

**beenden** to end

**Beere(n)** f berry (berries)

**Beförderung** f transport

**Begrenzung(en)** f limit(s)

**begrüßen** to greet; to welcome

**behalten** to keep

**Behälter** m container

**Behandlung** f treatment

**beheizt** heated

**Behinderung** f obstruction; **mit Behinderungen muß gerechnet werden** delays are to be expected

**Behörde** f authorities; office

**bei** near; at; on; during; care of; c/o; **bei mir** at my house

**beide** both

**Beifahrersitz** m passenger seat

**Beignet(s)** m fritter(s)

**Beilage** f side-dish; vegetables; side-salad

**Beispiel(e)** nt example(s); **zum Beispiel** for example

**Beitrag** m contribution; subscription *(to club)*

**Bekenntnis** nt denomination

**Bekleidung** f clothes

**beladen** to load *(truck, ship)*

**belasten** to burden

**Belastung** f load

**belegt** occupied; no vacancies; **belegtes Brötchen** open sandwich

**Beleuchtung** f lighting; **festliche Beleuchtung** illuminations

**Belichtungsmesser** m light meter

**beliebig** any; as you like; **beliebige Reihenfolge** in any order whatever

**Belohnung** f reward

**Bemerkung(en)** f comment(s); remark(s)

**benachrichtigen** to inform

**Benachrichtigung** f advice note

**benutzen** to use

**Benzin** nt petrol

**Benzinpumpe** f fuel pump

**Beratungsstelle** f advice centre

**berechtigt: berechtigt zu** entitled to

**Berechtigte(r)** m/f authorized person

**Bereich** m area; **im Bereich von** within the scope of

**bereit** ready

**Bereitschaftsdienst** m emergency service

**Berg(e)** m mountain(s)

**bergab** downhill

**bergauf** uphill

**Bergführer** m mountain guide

**Bergsteigen** nt mountaineering; **bergsteigen gehen** to go mountaineering

**Bergtour** f hillwalk; climb

**Bergwacht** f mountain rescue service

**Bergwanderung** f hike in the mountains

**Bericht(e)** m report(s); bulletin(s)

**berichtigen** to correct

**Berliner** m doughnut

**Berliner Weiße** f light, fizzy beer with fruit juice added

**Bernkasteler** m good Mosel white wine

**Beruf** m profession, occupation

**beruflich** professional

**Berufs-** professional *(not amateur)*

**Berufsverkehr** m rush-hour traffic

**Beruhigungsmittel** nt tranquillizer

**berühren** to handle; to touch

**beschädigen** to damage

**Beschäftigung** f employment; occupation

**Bescheinigung** f certificate

**Beschränkung(en)** f restriction(s)

**Beschreibung** f description

**Beschwerde(n)** f complaint(s)

**besetzt** engaged *(telephone)*

**Besetztzeichen** nt engaged signal

**Besichtigungen** pl sightseeing

**Besitzer** m owner

**besondere(r/s)** particular; special

**besonders** especially; extra

**besser** better

**Besserung(en)** f improvement(s); **gute Besserung** get well soon

**beständig** settled *(weather)*

**bestätigen** to confirm

**beste(r/s)** best

**besteigen** to board *(ship)*

**bestellen** to book; to order; **neu bestellen** to reorder *(goods)*

**Bestellformular** *nt* order-form

**Bestellung** *f* order

**bestimmt** definitely; certainly

**Bestimmungen** *pl* regulations

**Bestimmungsland** *nt* country of destination

**Bestimmungsort** *m* destination

**Besucher** *m* visitor

**Besuchszeit** *f* visiting hours

**Betrag** *m* amount; **Betrag (dankend) erhalten** payment received (with thanks)

**betreffs** concerning

**betreten** to enter; **Betreten verboten!** keep off

**Betrieb** *m* business; **außer Betrieb** out of order

**betriebsbereit** operational

**Bett(en)** *nt* bed(s)

**Bettkarte** *f* sleeper ticket

**Bettzeug** *nt* bedclothes

**bewacht** guarded

**bewegen** to move

**Beweis** *m* proof

**bewirtschaftet** serviced *(mountain shelter)*

**bewölkt** cloudy *(weather)*

**bezahlen** to pay (for); to settle *(bill)*

**bezahlt** paid

**Bezahlung** *f* payment

**Bezeichnung** *f* description; **genaue Bezeichnung des Inhalts** precise description of contents

**Bezirk** *m* district *(administrative)*

**Bibliothek** *f* library

**Bienenstich** *m* bee sting; cake coated with sugar and almonds and filled with custard or cream

**Bier(e)** *nt* beer(s); **Bier vom Faß** draught beer

**Biergarten** *m* beer garden

**Bierschinken** *m* ham sausage

**Bierstengel** *m* bread stick

**Bierstube** *f* pub which specializes in different types of beer

**Biersuppe** *f* beer soup

**Bierwurst** *f* slightly smoked pork sausage

**bieten** to offer

**Bild(er)** *nt* picture(s)

**Bildschirm** *m* screen *(TV)*

**billig** cheap; inexpensive

**Birne(n)** *f* pear(s); lightbulb(s)

**bis** until; **von Montag bis Freitag** Monday to Friday; **bis jetzt** up till now; **bis zu 6** up to 6; **bis bald** see you soon

**bisher** till now

**Biskuitrolle** *f* Swiss roll

**Bismarckheringe** *pl* soused herring with onions

**bißchen: ein bißchen** a little; a bit of

**bitte** please; **bitte?** pardon me?; (I beg your) pardon?

**Bitte** *f* request

**bitten** to ask

**bitter** bitter; **bittere Schokolade** plain chocolate

**Blatt (Blätter)** *nt* sheet(s) *(of paper)*; leaf (leaves)

**Blattsalat** *m* green salad

**Blattspinat** *m* leaf spinach

**blau** blue; au bleu *(fish)*

**Blaukraut** *nt* red cabbage
**Blauschimmelkäse** *m* blue cheese
**bleiben** to remain; to stay
**bleichen** to bleach
**bleifrei** unleaded; lead-free
**Blinkerhebel** *m* indicator switch
**Blitzlicht** *nt* flash *(on camera)*
**Blitzlichtbirne** *f* flashbulb
**Blitzlichtwürfel** *m* flashcube
**Blockschrift** *f* block letters
**Blumenkohl** *m* cauliflower
**Blut** *nt* blood
**Blutdruck** *m* blood pressure
**Blutgruppe** *f* blood group
**Blutprobe** *f* blood test
**Blutvergiftung** *f* blood poisoning
**Blutwurst** *f* blood sausage; black pudding
**Bockbier** *nt* bock (beer) *(strong beer)*
**Bocksbeutel** *m* dry (white) wine from Franconia
**Bockwurst** *f* boiled sausage
**Bohnen** *pl* beans; **grüne Bohnen** French beans
**Bohnensuppe** *f* (thick) bean soup
**Boiler** *m* immersion heater
**Boje** *f* buoy
**Bonbon** *nt* sweet
**Boot** *nt* boat
**Bootsverleih** *m* boat hire
**Bord** *nt* : **an Bord** on board *(ship, etc)*
**Bordkarte** *f* boarding pass
**Böschung** *f* embankment
**botanischer Garten** *m* botanical gardens
**Botschaft** *f* embassy

**Bouillon** *f* clear soup
**Bowle** *f* punch *(drink)*
**Brat-** fried; roast
**Bratapfel** *m* baked apple
**braten** to fry; to roast
**Braten** *m* roast meat; joint
**Bratensaft** *m* gravy
**Bratfett** *nt* fat for frying and roasting
**Brathähnchen** *nt* roast chicken
**Brathering** *m* fried herring *(eaten cold)*
**Bratkartoffeln** *pl* fried or sauté potatoes
**Bratspieß** *m* spit *(for roasting)*
**Bratwurst** *f* sausage
**Brauerei** *f* brewery
**Bräune** *f* tan *(on skin)*
**Brechreiz** *m* nausea
**breit** wide
**Breite** *f* width
**Bremsanlage** *f* braking system
**Bremse(n)** *f* brake(s)
**bremsen** to brake
**Bremsflüssigkeit** *f* brake fluid
**Bremslichter** *pl* stoplights
**Bremspedal** *nt* brake pedal
**brennen** to burn
**Brennspiritus** *m* methylated spirits
**Brennstoff** *m* fuel
**Brett** *nt* plank; board
**Brezel** *f* pretzel
**Brief** *m* letter *(message)*; **eingeschriebener Brief** registered letter
**Briefdrucksache** *f* circular *(letter)*
**Briefkasten** *m* letter box; mailbox
**Briefmarke(n)** *f* stamp(s)

**Briefmarkenautomat** *m* stamp machine

**Briefpapier** *nt* notepaper

**Briefumschlag(-schläge)** *m* envelope(s)

**britisch** British

**Brombeere(n)** *f* blackberry (-berries)

**Bronchialtee** *m* herbal tea to relieve bronchitis

**Brot** *nt* bread; loaf

**Brötchen** *nt* bread roll

**Brücke** *f* bridge

**Brüder (Brüder)** *m* brother(s)

**Brüderschaft** *f*: **Brüderschaft trinken** to agree to use the familiar 'du' over a drink

**Brühe** *f* stock *(for soup etc)*

**Brunnen** *m* well *(for water)*; fountain

**brutto** gross *(before deductions)*

**buchen** to book

**Büchersendung** *f* books (sent) at printed paper rate

**Buchhandlung** *f* bookshop

**Büchsen-** canned

**Büchsenöffner** *m* can-opener

**Buchstabe** *m* letter *(of alphabet)*; in **Buchstaben** in words

**Buchung** *f* booking

**Bügel** *m* coat hanger; **Bügel drücken!** press down!

**bügelfrei** drip-dry

**Bundes-** federal

**Bundesrepublik** *f* West Germany

**Bundesstraße** *f* 'A' road

**Bündnerfleisch** *nt* cured dried beef, thinly sliced

**bunt** coloured; **buntes Glasfenster** stained glass window

**Burg** *f* castle

**Burgenland** *nt* area in Austria renowned for its sweet red and white wines

**bürgerlich** middle-class; **bürgerliche Küche** good plain food

**Bürgermeister** *m* mayor

**Burgunder** *m* full-bodied red wine

**Büro** *nt* agency; office

**Bus(se)** *m* bus(es); coach(es)

**Bushaltestelle** *f* bus stop

**Buslinie** *f* bus route

**Bußtag** *m* day of repentance *(November 20th, public holiday)*

**Bustransfer** *m* transfer *(by coach)*

**Busverbindung** *f* bus service

**Butangas** *nt* Calor gas ®

**Butterkäse** *m* (full fat) cream cheese

**Buttermilch** *f* buttermilk

**Butterschmalz** *nt* clarified butter

**Campingführer** *m* camping guide(book)

**Champignon(s)** *m* mushroom(s)

**Charterflug(-flüge)** *m* charter flight(s)

**chemisch** chemical; **chemische Reinigung** dry cleaning; dry cleaner's

**Chinakohl** *m* Chinese cabbage

**Chinarestaurant** *nt* Chinese restaurant

**Chips** *pl* crisps; chips *(in poker etc)*

**Chorgestühl** *nt* choir stalls

**Christi Himmelfahrt** *f* Ascension

Day (public holiday)
**Cola** f Coke ®
**Cremespeise** f mousse
**Currywurst** f fried sausage with ketchup and curry

**da** there; **nicht da** out (not at home)
**Dach(gepäck)träger** m roof rack
**daheim** at home
**Dame** f lady; **meine Dame** madam; **'Damen'** 'Ladies'
**Damenbinde(n)** f sanitary towel(s)
**Damentoilette** f powder room
**dämpfen** to steam (food)
**Dampfer** m steamer
**Dampfnudeln** pl sweet yeast dumplings cooked in milk and sugar
**danach** afterward(s)
**danke** thank you; **danke gleichfalls** same to you; **nein danke** no thanks
**Darm** m intestines
**Darmgrippe** f gastric flu
**das** the; that; this; whom; **das heißt ...** that is (to say)
**Dattel(n)** f date(s) (fruit)
**Datum** nt date (day)
**Dauer** f duration
**Dauerwelle** f perm
**DB** f Federal Railway
**DDR** f East Germany
**Decke** f blanket; ceiling
**Deckel** m top; lid
**demnächst** very soon
**Denkmal(-mäler)** nt monument(s)
**Deponie** f disposal site
**der** the; who(m)

**Desinfektionsmittel** nt disinfectant
**desinfizieren** to disinfect
**deutlich** distinct
**deutsch** German
**Deutschland** nt Germany
**Devisen** pl foreign currency
**Dezember** m December
**Dia(s)** nt slide(s)
**Diabetiker(in)** m(f) diabetic
**Dichtung** f washer; sealing; gasket
**dick** thick; fat (person)
**Dickmilch** f soured milk
**die** the; who(m)
**Diebstahl** m theft
**Dienst** m service; **im Dienst** on duty
**Dienstag** m Tuesday
**dienstbereit** open (pharmacy); on duty (doctor)
**Dienstbereitschaft** f: **in Dienstbereitschaft** on stand-by duty; open (pharmacy)
**Dienstzeit** f office hours
**Diesel(kraftstoff)** m diesel oil
**Dieselmotor** m diesel engine
**Dieselöl** nt diesel fuel
**diese(r/s)** this (one); **diese** these
**Ding(e)** nt thing(s)
**direkt** direct; **eine direkte Verbindung nach** a through train/direct plane to
**Direktflug(-flüge)** m direct flight(s)
**Dolmetscher** m interpreter
**Dom** m cathedral
**Donnerstag** m Thursday
**Doppelbett** nt double bed
**doppelt** double
**Doppelzimmer** nt double room

**Dorf (Dörfer)** *nt* village(s)

**Dorsch** *m* Atlantic cod

**dort** there

**Dose** *f* box; tin; **in Dosen** tinned

**Dosenöffner** *m* tin-opener

**Dosis** *f* dosage; dose

**Drachen** *m* kite; hang-glider

**Draht** *m* wire

**Drahtseilbahn** *f* cable railway

**draußen** outdoors; **nach draußen gehen** to go outside

**drehen** to turn; to twist

**Drehzahlmesser** *m* rev counter

**drei** three

**Dreibettabteil** *nt* three-berth compartment

**Dreieck** *nt* triangle

**Dreikönigstag** *m* Epiphany (*public holiday*)

**Dreikornbrot** *nt* wholemeal bread containing three types of grain

**dringend** urgent

**drinnen** inside

**dritte(r/s)** third

**Droge** *f* drug

**Drogerie** *f* chemist's (shop) (*not for medicine and prescriptions*)

**drücken** to press; to push; **drücken Sie den Knopf** press the button

**Druckknopf** *m* press-stud; push-button

**Drucksache** *f* printed matter

**Druckschrift** *f* block letters

**du** you (*familiar form*)

**Düne(n)** *f* dune(s)

**dunkel** dark

**dünn** thin; weak (*tea*)

**durch** through; done (*meat*)

**Durchfahrt** *f* passage; transit; thoroughfare; **keine Durchfahrt/ Durchfahrt verboten** no through road

**Durchfall** *m* diarrhoea

**Durchgang** *m* way; passage; **kein Durchgang/Durchgang verboten or nicht gestattet** no right of way

**Durchgangsverkehr** *m* through traffic

**durchgebraten** well-done (*steak*)

**durchgehend: durchgehender Zug** *m* through train; **durchgehend geöffnet** open 24 hours

**Durchreise** *f*: **auf der Durchreise** passing through

**Durchsage** *f* announcement

**durchwählen** to dial direct

**dürfen** to be allowed; **dürfen überholt werden** overtaking (of specified vehicles) allowed

**Duschbad** *nt* shower lotion

**Dusche** *f* shower

**Dutzend** *nt* dozen

**D-Zug** *m* express or through train

**Ebbe** *f* low tide

**echt** real; genuine

**Ecke** *f* corner (*of streets*)

**Edamer** *m* German version of Edam, a mild hard cheese

**Edelstein** *m* jewel; gem

**ehemalig** ex-

**Ei(er)** *nt* egg(s); **ein weiches Ei** a soft-boiled egg

**Eiersalat** *m* egg mayonnaise salad

**Eigentum** *nt* property

**Eigentümer** *m* owner

**Eil-** urgent

**Eilbrief** *m* express letter

**Eilsendung** *f* express delivery

**Eilzug** *m* fast train which also stops at smaller stations

**Eilzustellung** *f* special delivery

**ein** a; one; **ein/aus** on/off

**ein(e)** a; an

**Einbahnstraße** *f* one-way street

**Einbettabteil** *nt* single-berth compartment

**einbiegen** to turn; **nach rechts/links einbiegen** turn right/left

**Einbruch** *m* burglary

**einchecken** to check in

**einfach** simple; **einfache Fahrkarte** single ticket

**Einfahrt** *f* entrance; drive; **keine Einfahrt** no entry

**Einfuhr** *f* import

**einführen** to insert; to import

**Eingang** *m* entrance; gate

**Eingangshalle** *f* lobby

**ein(geschaltet)** on *(machine)*

**eingeschlossen** included

**eingezogen: warten, bis die Banknote vollständig eingezogen ist** wait until the banknote has been completely drawn into the machine

**Einheit** *f* unit; **der Preis pro Einheit** unit price

**einige(r/s)** some

**Einkauf** *m* purchase; **Einkäufe** shopping

**einkaufen** to shop

**Einkaufszentrum** *nt* shopping centre

**Einladung** *f* invitation

**einlegen** to put in

**Einlieferungsschein** *m* certificate of posting

**einlösen** to cash *(cheque)*

**einordnen** to get in lane

**Einrichtungen** *pl* facilities

**eins** one

**einschalten** to switch on *(light, TV)*

**einschieben** to insert

**einschließlich** including

**Einschreiben** *nt* certified mail; **per Einschreiben** by recorded delivery

**einsteigen** to board *(train, bus)*

**einstellen** to adjust; to focus; to appoint; to stop

**Einstieg nur mit Fahrausweis** ticket-holders only (may enter)

**Eintopf** *m* stew

**eintreten** to come in

**Eintritt** *m* entry; admission *(fee)*; **Eintritt frei** admission free; **kein Eintritt/Eintritt verboten** no admittance

**Eintrittsgeld** *nt* entrance fee

**Eintrittskarte(n)** *f* ticket(s)

**Einwegmiete** *f* one-way rental

**einwerfen** to post; to insert

**Einwurf** *m* slot; slit; **Einwurf 2 Mark** insert 2 marks

**einzahlen** to pay in

**Einzahlung** *f* deposit

**Einzahlungsschein** *m* pay-in slip

**Einzelbett** *nt* single bed; **zwei Einzelbetten** twin beds

**Einzelfahrschein** *m* single ticket

**Einzelheit** *f* detail; **Einzelheiten**

siehe Rückseite see back for details
**Einzelkabine** f single cabin
**einzeln** single; individual
**Einzelreisende(r)** m/f person travelling alone
**Einzelzimmer** nt single room
**Eis** nt ice cream; ice; **Eis am Stiel** ice lolly
**Eisbahn** f skating rink
**Eisbecher** m sundae
**Eisbein** nt knuckle of pork (boiled and served with sauerkraut)
**Eisenbahn** f railway
**Eisenbahnfähre** f train ferry
**Eisenwaren** pl hardware
**Eiskaffee** m iced coffee
**Eistüte** f cornet (of ice cream)
**Eiswürfel** m ice cube
**Eiter** m pus
**Elastikbinde** f elastic bandage
**elektrisch** electric(al)
**Elektrizität** f electricity
**Element** nt unit; element
**Eltern** pl parents
**Emmentaler** m Swiss hard cheese
**Empfang** m welcome; reception
**empfangen** to receive (guest)
**Empfänger** m addressee
**Empfängerabschnitt** m receipt slip
**Empfangsschein** m receipt
**empfehlen** to recommend
**empfohlen** recommended
**Ende** nt bottom (of page, list); end
**Endstation** f terminal
**eng** narrow; tight (clothes)
**englisch** English; rare (steak); **auf englisch** in English

**Ente** f duck
**enteisen** to de-ice
**Entenbrust** f breast of duck
**entfernen** to remove
**entfernt** distant; **30 Kilometer entfernt** 30 kilometres away
**Entfernung** f distance
**Entfernungsmesser** m range finder
**entfrosten** to defrost
**Entgelt** nt : **Entgelt für Platzreservierung im Zuschlag enthalten** seat reservation included in supplement charge
**Enthaarungscreme** f depilatory cream
**enthalten** to contain; **enthalten Frühstück, Service und MwSt** includes breakfast, service and VAT
**Entlastungsroute** f relief road
**Entlastungszug** m relief train
**Entnahme** f ticket issue
**entnehmen** to take out
**entrahmt: entrahmte Milch** f skim(med) milk
**Entrecôte** nt sirloin steak
**Entschuldigung** f pardon; excuse me
**entsprechend** equivalent to
**entweder ... oder ...** either ... or ...
**Entwerter** m (ticket) cancelling machine
**entwickeln** to develop (photo)
**Entzündung** f inflammation
**Enzian** m gentian; spirit distilled from gentian roots
**er** he; it
**Erbsen** pl peas

**Erdäpfelknödel** pl potato and semolina dumplings
**Erdäpfelnudeln** pl fried potato balls in breadcrumbs
**Erdbeere(n)** f strawberry(-berries)
**Erdgeschoß** nt ground floor
**Erdnuß(-nüsse)** f peanut(s)
**Ereignis** nt incident; occasion
**erforderlich** necessary, required
**Erfrischungen** pl refreshments
**erhalten** to receive (letter)
**erhältlich** obtainable; available
**Erkältung** f cold (illness)
**Erklärung** f explanation
**erkundigen: sich erkundigen** to ask
**erlauben** to permit (something)
**Erlaubnis** f permission
**Erläuterung** f: **Erläuterung siehe Rückseite** for further information see over
**Erlebnis** nt experience (event)
**ermäßigt: ermäßigter Preis** m reduced price
**Ermäßigung** f reduction
**Ersatz** m substitute; replacement
**Ersatzrad** nt spare wheel
**Ersatzteil** nt spare (part)
**ersetzen** to replace (substitute)
**Erstattung** f: **Erstattung erhalten** refund received
**erste(r/s)** first; **Erste Hilfe** first aid
**Erste-Hilfe-Ausrüstung** f first-aid kit
**erstklassig** first class (work etc)
**Erwachsene(r)** m/f adult
**Erzeugnis** nt produce (products)
**es** it

**eßbar** edible
**essen** to eat
**Essen** nt food; meal
**Essig** m vinegar
**Eßlokal** nt restaurant
**Etage** f floor; storey
**Etagenbad** nt bathroom facilities on the same floor
**Etagenbetten** pl bunk beds
**Etagendusche** f shower facilities on the same floor
**etwa** around; about
**etwas** something
**europäisch** European
**Euroscheck** m Eurocheque
**eventuell** perhaps
**Exemplar** nt copy (of book etc)

**Fabrik** f works; factory
**Fach** nt: **Fach ziehen/schließen** pull out/push in drawer
**Facharzt** m consultant (doctor)
**Fachinhalt** m contents
**Fachnummer** f locker number
**Fahrausweis(e)** m ticket(s)
**Fahrausweisverkauf** m ticket sale
**Fahrbahn** f carriageway
**Fahrbahnverschmutzung** f mud on the road
**Fähre** f ferry
**fahren** to drive; to go
**Fahrer** m chauffeur; driver (of car)
**Fahrgast** m passenger
**Fahrgelderstattung** f refund of fare
**Fahrgestell** nt chassis
**Fahrkarte(n)** f ticket(s)
**Fahrkartenschalter** m ticket office

**Fahrplan** m timetable *(for trains etc)*

**Fahrplanauszüge** pl individual timetables

**Fahrplanhinweise** pl travel information

**Fahrpreis(e)** m fare(s)

**Fahrrad(-räder)** nt bicycle(s)

**Fahrschein(e)** m ticket(s); **Fahrscheine hier entwerten** please punch your ticket here

**Fahrscheinentwerter** m automatic ticket stamping machine

**Fahrspur(en)** f lane(s)

**Fahrstuhl** m lift

**Fahrt** f journey; drive; ride *(in vehicle)*; **während der Fahrt** while the train, etc is in motion; **gute Fahrt!** safe journey!

**Fahrtantritt** m : **vor Fahrtantritt** before commencing the journey

**Fahrtunterbrechung** f break in the journey

**Fahrzeug** nt vehicle

**Fahrziel** nt destination

**Fall** m instance; **im Falle von** in case of; **auf alle Fälle** in any case

**fällig** due *(owing)*

**falsch** false *(name etc)*; wrong; **falscher Hase** minced beef loaf

**Familie** f family

**Familienname** m surname

**Familienstand** m marital status

**Farbe** f colour; paint; suit *(cards)*

**farbecht** fast *(dye)*

**Farbfestiger** m setting lotion with a semi-permanent colourant

**Farbfilm** m colour film

**farbig** coloured

**Farbstoff** m dye

**Fasan** m pheasant

**Fasching** m carnival

**Faß** nt barrel; **vom Faß** on tap; on draught

**Faßbier** nt draught beer

**Fastnachtsdienstag** m Shrove Tuesday

**Februar** m February

**Feder** f spring *(coil)*; feather

**Federball** m badminton

**fehlen** to be missing

**Fehler** m fault; mistake

**Fehlzündung** f misfiring; backfiring

**feiern** to celebrate

**Feiertag** m holiday

**Feige(n)** f fig(s)

**Feinkostgeschäft** nt delicatessen

**Feinschmecker** m gourmet

**Feinwaschmittel** nt mild detergent

**Feldsalat** m corn salad; lamb's lettuce

**Felgenbremse(n)** f calliper brake(s)

**Fenchel** m fennel

**Fenster** nt window

**Fensterplatz** m seat by the window

**Ferien** pl holiday(s)

**Ferienhaus** nt (holiday) chalet

**Ferienwohnung** f holiday flat

**Fern-** long-distance

**Fernamt** nt telephone exchange

**Ferngespräch** nt trunk call

**Fernglas** nt binoculars

**Fernlicht** nt full or main beam

**Fernsehen** nt television

**Fernsprechamt** nt telephone exchange

**Fernsprecher** *m* (public) telephone
**fertig** ready; finished
**Fest** *nt* celebration; party
**festmachen** to fasten
**festsetzen** to arrange
**fett** greasy *(food)*
**Fett** *nt* fat; grease
**fettarm** low-fat
**feucht** damp
**Feuer** *nt* fire
**feuergefährlich** inflammable
**Feuerlöscher** *m* fire extinguisher
**Feuertreppe** *f* fire escape
**Feuerwehr** *f* fire brigade
**Feuerwerk** *nt* fireworks
**Feuerzeug** *nt* cigarette lighter
**Feuerzeugbenzin** *nt* lighter fuel
**Feuerzeuggas** *nt* lighter gas
**Fieber** *nt* fever
**Filet** *nt* sirloin; fillet *(of meat, fish)*
**Filetspitzen Stroganoff** beef
stroganoff
**Filetsteak** *nt* fillet steak
**Filiale** *f* branch *(of store, bank etc)*
**Filter-** tipped *(cigarettes)*
**Fisch** *m* fish
**Fischauflauf** *m* fish pudding
*(Austria)*
**Fischklöße** *pl* fish balls
**Fischstäbchen** *pl* fish fingers
**Fischsuppe** *f* fish soup
**Fitneßraum** *m* keep fit room
**Fitneßstudio** *nt* health studio
**Fläche** *f* area *(of surface)*
**flambiert** flambé
**Flamme** *f* flame
**Flasche** *f* bottle

**Flaschenbier** *nt* bottled beer
**Flaschenöffner** *m* bottle opener
**Flaschenweine** *pl* bottled wines
**Fleckenmittel/Fleckenwasser** *nt*
stain-remover
**Fleisch** *nt* meat; flesh
**Fleischbrühe** *f* bouillon; stock
**Fleischerei** *f* butcher's *(shop)*
**Fleischkäse** *m* meatloaf
**Fleischklößchen** *nt* meatball
**Fleischküchle** *nt* rissole
**Fleischsalat** *m* diced meat salad
with mayonnaise
**Fleischtopf** *m* meat pan
**Fleisch- und Wurstwaren** *pl* meat
counter
**Flickzeug** *nt* puncture repair kit
**Fliege** *f* bow tie; fly
**fliegen** to fly
**fließen** to flow
**fließend** fluently; **fließend warm und
kalt Wasser** hot and cold water
**Flohmarkt** *m* flea market
**Flug (Flüge)** *m* flight(s)
**Fluggast** *m* passenger
**Fluggesellschaft** *f* airline
**Flughafen** *m* airport
**Flughafenbus** *m* airport bus
**Flugnummer** *f* flight number
**Flugplan** *m* flight schedule
**Flugplanauskunft** *f* flight
information
**Flugschein(e)** *m* plane ticket(s)
**Flugscheinkontrolle** *f* ticket
control
**Flugsteig** *m* gate
**Flugstrecke** *f* route; flying distance

**Flugticket(s)** nt plane ticket(s)
**Flugverbindung** f air connection
**Flugverkehr** m air traffic
**Flugzeug** nt plane, aircraft
**Flunder** f flounder
**Fluß (Flüsse)** m river(s)
**Flüssigkeit** f liquid
**Flußkrebs** m crawfish; crayfish
**Flut** f flood; tide
**Flutlicht** nt floodlight
**Folge** f series; consequence
**folgen** to follow
**folgend** following
**Folie** f: **in der Folie** baked in foil
**Fönen** nt blow dry
**Forelle** f trout, **Forelle Steiermark**
  trout filled with bacon in white
  sauce
**Forellenfilet** nt fillet of smoked
  trout
**Form** f shape; form
**Format** nt size
**Formblatt** nt form
**Formular** nt form (document)
**fortsetzen** to continue
**Foto** nt photo
**Fotoapparat** m camera
**Fotogeschäft** nt photographic shop
**fotokopieren** to photocopy
**Fracht** f cargo; freight
**Frage** f question; **nicht in Frage** out
  of the question
**Fragebogen** m questionnaire
**fragen** to ask
**Frankenwein** m wine from
  Franconia (fairly dry)
**frankieren** to stamp (letter)

**Frankreich** nt France
**Franzose** m Frenchman
**Französin** f Frenchwoman
**französisch** French
**Frau** f Mrs; Ms; woman; wife
**Frauenarzt** m gynaecologist
**Fräulein** nt Miss
**frei** free; clear; vacant; **im Freien**
  outdoor; open-air
**Freibad** nt open-air swimming pool
**Freigepäck** nt baggage allowance
**freilassen** to leave blank
**freimachen** to stamp
**Freitag** m Friday
**Freizeichen** nt ringing tone
**Freizeit** f spare time; leisure
**Freizeitkleidung** f casual wear
**fremd** foreign; strange (unknown)
**Fremde(r)** m/f stranger
**Fremdenführer** m courier
**Fremdenverkehr** m tourism
**Fremdenverkehrsamt/Fremden-
  verkehrsbüro** nt tourist office
**Fremdenverkehrsverein** m tourist
  association
**Fremdenzimmer** nt guest room(s)
**Freund** m friend; boyfriend
**Freundin** f friend; girlfriend
**Friedhof** m cemetery
**Frikadelle(n)** f rissole(s)
**frisch** fresh; wet (paint)
**Frischhaltebeutel** m airtight bag
**Frischhaltefolie** f cling film
**Frischkäse** m cream cheese
**Frischwurst** f cold, unsmoked
  sausage
**Friseur** m hairdresser

**Frisiercreme** f hair cream
**Frist** f period; deadline
**Frisur** f hairstyle
**Fronleichnam** Corpus Christi (*public holiday*)
**Froschschenkel** pl frogs' legs
**Frostschutzmittel** nt antifreeze
**Früchte** pl fruit
**Fruchteis** nt water ice
**Früchtetee** m fruit tea
**Fruchtsaft** m fruit juice
**Fruchtsaftkonzentrat** nt cordial
**früh** early
**Frühling** m spring (*season*)
**Frühlingsrolle(n)** f spring or pancake roll(s)
**Frühlingssuppe** f spring vegetable soup with noodles
**Frühstück** nt breakfast
**Frühstücksbuffet** nt breakfast buffet
**Frühstücksgedeck** nt set breakfast
**Frühstücksraum** m breakfast room
**Führer** m leader; guide
**Führerschein** m driving licence
**Führung** f guided tour
**Füllung** f stuffing (*in chicken etc*)
**Fundbüro** nt lost property office
**Fundsachen** pl lost property
**fünf** five
**für** for; **Benzin für DM50** DM50 worth of petrol
**Fuß** m foot; **zu Fuß gehen** to walk
**Fußball** m football; soccer
**Fußbremse** f footbrake
**Fußgänger** m pedestrian
**Fußgängerüberweg** m pedestrian crossing
**Fußgängerunterführung** f pedestrian subway
**Fußgängerzone** f pedestrian precinct
**Fußweg** m footpath
**füttern: nicht füttern!** do not feed

**Gang** m course (*of meal*); passage; gear (*of car*)
**Gangschaltung** f gears
**Gans** f goose
**Gänsebraten** m roast goose
**Gänseleberpastete** f pâté de foie gras
**ganz** whole; quite
**ganztägig** full-time
**gar** done (*vegetables*); **nicht gar** undercooked
**Garantie** f guarantee; warrant(y)
**Garderobe** f cloakroom; wardrobe
**Garnele(n)** f prawn(s)
**Garnelencocktail** f shrimp cocktail
**Gartenlokal** nt garden café
**Gärtnerei** f market-garden
**Gaskocher** m camping stove
**Gasse** f alley; lane (*in town*)
**Gast** m guest; **für Gäste** patrons only
**Gästezimmer** nt guest-room
**Gasthaus** nt inn
**Gasthof** m inn
**Gaststätte** f restaurant
**Gaststube** f lounge
**geändert** altered; **geänderte Abfahrtszeiten/Vorfahrt** new departure times/right of way

**Gebäck** nt pastry (cake)

**gebackenes Goldbarschfilet** nt fried breaded perch fillet

**gebeizt** cured; marinated

**geben** to give

**Gebiet** nt region; area

**Gebirge** nt mountains

**Gebiß** nt dentures

**Gebläse** nt demister

**geboren** born; **geborene Schnorr** née Schnorr

**gebraten** fried; **gebratene Ente** roast duck

**Gebrauch** nt use

**gebrauchen** to use

**Gebrauchsanweisung** f instructions for use

**Gebraucht-** used (car etc)

**Gebühr** f fee; **Gebühr bezahlt Empfänger** postage to be paid by addressee; **Gebühren ablesen** read amount of charge

**gebührenfrei** free of charge; post free

**Gebührenordnung** f scale of charges

**gebührenpflichtig** subject to a charge; **gebührenpflichtige Verwarnung** fine; **gebühren-pflichtige Brücke** toll bridge

**Geburtsdatum** nt date of birth

**Geburtsort** m place of birth

**Geburtstag** m birthday

**Geburtsurkunde** f birth certificate

**Gedeck** nt place setting

**gedünstet** steamed

**geeignet** suitable

**Gefahr** f danger

**gefährlich** dangerous

**Gefälle** nt gradient

**Geflügel** nt poultry

**gefroren** frozen (food)

**gefüllt** stuffed; **gefüllte Kalbsbrust** stuffed roast breast of veal

**gegebenenfalls** if applicable

**gegen** versus; against; toward(s)

**Gegend** f district; region

**Gegenteil** nt opposite

**gegenüber** opposite; facing

**Gegenverkehr** m oncoming traffic

**gegrillt: gegrillter Lachs** m grilled salmon

**Gehacktes** nt mince

**gehen** to go; to walk; **wie geht es Ihnen?** how are you?

**gekocht** cooked; boiled

**gekühlt** cooled

**Gelände** nt grounds (land); site

**gelb** yellow

**Geld** nt money; **Geld einwerfen** insert money

**Geldautomat** m cash dispenser

**Geldeinwurf** m slot

**Geldrückgabe** f coin return

**Geldschein** m banknote

**Geldstrafe** f fine

**Geldstück** nt coin

**Geldwechsel** m exchange of money; bureau de change

**Geldwechselautomat/ Geldwechsler** m change machine

**gelten** to be worth; to be valid

**Geltungsbereich** m area within which a ticket is valid

**Geltungsdauer** f period of validity

**gemahlen** ground
**Gemeinde** f community
**gemeinsam** together
**gemischt** mixed; assorted;
**gemischter Salat** mixed (side) salad
**Gemüse** nt vegetables
**genau** accurate; precise; exact(ly)
**Genehmigung** f approval; permit
**Genuß** m enjoyment
**geöffnet** open
**Gepäck** nt luggage; **Gepäck einlegen** put in luggage
**Gepäckaufbewahrung** f left-luggage office
**Gepäckausgabe** f baggage claim
**Gepäckermittlung** f luggage desk
**Gepäcknetz** nt luggage rack (in train)
**Gepäckschein** m left-luggage ticket
**Gepäckschließfach** nt left-luggage locker
**Gepäckträger** m luggage rack (on car); porter
**Gepäckversicherung** f luggage insurance
**Gepäckwagen** m baggage car
**geradeaus** straight ahead
**Gerät** nt appliance; gadget
**geraucht/geräuchert** smoked
**Geräusch** nt noise; sound
**Gericht** nt court (law); dish (food)
**geröstet** sauté; fried; toasted;
**geröstete Mandeln** roasted almonds
**Geruch** m smell
**gesamt** entire; total
**Gesamt-Bruttogewicht** nt overall weight

**Geschäft(e)** nt shop(s)
**Geschäftsstunden** pl business hours
**Geschenk(e)** nt gift(s)
**Geschenkartikel** pl gifts
**Geschenkgutschein** m gift token
**geschieden** divorced
**Geschirrspülmittel** nt washing-up liquid
**Geschlecht** nt gender; sex
**geschlossen** closed
**Geschmack** m taste; flavour
**geschmort** braised
**Geschnetzeltes** nt meat cut into strips and stewed to produce a thick sauce
**Geschwindigkeit** f speed
**Geschwindigkeitsbegrenzung** f speed limit
**Geschwindigkeitsüberschreitung** f speeding
**Gesellschaft** f society
**Gesellschaftsraum** m lounge
**gesetzlich** legal; **gesetzlicher Feiertag** public holiday
**Gesichtscreme** f face cream
**Gesichtswasser** nt face lotion
**gesperrt** closed
**Gespräch** nt talk; (telephone) call
**gestattet** permitted
**gestern** yesterday
**gesund** healthy (person)
**Gesundheit** f health
**Getränk(e)** nt drink(s)
**Getränkekarte** f list of beverages; wine list
**getrennt** separately
**Getriebe** nt gearbox

**getrocknet** dried *(fruit, beans)*
**Gewähr** f: **ohne Gewähr** subject to change; no liability assumed
**Gewicht** nt weight
**Gewinn** m prize; winning ticket
**Gewürz** nt spice; seasoning; **Gewürze** condiments
**Gewürzgurke(n)** f gherkin(s)
**Gewürznelke(n)** f clove(s)
**Gewürztraminer** m full-bodied white wine
**Gezeiten** pl tide
**gibt: es gibt** there is; there are
**gießen** to pour
**Gift** nt poison
**giftig** poisonous
**Gitziprägel** nt baked rabbit in batter *(Switzerland)*
**Glas** nt glass; lens *(of glasses)*; jar
**Glatteisgefahr** f danger of black ice
**Gleis** nt track *(for trains)*; **der Zug fährt auf Gleis 3 ab** the train is leaving from platform 3
**Glocke** f bell
**Glück** nt happiness; luck
**Glückwunsch** m : **herzlichen Glückwunsch!** congratulations!
**Glückwunschtelegramm** nt greetings telegram
**Glühbirne** f light bulb
**Glühwein** m mulled wine
**Golfplatz** m golf course
**Golfschläger** m golf club
**Gondelbahn** f cable railway
**Gottesdienst** m service *(in church)*
**Grad** m degree
**Gräte** f bone *(of fish)*

**gratis** free of charge
**Graubrot** nt bread made from a mixture of types of flour
**Grenze** f frontier; border
**Grenzübergang** m border crossing-point
**Griebenschmalz** nt dripping with crackling
**Grieß** m semolina
**Grießklößchen** pl semolina dumplings
**Grießnockerlsuppe** f beef broth with chives and dumplings
**Griff** m handle; knob
**Grill** m grill; **vom Grill** grilled; barbecued
**Grillspieß** m (shish) kebab
**Grillteller** m mixed grill
**Grippe** f flu
**grob** roughly; coarse *(texture)*
**groß** tall; great; big; wide *(range)*
**Großbritannien** nt Great Britain
**Großbuchstabe(n)** m capital letter(s)
**Größe** f size; height
**Großstadt** f city
**grün** green; fresh *(fish)*
**Grünanlage** f park
**Grund** m ground; reason
**Gründonnerstag** m Maundy Thursday
**Grundstück** nt land *(property)*
**grüner Salat** lettuce salad with French dressing
**Grünkernsuppe** f green corn soup with cream
**Gruppenreise** f group travel
**Gruß** m greeting

**Grütze** *f*: **rote Grütze** fruit jelly
**Gulasch** *nt* goulash
**gültig** valid; **gültig ab 10. Februar** effective February 10th
**Gummi** *m* rubber; elastic
**günstig** favourable; convenient
**gurgeln** to gargle
**Gurke(n)** *f* cucumber(s); gherkin(s)
**Gürtel** *m* belt
**Gürtelreifen** *m* radial (tyre)
**Gußeisen** *nt* cast iron
**gut** good; well; all right *(yes)*; **guten Appetit** enjoy your meal; **alles Gute** all the best; with best wishes
**Gutedel** *m* very dry white wine
**Güter** *pl* goods
**Güterzug** *m* freight train
**Guthaben** *nt* credit
**Gutschein** *m* voucher; coupon
**Gutscheinwert** *m* voucher value

**Haar** *nt* hair
**Haarfestiger** *m* setting lotion
**Haarkur** *f* conditioner
**Haarnadelkurve** *f* hairpin bend
**Haarschnitt** *m* haircut
**Haartrockner** *m* hairdrier
**Haarwaschmittel** *m* shampoo
**Haarwasser** *nt* hair lotion
**haben** to have
**Hackbraten** *m* meat loaf
**Hackfleisch** *nt* mince
**Hacksteak** *nt* hamburger
**Hafen** *m* harbour; port
**Hafenrundfahrt** *f* trip round the harbour
**Haferflocken** *pl* rolled oats

**Haftpflichtdeckung** *f* public liability
**Haftpflichtversicherung** *f* third party insurance
**Haftpulver** *nt* dental adhesive
**Haftung** *f* liability
**Haftungsbeschränkung** *f* collision damage waiver
**Hagebuttentee** *m* rosehip tea
**Hahn** *m* tap *(for water)*; cock(erel)
**Hähnchen** *nt* chicken
**halb** half; **zum halben Preis** half-price
**halbdurch** medium *(steak)*
**Halbpension** *f* half board
**Hälfte** *f* half
**Hallenbad** *nt* indoor pool
**Hals** *m* neck; throat
**Halskette** *f* necklace
**Hals-Nasen-Ohren-Arzt** *m* ear, nose and throat specialist
**Halsschmerzen** *pl* sore throat
**halt** stop
**haltbar** durable
**halten** to hold; to keep; **Halten verboten** no waiting *(road sign)*
**Haltestelle** *f* bus stop
**Hammelfleisch** *nt* mutton
**Handbremse** *f* handbrake
**Handel** *m* trade; commerce
**handgemacht** handmade
**Handgepäck** *nt* hand-luggage
**Handschuhe** *pl* gloves
**Handtasche** *f* handbag
**Handtuch** *nt* towel
**Handwerker** *m* craftsman
**Hang** *m* slope; hill

**Hängematte** *f* hammock
**hartgekocht** hard-boiled
**Hase** *m* hare
**Haselnuß(-nüsse)** *f* hazelnut(s)
**häufig** frequent; common
**Haupt-** major; main
**Hauptbahnhof** *m* main station
**Haupteingang** *m* main entrance
**Hauptgericht(e)** *nt* main course(s)
**Hauptsaison** *f* high season
**Hauptstadt** *f* capital *(city)*
**Hauptverkehrszeit** *f* peak hours
**Haus** *nt* house; home; **zu Hause** at home
**Hausdiener** *m* valet *(in hotel)*
**hauseigen** belonging to the hotel
**Haushaltswaren** *pl* household goods
**Hausmeister** *m* caretaker
**Hausnummer** *f* street number
**Hausordnung** *f* house regulations
**Hausschlüssel** *m* house key
**Hauswein** *m* house wine
**Haut** *f* hide *(leather)*; skin
**Hautarzt** *m* dermatologist
**Haxe** *f* leg *(joint)*
**Hebel** *m* lever
**Hecht** *m* pike
**Hecktürmodell** *nt* hatchback *(car)*
**Hefe** *f* yeast
**Heftpflaster** *nt* sticking plaster
**Heilbutt** *m* halibut
**Heiligabend** *m* Christmas Eve
**Heilmittel** *nt* remedy
**Heilpraktiker** *m* non-medical practitioner
**Heim** *nt* home *(institution)*; hostel

**Heimatadresse** *f* home address
**Heimatmuseum** *nt* museum of local history
**Heimreise** *f* return journey
**heiß** hot
**heißen** to be called; **wie heißen Sie?** what is your name?
**Heißwassergerät** *nt* water heater
**Heizdecke** *f* electric blanket
**Heizgerät** *nt* heater
**Heizkörper** *m* radiator
**Heizung** *f* heating
**helfen** to help
**hell** light *(pale)*; bright
**Helm** *m* helmet
**Hemd(en)** *nt* shirt(s)
**herausziehen** to pull out
**Herbst** *m* autumn
**herein** in; come in
**Hering** *m* herring; peg
**Heringstopf** *m* pickled herrings in soured cream
**Herr** *m* gentleman; master; Mr; **mein Herr** sir; 'Herren' 'Gents'
**Herrenbekleidung** *f* menswear
**Herrentoilette** *f* gents' toilet
**Herz** *nt* heart
**Herzmuschel(n)** *f* cockle(s)
**Heuriger** *m* Austrian term for Neuer Wein
**Heuschnupfen** *m* hay fever
**heute** today; **heute abend** tonight
**hier** here
**hierher** this way
**hiesig** local
**Hilfe** *f* help; **Hilfe!** help!
**Himbeere(n)** *f* raspberry(-berries)

**Himbeergeist** *m* raspberry brandy
**hin** there
**hinab** down
**hinauf** up
**hinaus** out
**hinein** in
**hineinstecken** to put in; to plug in
**hinten** behind; **nach hinten** back
**hinter** behind
**Hinter-** rear
**hinterlassen** to leave
**Hinterradantrieb** *m* rear wheel drive
**hinüber** across; over
**Hin- und Rückfahrt** *f* round trip
**hinunter** down
**Hinweis** *m* notice
**Hinweisschild** *nt* sign
**Hirn** *nt* brains (as food)
**Hirsch** *m* venison
**Hitze** *f* heat
**hoch** high
**Hoch-** overhead (railway)
**Hochsaison** *f* high season
**Hochspannung** *f* high tension
**Höchst-** maximum
**Höchstgeschwindigkeit** *f* maximum speed
**Höchstmietdauer** *f* maximum rental period
**Höchstparkdauer** *f* waiting limited to
**Hochwasser** *nt* high tide; flood
**Hof** *m* yard (of building); courtyard
**Höhe** *f* altitude; height (of object)
**höher** higher; **höher stellen** to turn up (heat, volume)

**Höhle** *f* cave
**holen** to get; to fetch
**holländisch** Dutch
**Holz** *nt* wood (material)
**Holzkohlenbrot** *nt* bread baked in a wood-fired oven
**Honig** *m* honey
**Honigmelone** *f* honey melon
**hören** to hear
**Hörer** *m* receiver (phone)
**Hörgerät** *nt* hearing aid
**Hörnchen** *nt* croissant
**Höschenwindeln** *pl* disposable nappies
**Hose** *f* trousers; **kurze Hose** shorts
**Hotelführer** *m* hotel guide
**Hotel garni** *nt* bed and breakfast hotel
**Hotelverzeichnis** *nt* list of hotels
**Hubraum** *m* cubic capacity
**Hubschrauber** *m* helicopter
**Huhn** *nt* chicken
**Hühnerauge** *nt* corn (on foot)
**Hühnerbrühe** *f* clear chicken broth
**Hühnerbrust** *f* chicken breast
**Hühnerfrikassee** *nt* chicken fricassee
**Hühnerkeule** *f* chicken leg
**Hummer** *m* lobster
**Hund** *m* dog
**hundert** hundred
**Hupe** *f* horn (of car)
**Husten** *m* cough
**Hustensaft** *m* cough medicine
**Hustentee** *m* tea which is good for coughs

**Hütte** f hut; mountain shelter
**Hüttenkäse** m cottage cheese
**Hüttenruhe** f lights out (in mountain shelter)

**ich** I
**IC-Zuschlag** m Intercity supplement
**Idiotenhügel** m nursery slope
**ihr** you (plural familiar form)
**Imbiß** m snack
**Imbißstube** f snack bar
**immer** always
**Impfung** f vaccination
**in** in; into
**inbegriffen** included
**Industriegebiet** nt industrial area
**Informationszentrum** nt information centre
**Ingwer** m ginger
**Inhalt** m contents
**inklusive** inclusive
**Inklusivpreise** pl prices inclusive of VAT and service charge
**Inland** nt inland
**Inlandsgespräch(e)** nt national call(s)
**innen** inside
**Innen-** interior
**Innenraum** m inner zone
**Innenstadt** f city centre
**innere(r/s)** internal
**innerhalb** within
**innerlich** for internal use (medicine)
**Insassen(unfall)versicherung** f passenger insurance
**Insektenschutzmittel** nt insect repellent
**Insel** f island
**insgesamt** altogether
**irgendwo** somewhere
**Irrtum** m mistake
**Italien** nt Italy
**italienisch** Italian

**ja** yes
**Jacke** f jacket; cardigan
**Jägerschnitzel** nt pork escalope with mushrooms
**Jahr** nt year
**Jahreszeit** f season
**Jahrgang** m vintage
**Jahrhundert** nt century
**jährlich** annual; yearly
**Jahrmarkt** m fair
**Jakobsmuschel(n)** f scallop(s)
**Januar** m January
**jede(r/s)** each; every
**jemand** somebody; someone
**jetzt** now
**Jod** nt iodine
**Joghurt** m yoghurt
**Johannisbeere(n)** f currant(s); **rote Johannisbeere** redcurrant; **schwarze Johannisbeere** blackcurrant
**Johannisberg** m medium-dry white wine
**Jubiläum** nt jubilee
**Juckreiz** m itch
**Jugend** f youth (period)
**Jugendherberge** f youth hostel
**Jugendherbergsausweis** m youth hostel membership card
**Jugendliche(r)** m/f teenager

**Jugoslawien** nt Yugoslavia
**Juli** m July
**jung** young
**Junge** m boy
**Junggeselle** m bachelor
**Juni** m June
**Jura Omelette** f omelette with
  Emmental cheese, bacon, potato,
  onion, tomato

**Kabel** nt cable; lead *(electrical)*
**Kabeljau** m cod
**Kabine** f cubicle; cabin *(on ship)*
**Kabinenbahn** f cable railway
**Kaffee** m coffee
**Kaffeekanne** f coffeepot
**Kaffeemaschine** f percolator
**Kaffeepause** f coffee break
**Kai** m quayside
**Kaiserschmarren** m shredded
  pancake with raisins and syrup
**Kajüte** f cabin *(on ship)*
**Kakao** m cocoa
**Kalb** nt calf
**Kalbfleisch** nt veal
**Kalbsbries** nt calf's sweetbread
**Kalbsleber** f calf's liver
**Kalbsrückensteak** nt veal steak
**Kalbsschnitzel** nt veal escalope
**Kaldaunen** pl tripe
**kalt** cold; **kalte Speisen** cold dishes;
  snacks
**Kalterersee** m light red wine
**Kaltstartautomatik** f cold weather
  automatic starter
**Kamillentee** m camomile tea
**Kamin** m fireplace

**Kamm** m comb; ridge
**Kanada** nt Canada
**kanadisch** Canadian
**kandiert** glacé
**Kandis(zucker)** m rock *(sweet)*
**Kaninchen** nt rabbit
**Kanister** m (petrol) can
**Kännchen Kaffee** nt pot of coffee
**Kanu** nt canoe
**Kapelle** f chapel; orchestra
**Kapern** pl capers
**Kapsel** f capsule *(of medicine)*
**kaputt** broken; out of order
**Karaffe** f decanter; carafe
**Karamelbonbon(s)** nt toffee(s)
**Karfreitag** m Good Friday
**Karotten** pl carrots
**Karpfen** m carp
**Karte** f card; ticket; chart; menu
**Kartentelefon** nt cardphone
**Kartenvorverkauf** m advance
  booking
**Kartoffel(n)** f potato(es); **gebackene
  Kartoffeln/Kartoffeln in der Schale**
  baked potatoes
**Kartoffelbrei** m mashed potatoes
**Kartoffelklöße** pl potato dumplings
**Kartoffelpuffer** m potato fritter
**Kartoffelpüree** nt mashed potatoes
**Kartoffelsalat** m potato salad
**Käse** m cheese
**Käsekuchen** m cheesecake
**Käseplatte** f (plate of) assorted
  cheeses
**Kasse** f cash desk; box office
**Kasseler Rippenspeer** m pickled,
  smoked pork chops

**Kassette** *f* cassette; cartridge
**Kassettenfilm** *m* cartridge film
**Kassierer** *m* teller; cashier
**Kassler** *nt* lightly smoked pork loin
**Kastanie** *f* chestnut
**Katalysator** *m* catalytic converter
**kaufen** to buy
**Käufer** *m* buyer
**Kaufhaus** *nt* department store
**Kaugummi** *nt* chewing gum
**Kaution** *f* deposit
**Kefir** *m* fermented milk
**Kegelbahn** *f* bowling alley
**Keilriemen** *m* fan belt
**kein(e)** no; not a(n); **kein Zutritt** no entry; **keine Einfahrt** no entry
**Keks(e)** *m* biscuit(s) *(sweet)*
**Keller** *m* cellar
**Kellner** *m* waiter; steward *(at club)*
**Kennzeichen** *nt* registration number; **besondere Kennzeichen** distinguishing marks
**Keramik** *f* pottery
**Kette** *f* chain
**Keule** *f* drumstick *(of chicken)*
**Kilometer** *m* kilometre; **Kilometer pro Stunde** kilometres per hour
**Kilometerzähler** *m* ≈ milometer
**Kind(er)** *nt* child(ren)
**Kinderarzt** *m* paediatrician
**Kinderbett** *nt* cot
**Kinderfahrkarte** *f* child's ticket
**Kindersicherung** *f* childproof safety catch
**Kinderteller** *m* child's helping
**Kino** *nt* cinema
**Kinoprogramme** *pl* film guide

**Kirche** *f* church
**Kirsche(n)** *f* cherry (cherries)
**Kirschkuchen** *m* cherry cake
**Kirschlikör** *m* cherry brandy
**Kirschwasser** *nt* kirsch
**Klage** *f* complaint
**klar** clear; plain; definite; **klare Brühe** clear stock
**Klarer** *m* schnapps
**Klasse** *f* class; grade; **erster Klasse fahren** to travel first class; **zweite Klasse** second-class; **ein Fahrschein zweiter Klasse** a second-class ticket
**Klebestreifen** *m* adhesive tape
**Klebstoff** *m* glue
**Kleid(er)** *nt* dress(es)
**Kleider** *pl* clothes
**Kleiderbügel** *m* coat hanger
**Kleidung** *f* outfit
**Kleidungsstück** *nt* garment
**klein** short *(person)*; small
**Kleinbus** *m* minibus
**Kleingeld** *nt* change *(money)*
**Kleinkunstbühne** *f* cabaret
**Klettern** *nt* rock climbing
**Klima** *nt* climate
**Klimaanlage** *f* air-conditioning
**klimatisiert** air-conditioned
**Klingel** *f* bell
**Klinke** *f* handle *(of door)*
**klopfen** to knock
**Kloß** *m* dumpling
**Kloster** *nt* monastery; convent
**Knäckebrot** *nt* crispbread
**Knoblauch** *m* garlic
**Knochen** *m* bone
**Knödel** *m* dumpling

**Knopf** m button; knob (on radio etc); **Knopf drücken** press button
**kochen** to boil; to cook
**Kocher** m cooker; stove
**Kochgelegenheit** f cooking facilities
**Kochtopf** m saucepan
**koffeinfrei** decaffeinated
**Koffer** m suitcase
**Kofferanhänger** m luggage tag
**Kofferraum** m boot (of car)
**Kohl** m cabbage
**Kohlroulade** f stuffed cabbage
**Kohlrübe** f swede
**Koje** f berth (in ship); bunk
**Kokosnuß** f coconut
**Kölnischwasser** nt cologne
**Kölsch** nt strong lager
**Kombiwagen** m estate (car)
**kommen** to come
**Kommißbrot** nt rye bread
**Komödie** f comedy
**Kompott** nt stewed fruit
**Kondensmilch** f condensed milk
**Konditorei** f cake shop; café
**Kondom** nt condom
**Konfektions-** ready-made (clothes)
**Konfession** f denomination
**Konfitüre** f jam
**König** m king
**Königin** f queen
**Königinpastete** f vol-au-vent
**königlich** royal
**Königsberger Klopse** pl meat dumplings in a white sauce with capers
**können** to be able; to know

**Konserven** pl tinned goods
**Konservierungsmittel** nt preservative
**Konsulat** nt consulate
**Kontaktlinsen** pl contact lenses
**Konto (Konten)** nt account(s)
**Kontrollabschnitt** m counterfoil
**Kontrolle** f check; control
**Kontrolleuchte** f warning light
**Kontrolleur** m inspector (of tickets)
**kontrollieren** to check (ticket, etc)
**Konzertsaal** m concert hall
**Kopfhörer** m headphones
**Kopfkissen** nt pillow
**Kopfsalat** m lettuce
**Kopfschmerzen** pl headache
**Kopfstütze** f headrest
**Korb** m hamper; basket
**Kordsamt** m cord; corduroy
**Korinthe(n)** f currant(s)
**Korken** m cork (of bottle)
**Korkenzieher** m corkscrew
**Korn** m corn schnapps
**Körper** m body
**körperbehindert** disabled
**Körperlotion** f body lotion
**Kosmetika** pl cosmetics
**Kosmetiktücher** pl paper tissues
**kosten** to cost
**Kosten** pl cost; expense
**kostenlos** free (costing nothing)
**Kotelett** nt cutlet
**Krabben** pl shrimps
**Krabbencocktail** m prawn cocktail
**Kräcker** m biscuit (savoury); cracker
**Kraftbrühe** f consommé

**Kraftfahrzeugbrief** m logbook

**Kraftfahrzeugkennzeichen** nt registration number

**Kraftfahrzeugschein** m registration document

**Kraftstoff** m fuel

**Kraftstoffverbrauch** m fuel consumption

**Krampfadern** pl varicose veins

**krank** ill; sick

**Krankenhaus** nt hospital

**Krankenkasse** f medical insurance

**Krankenschein** m medical insurance record card

**Krankenwagen** m ambulance

**Krankheit** f disease; illness

**Kräuter** pl herbs

**Kräuterbutter** f herb butter

**Kräuterlikör** m herb liqueur

**Kräutertee** m herbal tea

**Krautsalat** m coleslaw

**Krawatte** f (neck)tie

**Krebs** m crab

**Kreditkarte** f credit card

**Kreis** m circle; round

**Kreisverkehr** m roundabout

**Kresse** f watercress; cress

**Kreuz** nt cross

**Kreuzfahrt** f cruise

**Kreuzgang** m cloister

**Kreuznacher** m good quality white wine from the Nahe region

**Kreuzschlüssel** m wheel brace

**Kreuzung** f junction; crossroads

**Krevetten** pl shrimps

**Kriechspur** f crawler lane

**Krieg** m war

**Krokette(n)** f croquette(s)

**Küche** f kitchen; cooking; **warme/ kalte Küche** hot meals/snacks

**Kuchen** m flan; cake

**Kugel** f ball; scoop (of ice cream)

**Kugelschreiber** m pen

**kühl** cool

**kühlen** to chill (wine, food)

**Kühler** m radiator (of car)

**Kühlschrank** m fridge

**Kühlung** f cooling system

**Kühlwasser** nt radiator water

**Kümmel** m caraway seed; schnapps

**Kümmelbraten** m roast beef flavoured with caraway (Austria)

**Kümmelkäse** m cheese with caraway seeds

**Kunde** m customer; client

**Kundendienst** m after-sales service

**Kunst-** synthetic

**Kunstgalerie** f art gallery

**Künstler** m artist

**künstlich** artificial; man-made

**Kunststoff** m synthetic material

**Kupfer** nt copper

**Kupplung** f clutch (of car)

**Kurbel** f handle (for winding)

**Kürbis** m squash; pumpkin

**Kurfestiger** m setting lotion with conditioner

**Kurmittelhaus** nt spa centre

**Kurort** m spa

**Kurpackung** f conditioner

**Kurs** m course; exchange rate

**Kurswagen** m through coach

**Kurve** f curve; corner; turn

**kurvenreich: kurvenreiche Strecke 200M** bends for 200m
**Kurverwaltung** f management of the health resort
**kurz** short; brief
**Kurzschluß** m short-circuit
**Kurz(zeit)parken** nt short-stay car park
**Küste** f coast; seaside
**Küstenwache** f coastguard
**Kutteln** pl tripe

**Labskaus** nt cured pork, herring, potatoes and cabbage
**Lachs** m salmon
**Lack** m varnish
**Laden** m shop; store
**Ladendiebstahl** m shoplifting
**Lage** f position; situation
**Lager** nt camp; store (warehouse); **die Lager** the bearings (in car)
**Lakritze** f liquorice
**Lamm** nt lamb
**Lammkeule** f leg of lamb
**Lammrücken** m saddle of lamb
**Lampe** f lamp
**Land** nt country; land
**landen** to land (plane)
**Landjäger** m pressed, smoked sausage
**Landkarte** f map (of country)
**Landschaft** f countryside
**Landstraße** f highway
**Landung** f landing (of plane)
**Landwein** m table wine
**lang** long
**Länge** f length

**Langlauf** m cross-country skiing
**langsam** slow; **langsamer fahren** to slow down
**Languste** f crayfish
**Langzeitparken** nt long-stay car park
**lassen** to let (allow)
**Last** f load
**Lastschriftzettel** m statement of debit
**Lastwagen** m truck
**Laterne** f streetlight
**Lauch** m leek
**laufen** to run
**Laugenbrezel** f soft pretzel
**Laugenstange** f bread stick with a coating similar to pretzels
**laut** noisy; loud(ly); aloud
**läuten** to ring (doorbell)
**Lautsprecher** m (loud)speaker
**Lautstärke** f volume (of sound)
**Lawine** f avalanche
**Lawinengefahr** f danger of avalanches
**Lebensgefahr** f danger
**Lebensmittel** pl groceries
**Lebensmittelgeschäft** nt grocer's
**Lebensmittelvergiftung** f food poisoning
**Leber** f liver
**Leberkäse** m meat loaf
**Leberknödel** m liver dumpling
**Leberpastete** f liver pâté
**Leberwurst** f liver sausage
**Lebkuchen** m gingerbread
**Lederwaren** pl leather goods
**ledig** single (not married)

**leer** empty; flat *(battery)*; blank
**Leerlauf** *m* neutral *(gear)*
**Leerung** *f* collection *(of mail)*
**legen** to lay; **sich die Haare legen lassen** to have one's hair set
**leicht** light *(not heavy)*; easy; easily
**Leid** *nt* grief; **es tut mir leid** (I'm) sorry
**leider** unfortunately; **leider nicht** I'm afraid not
**leihen** to rent *(car)*; to lend
**Leihgebühr** *f* rental
**Leinen** *nt* linen *(cloth)*
**Leinenschlafsack** *m* canvas sleeping bag
**Leipziger Allerlei** *nt* peas, carrots, cauliflower and cabbage
**leise** quietly; soft; faint; **leiser stellen** to turn down *(volume)*
**Leitplanke** *f* crash barrier
**Lendchen** *nt* fillet of pork
**Lendenschnitten** *pl* tournedos
**Lenkrad** *nt* steering wheel
**Lenkradschloß** *nt* steering wheel lock
**Lenkstange** *f* handlebar(s)
**lernen** to learn
**lesen** to read
**letzte(r/s)** last; final; **letzte Nacht/Woche** last night/week
**Leuchtturm** *m* lighthouse
**Leute** *pl* people
**Licht** *nt* light; **Licht anschalten** switch on headlights
**Lichthupe** *f* flash of the headlights
**Lichtschalter** *m* light switch
**Lichtschutzfaktor** *m* protection factor

**Lidschatten** *m* eye shadow
**liebenswürdig** kind
**lieber** rather
**Liebfraumilch** *f* blended, mild, sweet Rhine wines
**Lied** *nt* song
**Liegekarte** *f* couchette ticket
**Liegestuhl** *m* deckchair
**Liegewagenplatz** *m* couchette
**Liegewiese** *f* lawn for sunbathing
**Lift** *m* elevator; ski lift
**Likör** *m* liqueur
**Limburger** *m* strong cheese with herbs
**Limonade** *f* lemonade
**Limone** *f* lime *(fruit)*
**Lindenblütentee** *m* lime blossom tea
**Linie** *f* line; **punktierte Linie** dotted line
**Linienflug** *m* scheduled flight
**Linienmaschine** *f* scheduled plane
**linke(r/s)** left(-hand)
**links** (to the) left; on the left; **links abbiegen** to turn left
**Linkssteuerung** *f* left-hand drive
**Linsen** *pl* lentils
**Linsensuppe** *f* lentil soup
**Linzer Torte** *f* jam tart
**Lippe** *f* lip
**Lippenstift** *m* lipstick
**Liptauer** *m* cream cheese with paprika and herbs *(Austria)*
**Liter** *m* litre
**LKW** *m* heavy goods vehicle
**Loch** *nt* hole
**lochen** to punch *(ticket etc)*

**Locke** f curl
**Loge** f box *(in theatre)*
**Loipe** f cross-country ski run
**lokal: lokale Adresse** f contact address
**Lokal** nt pub; restaurant
**Lorbeer** m bayleaf
**los** loose; **was ist los?** what's wrong?
**Los** nt lot *(at auction)*; ticket *(lottery)*
**lösen** to buy *(ticket)*
**Luft** f air
**Luftdruck** m air pressure
**Luftfilter** m air filter
**Luftfracht** f air freight
**Luftkissenfahrzeug** nt hovercraft
**Luftmatratze** f air bed; air mattress
**Luftpost** f: **per Luftpost** by air mail
**Lunge** f lung
**Luxus** m luxury
**Lyoner** f veal sausage

**machen** to make; to do
**Mädchen** nt girl
**Mädchenname** m maiden name
**Magen** m stomach
**Magenbeschwerden** pl stomach trouble
**Magenbitter** m bitters
**mager** lean *(meat)*
**Mahlzeit** f meal
**Mai** m May
**Maifeiertag** m Mayday
**Mais** m sweet corn
**Maiskolben** m corn on the cob
**Makrele** f mackerel
**Mal** nt time
**Maler** m painter

**Maluns** pl sliced, grated potatoes fried in lard
**Malventee** m hollyhock tea
**Malzbier** nt malt beer
**man** one
**manchmal** sometimes
**Mandarine** f tangerine
**Mandel** f almond
**Mandelentzündung** f tonsillitis
**Mann** m man; husband
**Männer** pl men
**männlich** masculine; male
**Marke** f brand *(of product)*; token *(for machine)*
**Markklößchen** pl small beef-marrow dumplings
**Markt** m market
**Marktplatz** m market-place
**Marmelade** f jam
**Marmor** m marble *(material)*
**März** m March
**Masern** pl measles
**Maße** pl measurements
**maßgeschneidert** made-to-measure
**Maßstab** m scale *(of map)*
**Matetee** m Paraguay tea
**Matjeshering** m salted young herring
**Maultaschen** pl king-size ravioli
**Mautstelle** f toll
**Mechaniker** m mechanic
**Medikament** nt drug; medicine
**medizinisch** medical
**Meer** nt sea
**Meeresfische** pl sea fish
**Meeresfrüchte** pl seafood

**Meeresspiegel** m  sea level
**Meerrettich** m  horseradish
**Mehl** nt  flour
**mehr**  more
**mehrere**  several
**Mehrfahrtenkarte** f  ticket valid for several journeys
**Mehrwertsteuer** f  value-added tax
**meister(r/s)**  most
**melden**  to report (tell about)
**Meldeschlußzeit** f  latest check-in time
**Melone** f  melon; bowler hat
**Menthol-**  mentholated
**merken**  to notice
**Messe** f  fair (commercial); mass (church)
**Messing** nt  brass
**Meßgerät** nt  gauge
**Metzgerei** f  butcher's shop
**Miederwaren** pl  corsetry
**Miesmuschel(n)** f  mussel(s)
**Mietbedingungen** pl  conditions of rental
**Mietdauer** f  duration of rental
**Miete** f  lease; rent
**mieten**  to hire; to rent (house etc)
**Mieter** m  renter (of car)
**Mietfahrzeug** nt  rented car
**Mietgebühr** f  rental (amount)
**Mietvertrag** m  rental agreement
**Mietwagen** m  rented car
**Milch** f  milk
**Milchkaffee** m  white coffee
**Milchmixgetränk** nt  milkshake
**Milchpulver** nt  dried milk
**Milchreis** m  rice pudding

**minderjährig**  under age
**Mindest-**  minimum
**Mindestalter** nt  required minimum age
**mindestens**  at least
**Mindestpreis** m  reserve price
**Mineralbad** nt  mineral bath; spa
**Mineralwasser** nt  mineral water
**Minute(n)** f  minute(s)
**Minze** f  mint (herb)
**Mirabelle(n)** f  small yellow plum(s)
**Mischbrot** nt  bread made from a mixture of types of flour
**Mischung** f  mixture
**Mißbrauch** m  abuse; **vor Mißbrauch wird gewarnt** use only as directed; do not misuse
**mit**  with
**Mitglied** nt  member; **Mitglied werden von** to join (club)
**Mitgliedsausweis** m/ **Mitgliedskarte** f  membership card
**mitnehmen**  to give a lift to; **zum Mitnehmen** takeaway (food)
**Mittag** m  midday
**Mittagessen** nt  lunch
**mittags**  at midday
**Mitte** f  middle
**mitteilen**  to inform
**Mitteilung** f  message
**Mittel** nt  means; **ein Mittel gegen** a remedy for
**Mittelalter** nt  Middle Ages
**Mittelmeer-**  Mediterranean
**mittels**  by means of
**Mittelstreifen** m  central reservation

**mittlere(r/s)** medium
**Mittwoch** m Wednesday
**Mode** f fashion
**Modeschmuck** m costume
  jewellery
**modisch** fashionable
**Mofa** nt small moped
**mögen** to like
**möglich** possible
**Mohn** m poppy seed
**Möhre(n)** f carrot(s)
**Monat** f month
**monatlich** monthly
**Monatskarte** f monthly season
  ticket
**Montag** m Monday
**Morcheln** pl morels
**morgen** tomorrow
**Morgen** m morning
**Moselwein** m moselle (wine)
**Motor** m motor; engine
**Motorboot** nt motor boat
**Motorjacht** f cabin cruiser
**Motorrad** nt motorbike
**Motorroller** m scooter
**Motorschaden** m engine trouble
**Motosport** m motor-racing
**Mücke(n)** f gnat(s), midge(s)
**müde** tired
**Mühe** f bother (effort)
**Mullbinde** f gauze bandage
**Mülleimer** m bin (for refuse)
**Müllerin Art** meunière
**Müller-Thurgau** m light, fruity
  white wine
**München** nt Munich
**Mund** m mouth

**mündlich** verbal (agreement)
**Mundwasser** nt mouthwash
**Münster** nt cathedral
**Münze(n)** f coin(s)
**Münzfernsprecher** m pay phone
**Münzgeld** nt : **Münzgeld einwerfen**
  insert coins
**Münzwechsler** m change machine
**Muscheln** pl mussels
**Muskatnuß** f nutmeg
**müssen** to have to
**Mutter** f mother
**MwSt** f VAT

**nach** after; according to; **nach**
  **London gehen** to go to London;
  **nach Frankreich** to France; **nach**
  **London abreisen** to leave for
  London
**nacheinander** one after the other
**Nachmittag** m afternoon
**nachmittags** p.m.; in the afternoon
**Nachnahme** f : **per Nachnahme**
  cash on delivery
**Nachname** m surname
**Nachricht** f note (letter); message
**Nachrichten** pl news
**Nachsaison** f : **in der Nachsaison**
  after the season
**nachsenden** to forward (letter)
**Nachspeise** f dessert
**nächste(r/s)** next; **der nächste**
  **Verwandte** the next of kin
**Nacht** f night; **von einer Nacht**
  overnight (a stay); **über Nacht**
  overnight
**Nachtdienst** m all-night service
**Nachtisch** m dessert

**Nachtleben** *nt* nightlife
**Nachtlokal** *nt* night club
**Nachtportier** *m* night porter
**Nachtschalter** *m* night counter
**Nachtzug** *m* night train
**nachzahlen** to pay extra
**nackt** nude; naked; bare
**Nagellackentferner** *m* nail varnish remover
**nahe** close *(near)*
**Nähe** *f* proximity; **in der Nähe** nearby
**Nahverkehrsnetz** *nt* suburban public transport system
**Name** *m* name; surname
**Narkose** *f* anaesthetic
**Nase** *f* nose
**naß** wet
**Nationalitätskennzeichen** *nt* nationality plate
**natur** not in breadcrumbs
**Natur-** natural
**Nebel** *m* mist; fog
**Nebelscheinwerfer** *m* fog lamp
**neben** by *(next to)*; beside
**Neben-** minor *(road)*
**neblig** foggy
**nehmen** to take *(remove, acquire)*; **nehmen Sie sich** help yourself
**nein** no *(as answer)*
**Nelke(n)** *f* carnation(s); clove(s)
**nennen** to quote *(price)*
**Nesselschlafsack** *m* cotton sleeping-bag
**Netto-** net *(income, price)*
**Nettogewicht** *nt* net weight
**Netz** *nt* net; network

**neu** new
**Neuer Wein** *m* first wine drunk after new harvest
**neueste(r/s)** recent
**Neujahrstag** *m* New Year's Day
**neun** nine
**nicht** not
**nicht-** non-
**Nichtraucher** *m* non-smoker
**nichts** nothing
**Nichtschwimmer** *m* non-swimmer
**nie** never
**Niederlande** *pl* Netherlands
**niedrig** low
**Niedrigwasser** *nt* low tide
**niemand** no one
**Niere(n)** *f* kidney(s)
**Niersteiner** *m* medium-dry to sweet white Rhine wine
**Nieselregen** *m* drizzle
**nirgends** nowhere
**Nizzasalat** *m* salad niçoise
**noch** still *(up to this time)*; yet
**Nockenwelle** *f* camshaft
**Nockerl** *pl* small dumplings
**Norden** *m* north
**nördlich** north; northern
**Nordsee** *f* North Sea
**Norm** *f* standard
**Normal-** standard *(size)*
**Normal(benzin)** *nt* regular *(petrol)*
**Notarzt** *m* doctor on emergency call
**Notausgang** *m* emergency exit
**Notbremse** *f* emergency brake
**Notdienstapotheke** *f* on-duty chemist

**Notfall** m emergency
**notieren** to make a note of
**nötig** necessary
**Notruf** m emergency number
**Notrufsäule** f emergency telephone
**Notsignal** nt distress signal
**notwendig** essential
**November** m November
**nüchtern** sober; **auf nüchternen Magen** on an empty stomach
**Nudeln** pl pasta; noodles
**Null** f nil; zero; nought
**numerieren** to number
**Nummer** f number; act
**Nummernschild** nt number plate
**nur** only
**Nuß (Nüsse)** f nut(s)
**nützlich** useful

**ob** whether
**oben** upstairs; overhead; this side up; **oben sehen Sie ...** above, you can see ...
**Obst** nt fruit
**Obstkuchen** m fruit tart
**Obstler** m fruit schnapps
**Obstsalat** m fruit salad
**Obstwasser** nt fruit schnapps
**Ochsenschwanzsuppe** f oxtail soup
**oder** or
**offen** open; **offene Weine** wine served by the glass
**öffentlich** public
**Öffentlichkeit** f the public
**öffnen** to open; to undo

**Öffnungszeiten** pl hours of business
**oft** often
**ohne** without
**Ohnmacht** f faint
**Ohr(en)** nt ear(s)
**Ohrentropfen** pl ear drops
**Oktanzahl** f octane rating
**Oktober** m October
**Öl** nt oil
**Ölstand** m oil level
**Ölverbrauch** m oil consumption
**Ölwechsel** m oil change
**Oppenheimer** m good medium-dry to sweet Rhine wine
**Optiker** m optician
**Orangenmarmelade** f marmalade
**Orangensaft** m orange juice
**Ort** m place; **an Ort und Stelle** on the spot
**örtlich** local
**Ortschaft** f village; town; **geschlossene Ortschaft** built-up area
**Ortsgespräch** nt local call
**Ortsmitte** f (town) centre
**Ortszeit** f local time
**Osten** m east
**Ostermontag** m Easter Monday
**Ostern** nt Easter
**Österreich** nt Austria
**österreichisch** Austrian
**Ostersonntag** m Easter Sunday
**östlich** eastern

**Paar** nt pair; couple *(persons)*; **ein paar** a couple of *(a few)*
**Päckchen** nt packet; small parcel

**Paket** nt parcel; packet
**Paketannahme/Paketausgabe** f parcels office
**Paketkarte** f dispatch form
**Palatschinken** pl pancakes filled with curd cheese or jam
**Pampelmuse(n)** f grapefruit(s)
**paniert** coated with breadcrumbs
**Panne** f breakdown (of car)
**Pannenhilfe** f breakdown service
**Papier(e)** nt paper(s)
**Papiertaschentuch** nt tissue
**Paprikaschote** f pepper (capsicum)
**Parfümerie** f perfumery
**Parkdeck** nt deck (in car park)
**parken** to park; **Parken verboten** no parking
**Parkett** nt stalls (in theatre)
**Parkhaus** nt multi-storey car park
**Parkmöglichkeit** f parking facilities
**Parkplatz** m car park; parking space; lay-by
**Parkscheibe** f parking disc
**Parkschein** m parking ticket
**Parkuhr** f parking meter
**Parkverbot** nt : **Parkverbot Ende** end of parking restrictions
**Partnerstädte** pl twin towns
**Paß** m passport; pass (in mountains)
**Passagier** m passenger; **nur für Passagiere** passengers only
**Passagierschiff** nt liner (ship)
**passen** to fit; to suit
**Paßkontrolle** f passport control
**Pastete** f pâté; pie (meat)
**Patrone** f cartridge

**pauschal** flat-rate; **bis 10 km pauschal** up to 10 kms inclusive
**Pauschale** f/**Pauschalpreis** m flat rate
**Pauschalreise** f package holiday
**Pauschaltarif** m flat-rate tariff
**Pause** f pause; break; interval
**Pellkartoffeln** pl potatoes boiled in their jackets
**Pelzwaren** pl furs
**Pendelverkehr** m shuttle (service)
**Pension** f boarding house
**Personal** nt staff
**Personalien** pl particulars
**Personenzug** m stopping train
**persönlich** personal(ly)
**Petersilie** f parsley
**Pfandflasche** f bottle with deposit
**Pfannengerichte** pl fried dishes
**Pfannkuchen** m pancake
**Pfeffer** m pepper
**Pfefferkuchen** m gingerbread
**Pfefferminz** nt (pepper)mint
**Pfefferminzlikör** m crème de menthe
**Pfefferminztee** m mint tea
**Pfeffersteak** m steak sprinkled with crushed black peppercorns
**Pfeil** m arrow; dart
**Pferderennen** nt horse-racing
**Pfifferlinge** pl chanterelles
**Pfingsten** nt Whitsun
**Pfingstmontag** m Whit Monday
**Pfingstsonntag** m Whitsunday
**Pfirsich(e)** m peach(es)
**Pflaster** nt plaster (for wound)
**Pflaume(n)** f plum(s)

**Pflicht** f duty
**Pforte** f gate
**Pförtner** m porter *(doorkeeper)*
**Pfund** nt pound
**pikant** savoury *(not sweet)*
**Pils/Pilsner** nt lager
**Pilz(e)** m mushroom(s)
**Piste** f runway; ski run
**Plakette** f badge *(of metal)*
**planmäßig** scheduled
**Platte** f plate; dish; record
**Plattfuß** m flat foot; flat tyre
**Platz** m place *(seat)*; room *(space)*; square *(in town)*; court *(tennis etc)*; course *(for golf)*; field *(for football etc)*; **Platz nehmen** to take a seat
**Platzbuchung** f reservations
**Plätzchen** nt biscuit(s)
**Platzkarte** f seat reservation *(ticket)*
**Platzreservierungen** pl seat reservations
**Plombe** f filling *(in tooth)*
**pochiert** poached
**Pol** m terminal *(electricity)*
**Police** f policy *(insurance)*
**Polizei** f police
**Polizeibeamte(r)** m (police) officer
**Polizeiwache** f police station
**Polizist** m policeman
**Pommes frites** pl chips
**Porree** m leek
**Portier** m doorman
**Portion** f helping
**Porto** nt postage
**Post** f post; Post Office; **mit der Post schicken** to post
**Post-** postal

**Postamt** nt post office
**Postanweisung** f postal order
**Postfach** nt post-office box
**Postgiroamt** nt main post office which acts as clearing house for giro accounts
**Postkarte** f postcard
**postlagernd** poste restante
**Postleitzahl** f postcode
**Postüberweisung** f post-office transfer
**Postvermerk** m note from the post office
**Postwertzeichen** nt postage stamp
**Poulardenbrust** f chicken breast
**praktisch** handy; practical; **praktischer Arzt** general practitioner
**Pralinen** pl chocolates
**Präservativ** nt condom
**Praxis** f doctor's surgery
**Preis** m prize; price; **Preise schließen ein** prices are inclusive of
**Preisänderung** f: **Preisänderungen vorbehalten** rates are subject to change without notice
**Preiselbeere(n)** f cranberry(-berries)
**Prinzeßbohnen** pl French beans
**Privatgrundstück** nt private property
**Privatweg** m private way
**pro** per; **pro Stunde** per hour; **zweimal pro Tag** twice a day; **pro Kopf** per person; **pro Jahr** per annum
**probieren** to taste; to sample
**Programmübersicht** f summary of what's on
**prost!** cheers!

**Proviant** *m* provisions
**Provision** *f* commission *(sum received)*; bank charges
**Prozent** *nt* per cent
**prüfen** to check *(oil, water etc)*
**Pudding** *m* blancmange
**Puder** *m* powder *(cosmetic)*
**Pulver** *nt* powder
**Pulverkaffee** *m* instant coffee
**pünktlich** on schedule *(train)*, punctual
**pur** straight *(drink)*
**Pute** *f* turkey *(hen)*
**Putenschnitzel** *nt* turkey breast
**Puter** *m* turkey *(cock)*
**Putzdienst** *m* cleaning duty

**Qualität** *f* quality
**Qualitätswein** *m* good quality wine; **Qualitätswein mit Prädikat** best quality wine
**Qualle** *f* jellyfish
**Quark** *m* soft curd cheese
**Quarktasche** *f* curd cheese turnover
**Quelle** *f* spring *(of water)*; source
**Quetschung** *f* bruise
**Quittung** *f* receipt

**Rabatt** *m* discount
**rabattfähig** discountable
**Raclette** *nt* Swiss dish of melted cheese and potatoes
**Rad** *nt* wheel; bicycle
**Radarkontrolle** *f* radar speed check
**Räder** *pl* wheels

**Radfahrer** *m* cyclist
**Radfahrweg** *m* cycle track
**Radieschen** *nt* (small red) radish(es)
**Radlermaß** *f* shandy
**Radwechsel** *m* wheel change
**Rahmgeschnetzeltes** *nt* sliced pork in a cream sauce
**Rand** *m* verge; border; edge
**Randstein** *m* kerb
**Rang** *m* circle *(in theatre)*; rank
**Rasen** *m* lawn
**Rasierapparat** *m* shaver; razor
**Rasiercreme** *f* shaving cream
**Rasierklinge** *f* razor blade
**Rasierpinsel** *m* shaving brush
**Rasierschaum** *m* shaving foam
**Rasierseite** *f* shaving soap
**Rasierwasser** *nt* aftershave (lotion)
**Rastplatz** *m* picnic area
**Raststätte** *f* service area
**Rathaus** *nt* town hall
**Ratskeller** *m* restaurant under the town hall
**rauchen** to smoke; **Rauchen verboten** no smoking
**Raucher** *m* smoker *(person)*
**Räucheraal** *m* smoked eel
**Räucherlachs** *m* smoked salmon
**Räucherplatte** *f* smoked fish/meat platter
**Rauchfleisch** *nt* smoked meat
**Raum** *m* space *(room)*
**räumen** to clear *(road)*
**Räumlichkeiten** *pl* premises
**Rebhuhn** *nt* partridge
**rechnen** to calculate; **rechnen Sie**

**mit 10 Minuten, um dort hinzukommen** allow 10 minutes to get there

**Rechnung** f bill *(account)*

**Rechnungsbetrag** m total *(charges)*

**rechte(r/s)** right *(not left)*

**rechts** (to the) right; on the right; **rechts abbiegen** to turn right; **rechts fahren** keep right; **rechts vor links** give way to traffic coming from the right

**Rechtsanwalt** m lawyer; solicitor

**rechtzeitig** on time; **gerade noch rechtzeitig** just in time

**reden** to speak

**Reformationsfest** nt Reformation Day *(October 31st, public holiday)*

**Reformhaus** nt health food shop

**Reformkost** f health foods

**regelmäßig** regular

**Regen** m rain

**Regenbekleidung** f rainwear

**Regenmantel** m raincoat

**Regenschirm** m umbrella

**regnen** to rain; **es regnet** it's raining

**Reh** nt deer

**Rehfleisch** nt venison

**Rehkeule** f haunch of venison

**Rehrücken** m saddle of venison

**Reibekuchen** m potato fritter

**Reich** nt empire

**reichen** to pass *(hand on: object)*; **reicht es?** will it do? *(be enough)*

**reif** ripe; mature *(cheese)*

**Reifen** m tyre

**Reifen(füll)druck** m tyre pressure

**Reifenpanne** f blowout; puncture

**Reihe** f row; **Sie sind an der Reihe** it's your turn

**Reihenfolge** f order *(in series)*

**rein** pure

**reinigen** to clean

**Reinigung** f cleaner's; **die chemische Reinigung** dry-cleaner's

**Reinigungsmilch** f cleansing milk

**Reis** m rice

**Reise** f trip *(journey)*; **gute Reise!** have a good journey!

**Reiseandenken** pl souvenirs

**Reisebüro** nt travel agency

**Reiseführer** m guidebook

**Reisegepäck** nt luggage

**Reisekrankheit** f travel sickness

**reisen** to travel

**Reisende(r)** m/f traveller

**Reisepaß** m passport

**Reiseproviant** m food for the journey

**Reiseroute** f itinerary

**Reisescheck** m traveller's cheque

**Reiseveranstalter** m travel agent

**Reisewetterbericht** m/ **Reisewettervorhersage** f holiday weather forecast

**Reiseziel** nt destination

**Reiten** nt riding

**Remouladensoße** f tartar sauce

**Rennbahn** f racecourse; track

**Rennen** nt race *(sport)*

**Rentner** m pensioner

**Reparatur** f: **in Reparatur** under repair

**Reparaturwerkstatt** f garage

**reparieren** to repair

**Reserverad** nt spare wheel

**reservieren: reservieren lassen** to book *(seat)*
**Reservierung** *f* booking
**Restbetrag** *m* unused coins; remainder to be carried over
**Restgeld** *nt* **: Restgeld wird erstattet** change given
**Rettich** *m* (large white) radish
**Rettungsboot** *nt* lifeboat
**Rettungsflugwacht** *f* air-rescue service
**Rezept** *nt* prescription; recipe
**rezeptpflichtig** available only on prescription
**Rhabarber** *m* rhubarb
**Rhein** *m* Rhine
**Rheinwein** *m* Rhine wine; **der weiße Rheinwein** hock
**Richtgeschwindigkeit** *f* recommended speed
**richtig** correct; right; proper
**Richtung** *f* direction
**Riesling** *m* medium-dry to semi-sweet white wine
**Rinderbraten** *m* roast beef
**Rindfleisch** *nt* beef
**Rindsrouladen** *pl* beef olives
**Ringstraße** *f* ring road
**Rippchen** *nt* slightly cured pork rib
**Rochen** *m* skate *(fish)*
**Rock** *m* skirt
**Roggenbrot** *m* rye bread
**roh** raw
**Rohkost** *f* raw fruit and vegetables
**Rollbraten** *m* rolled pork roast
**Rollschuhe** *pl* roller skates
**Rollstuhl** *m* wheelchair

**Rolltreppe** *f* escalator
**romanisch** romanesque
**Röntgenaufnahme** *f* X-ray *(photo)*
**Rosenkohl** *m* Brussels sprouts
**Rosine(n)** *f* raisin(s)
**Rost** *m* rust; grill
**Rostbraten** *m* roast
**Rostbratwürstchen** *pl* grilled sausages
**rosten** to rust
**rostfrei** stainless *(steel)*
**Rösti** *pl* grated roast potatoes
**Röstkartoffeln** *pl* sauté potatoes
**Röstzwiebeln** *pl* fried onions
**rot** red; **rote Bete** *or* **Rübe** beetroot; **das Rote Kreuz** the Red Cross
**Rotbarsch** *m* red snapper
**Röteln** *pl* German measles
**Rotkohl** *m*/**Rotkraut** *nt* red cabbage
**Rotwein** *m* red wine
**Rotzunge** *f* witch flounder
**Roulade(n)** *f* beef olive(s)
**Rübe** *f* turnip
**Rückenschmerzen** *pl* backache
**Rückfahrkarte** *f* return ticket
**Rückfahrt** *f* return journey
**Rückflug** *m* return flight
**Rückfrage** *f* question; query
**Rückführgebühr** *f* drop-off charge; collection charge
**Rückgabe** *f* return
**Rückgabeknopf** *m* coin return (button)
**Rückkehr** *f* return *(going/returning)*
**Rücklicht** *nt* rear light
**Rucksack** *m* rucksack

**Rückseite** f back (reverse side)
**Rücksitz** m back seat; pillion
**Rückspiegel** m rear-view mirror
**Rückstrahler** m reflector
**rückwärts** backwards
**Rückwärtsgang** m reverse (gear)
**Rückzahlung** f repayment
**Rückzahlungsbetrag** m amount to be withdrawn
**Rückzahlungsschein** m withdrawal slip
**Ruderboot** nt rowing boat
**Rüdesheimer** m good quality dry wine from the Rheingau region
**Rufnummer** f telephone number
**Ruhe** f rest (repose); peace (calm); **Ruhe!** be quiet!
**ruhig** calm; quiet; peaceful; quietly
**Rührei** nt scrambled eggs
**Ruländer** m full-bodied sweetish white wine
**Rummelplatz** m fairground
**Rumtopf** m soft fruit in rum
**rund** round; **rund um Stuttgart** Stuttgart and surroundings
**Rundfahrt** f tour; round trip
**Rundflug** m sightseeing flight
**Rundfunk** m radio
**Rundgang** m tour
**Rundreise** f round trip
**Rundwanderweg** m circular trail for ramblers
**russisch** Russian; **russische Eier** egg(s) mayonnaise
**Rutschbahn** f slide (chute)
**rutschig** slippery

**Saal** m hall (room)

**Sache** f thing
**Sachen** pl stuff (things); belongings
**Sachertorte** f rich chocolate cake
**Sackgasse** f dead end; cul-de-sac
**Saft** m juice
**saftig** juicy
**sagen** to say; to tell (fact, news)
**Sahne** f cream; **mit Sahne** with whipped cream; **saure Sahne** sour cream
**Sahnequark** m cream cheese
**Sahnetorte** f cream gâteau
**Saison** f season; **außerhalb der Saison** in the off-season
**Saitenwurst** f type of frankfurter sausage
**Salat** m salad
**Salatplatte** f salad (main dish)
**Salbe** f ointment
**Salbei** m sage (herb)
**Salz** nt salt
**salzig** salty
**Salzkartoffeln** pl boiled potatoes
**Salzstangen** pl pretzel sticks
**Sammelfahrschein** m group ticket
**Samstag** m Saturday
**Sardelle(n)** f anchovy (anchovies)
**satt** full
**Satz** m set (collection); grounds (of coffee); sentence
**sauber** clean
**Sauerbraten** m braised beef marinated in vinegar
**Sauerkraut** nt shredded pickled white cabbage
**Sauerrahm** m sour cream
**Sauerstoff** m oxygen
**S-Bahn** f suburban railway

# SCH – SCH

**Schach** nt chess
**schade** a pity
**Schaden** m damage
**Schadensersatz** m damages; compensation
**Schadensersatzverpflichtung** f liability for damages
**schädlich** harmful
**Schaffner** m conductor; guard
**Schalldämpfer** m silencer (on car)
**Schallplatte** f record
**schalten** to shift gear
**Schalter** m switch; counter
**Schalterhalle** f booking hall
**Schalthebel** m switch lever; gear lever
**Schaltiere** pl shellfish (on menu)
**Schaltknüppel** m gear lever; gearshift
**scharf** hot (spicy); sharp
**Schaschlik** nt (shish) kebab
**schattig** shady
**Schatz** m treasure; darling
**schätzen** to value; to estimate; **zu schätzen wissen** to appreciate
**Schaufenster** nt shop window
**Schaufensterbummel** m window shopping
**Schaum** m foam
**Schaum-** sparkling (wine)
**Schaumbad** nt foam bath
**Schaumfestiger** m setting foam
**Schaumkur** f foam conditioner
**Schauspiel** nt play
**Scheck** m cheque; **einen Scheck einlösen** to cash a cheque
**Scheckbuch** nt cheque book

**Scheckkarte** f cheque card
**Schein(e)** m banknote(s)
**scheinen** to shine (sun etc); to seem
**Scheinwerfer** m headlight; floodlight; spotlight
**Schellfisch** m haddock
**Schere** f (pair of) scissors
**Schi-** see Ski
**schicken** to send
**Schiene** f splint
**Schienen** pl rails (for train)
**Schiff** nt ship; **mit dem Schiff fahren** to go by sea
**Schiffahrtsgesellschaft** f shipping company
**Schiffskarte** f boat ticket
**Schiffsverbindungen** pl connecting boat service
**Schild** nt sign (notice)
**Schildkrötensuppe** f turtle soup
**Schinken** m ham; **roher/gekochter/geraucher Schinken** raw ham (smoked)/cooked ham/smoked ham
**Schinkenhäger** m type of schnapps
**Schinkenwurst** f ham sausage
**Schirm** m umbrella; screen
**Schlacht(e)platte** f ham and sausage served with sauerkraut
**Schlachterei** f butcher's shop
**schlafen** to sleep; **haben Sie gut geschlafen?** did you sleep well?; **schlafen Sie gut!** sleep well!
**Schlaflosigkeit** f insomnia
**Schlafmittel** nt sleeping drug
**Schlafsaal** m dormitory (room)
**Schlafsack** m sleeping bag
**Schlaftablette** f sleeping pill

173

**Schlafwagen** m sleeping car

**Schlafwagenkarte** f sleeper reservation ticket

**Schlafwagenplatz** m berth (in train)

**Schlagsahne** f whipped cream

**Schlange** f queue; snake

**Schlauch** m hose; tube (of tyre)

**Schlauchboot** nt dinghy (inflatable)

**schlauchlos** tubeless

**schlecht** bad; badly

**Schleie** f tench

**Schlepplift** m ski tow

**Schleudergefahr** f slippery road

**Schleuse** f lock (in canal)

**schließen** to shut

**Schließfach** nt locker

**Schlitten** m sleigh; sledge

**Schlittschuh(e)** m skate(s)

**Schlitz** m slot

**Schloß** nt castle; lock (on door)

**Schlummertaste** f snooze button

**Schluß** m end

**Schlüssel** m key; **Schlüssel abziehen** remove key

**Schlüsseldienst** m locksmith emergency service

**Schlußleuchte** f rear light

**Schlußverkauf** m clearance sale

**Schmalz** nt lard; dripping

**schmecken** to taste

**Schmerz** m pain; ache

**schmerzhaft** painful

**schmerzstillendes Mittel** nt / **Schmerztablette** f painkiller

**schmieren** to lubricate

**Schmierfett** nt grease (lubricant)

**Schmortopf** m casserole (dish)

**Schmuck** m jewellery; decorations

**Schnaps** m schnapps; spirits

**Schnecke** f snail

**Schnee** m snow

**Schneebrille** f snow goggles

**schneefrei** free of snow

**Schneeketten** pl snow chains

**Schneepflug** m snowplough

**Schneesturm** m blizzard

**Schneewehe** f snowdrift

**schneiden** to cut

**schneien: es schneit** it's snowing

**schnell** fast

**Schnell-** high-speed

**Schnellgang** m overdrive

**Schnellstraße** f dual carriageway

**Schnellzug** m express train

**Schnittlauch** m chives

**Schnittwunde** f cut (wound)

**Schnitzel** nt escalope

**Schnuller** m dummy (baby's)

**Schnupfen** m cold

**Schnürsenkel** pl shoelaces

**Scholle** f plaice

**schön** lovely; fine; beautiful

**Schonkost** f light diet

**Schorle** nt wine and soda water mix; **Schorle süss** wine and lemonade

**Schranke** f barrier

**Schraubenschlüssel** m spanner

**Schraubenzieher** m screwdriver

**schreiben** to write

**Schreibmaschine** f typewriter

**Schreibwarengeschäft** nt stationer's (shop)

**schriftlich** in writing

**Schritt** m pace; step; **Schritt fahren!** dead slow

**Schrittempo** nt walking speed; dead slow

**Schuh(e)** m shoe(s)

**Schuhgeschäft** nt shoeshop

**Schuhputzmittel** nt shoe polish

**schuld: schuld sein** to be to blame; **wer ist schuld daran?** whose fault is it?

**Schuld** f debt; guilt; fault; **die Schuld geben** to blame

**Schüler** m pupil

**Schulter(n)** f shoulder(s)

**Schuppen** pl scales (of fish); dandruff

**Schüssel** f basin; bowl (for food)

**Schutt** m : **Schutt abladen verboten** no tipping

**schütteln** to shake

**Schutz** m safeguard

**Schutzbrille** f goggles

**schützen** to guard (protect)

**Schutzhütte** f shelter; refuge

**Schutzimpfung** f vaccination

**schwanger** pregnant

**schwarz** black

**Schwarztee** m tea

**Schwarzwälder Kirschtorte** f Black Forest gâteau

**Schwarzweißfilm** m black and white film

**Schwein** nt pig

**Schweinebraten** m roast pork

**Schweinefleisch** nt pork

**Schweinehals** m neck of pork

**Schweinekotelett** nt pork chop

**Schweinelendchen** nt pork fillet

**Schweinerippchen** nt cured pork chop

**Schweinerückensteak** nt pork steak

**Schweineschmalz** nt lard

**Schweinshaxe** f knuckle of pork

**Schweinsleder** nt pigskin

**Schweiß** m sweat

**Schweiz** f Switzerland

**schweizerisch** Swiss

**Schwellung** f swelling

**Schwenkkartoffeln** pl sauté potatoes

**Schwerbehinderte** pl severely disabled persons

**Schwester** f sister; nurse; nun

**schwierig** hard; difficult

**Schwierigkeit** f difficulty; **Schwierigkeiten** trouble (problems)

**Schwimmbad/Schwimmbecken** nt swimming pool

**schwimmen** to swim

**Schwimmflossen** pl flippers

**Schwimmgürtel** m swimming belt

**Schwimmweste** f life jacket

**sechs** six

**See**[1] f sea

**See**[2] m lake

**seekrank** seasick

**Seelachs** m pollack

**Seeteufel** m monkfish

**Seezunge** f sole (fish)

**Segel** nt sail

**Segelboot** nt sailing boat

**Segelfliegen** nt gliding (sport)

**Segelflugzeug** nt glider

**segeln** to sail

**Segeln** *nt* yachting
**sehen** to see
**Sehenswürdigkeiten** *pl* sights
**Seife** *f* soap
**Seifenpulver** *nt* soap powder
**Seil** *nt* rope
**Seilbahn** *f* cable railway; funicular
**sein** to be; *see* **GRAMMAR**
**seit** since
**seitdem** since
**Seite** *f* page; side
**Seitenstraße** *f* side road; side street
**Seitenstreifen** *m* hard shoulder;
  **Seitenstreifen nicht befahrbar** soft
  verges
**Sekt** *m* sparkling wine
**Selbstbedienung** *f*: **mit**
  **Selbstbedienung** self-service
**Selbstbedienungsrestaurant** *nt*
  cafeteria
**Selbstbeteiligung** *f* (percentage)
  excess
**Selbstbräuner** *m* fake tan
**selbsttanken** self-service
**Selbstversorger** *m* self-caterer
**Selbstwählfernverkehr** *m* STD
**Sellerie** *f* celeriac
**Semmelknödel** *m* bread dumpling
**senden** to broadcast; to send
**Sendung** *f* programme; shipment
**Senf** *m* mustard
**September** *m* September
**servieren** to serve *(food)*
**Servobremse** *f* power-assisted
  brake
**Servolenkung** *f* power-assisted
  steering

**Sesambrötchen** *nt* sesame roll
**Sessellift** *m* chairlift
**setzen** to place; to put; **sich setzen**
  to sit down; **setzen Sie sich bitte**
  please take a seat
**sicher** sure; safe; definite
**Sicherheit** *f* safety
**Sicherheitsgurt** *m* seat belt; safety
  belt
**Sicherung** *f* fuse
**Sicht** *f* sight; view
**Sichtvermerk** *m* endorsement; visa
**sie** she; they
**Sie** you *(polite form)*
**sieben** seven
**Silber** *nt* silver
**Silvester** *nt* New Year's Eve
**Sitz** *m* seat
**sitzen** to sit
**Sitzplatz** *m* seat
**Ski(er)** *m* ski(s); **Ski fahren** to ski
**Skifahren** *nt* skiing
**Skihalter** *m* ski rack
**Skihose** *f* ski pants
**Skiläufer** *m* skier
**Skilehrer** *m* ski instructor
**Skilift** *m* ski lift
**Skipaß** *m* ski pass
**Skipiste** *f* ski run
**Skischule** *f* ski school
**Skistiefel** *m* ski boot(s)
**S-Kurve** *f* double bend
**Slipeinlagen** *pl* panty liners
**Smoking** *m* /**Smokingjacke** *f*
  dinner jacket
**Sodbrennen** *nt* heartburn
**sofort** at once; immediately

**Sohlen** *pl* soles
**Sojabrot** *nt* soya bread
**sollen** to be (supposed) to
**Sommer** *m* summer
**Sommerfahrplan** *m* summer railway timetable
**Sommerreifen** *pl* normal tyres
**Sonder-** special
**Sonderfahrt** *f* special excursion
**Sonderpreis** *m* special reduced price
**Sonderzug** *m* special train
**Sonnabend** *m* Saturday
**Sonne** *f* sun
**Sonnen-** solar
**Sonnenaufgang** *m* sunrise
**Sonnenbrand** *m* sunburn *(painful)*
**Sonnenbrille** *f* sunglasses
**Sonnenmilch** *f* sun lotion
**Sonnenöl** *nt* suntan oil
**Sonnenschirm** *m* parasol; umbrella
**Sonnenstich** *m* sunstroke
**Sonnenuntergang** *m* sunset
**Sonntag** *m* Sunday
**sonn- und feiertags** Sundays and public holidays
**sonstig** other; **sonstige Abzüge** miscellaneous deductions
**sorgen: sorgen für** to look after; to take care of
**sorgfältig** careful; **sorgfältig aufbewahren** keep in a safe place; do not discard
**Soße** *f* dressing *(salad)*; sauce; gravy
**Spannung** *f* voltage
**Sparbuch** *nt* bankbook
**Spargel** *m* asparagus

**Spargelspitzen** *pl* asparagus tips
**Sparkasse** *f* savings bank
**Sparpreis** *m* economy fare
**sparsam** economical
**Spaß** *m* fun; joke; **viel Spaß!** have a good time!
**spät** late
**Spätburgunder Rotwein** *m* full-bodied red wine
**Spätvorstellung** *f* late show
**Spätzle** *pl* home-made noodles
**Spaziergang** *m* stroll; walk
**Speck** *m* bacon
**Speise** *f* dish; food
**Speiseeis** *nt* ice cream
**Speisekarte** *f* menu; **nach der Speisekarte** à la carte
**Speiselokal** *nt* restaurant
**Speisequark** *m* curd cheese
**Speisesaal** *m* dining room
**Speisewagen** *m* dining car
**Spende** *f* donation
**Sperre** *f* barrier *(fence)*
**sperren** to close *(road)*
**Spezi** *nt* mixture of Coke and Fanta
**Spezialitäten** *pl* special dishes
**Spezialitäten-Restaurant** *nt* restaurant offering special or ethnic food
**Spickbraten** *m* larded roast of beef
**Spiegel** *m* mirror
**Spiegelei** *nt* fried egg
**Spiegelreflexkamera** *f* reflex camera
**Spiel** *nt* pack *(of cards)*; game
**Spielautomat** *m* slot machine *(for gambling)*

**Spielbank** f casino
**spielen** to gamble; to play
**Spielfilm** m feature film
**Spielplan** m (theatre) programme
**Spielwarenladen** m toyshop
**Spieß** m skewer; **am Spieß** barbecued
**Spinat** m spinach
**Spirituosen** pl spirits (alcohol)
**Spirituskocher** m spirit stove
**Spitze** f lace; point (tip)
**Sport(arten)** m sport(s)
**Sportartikel** pl sports equipment
**Sportkleidung** f sportswear
**Sportplatz** m playing field
**Sportwagen** m push chair; sports car
**Sprache** f speech; language
**Sprachführer** m phrase book
**sprechen** to speak
**Sprechstunde** f consultation (hour); surgery (hour)
**Sprechzimmer** nt consulting room; doctor's office
**Sprengarbeiten** pl blasting operations
**Spritze** f injection
**spülen** to flush the toilet; to rinse
**Spülmittel** nt washing-up liquid
**Spülung** f rinse (hair conditioner)
**Spur** f trace; track; lane (of road)
**Staatsangehörigkeit** f nationality
**Stachelbeeren** pl gooseberries
**Stadion** nt stadium
**Stadium** nt stage (period)
**Stadt (Städte)** f town(s)
**Stadtbüro** nt city-centre branch

**Stadtführung** f guided tour of the town
**städtisch** urban; municipal
**Stadtmitte** f city centre
**Stadtplan** m map (of town)
**Stadtrundfahrt** f sightseeing tour of the town
**Stadtteil** m district (of town)
**Stadtzentrum** nt town centre
**Stand** m stall; taxi rank
**ständig** permanent(ly); continuous(ly)
**Standlicht** nt sidelights
**Standort** m (present) location
**Stangenbohnen** pl runner beans
**Stangenbrot** nt French loaf
**Stangensellerie** f celery
**Starthilfekabel** pl jump leads
**Station** f station; stop; ward
**Stativ** nt tripod
**statt** instead of
**stattfinden** to take place
**Stau** m tailback
**Staudensellerie** f celery
**Staugefahr** f possibility of tailbacks
**Stechmücke** f mosquito; gnat
**Steckdose** f socket (electrical)
**Stecker** m plug (electric)
**stehen** to stand
**Stehplätze** pl standing room
**Steigung** f gradient
**steil** steep
**Steinbutt** m turbot
**Steinpilz** m type of wild mushroom
**Steinschlag** m falling stones
**Stelle** f place; point (in space)

**stellen** to set *(alarm)*; to put
**Stempel** *m* hallmark; stamp *(rubber)*
**stempeln** to stamp *(visa)*
**Steppdecke** *f* quilt
**Stern** *m* star
**Sternwarte** *f* observatory
**Steuer** *f* tax
**steuerfrei** tax-free
**steuern** to steer
**steuerpflichtig** taxable
**Steuerung** *f* controls
**Stich** *m* bite *(by insect)*; stitch *(sewing)*; sting
**Stiefel** *pl* boots
**Stil** *m* style
**Stimmung** *f* mood; atmosphere
**Stirn** *f* forehead
**Stock** *m* cane *(walking stick)*; stick; floor; **der erste Stock** the first floor
**Stockung** *f* hold-up *(traffic)*
**Stockwerk** *nt* storey
**Stör** *m* sturgeon
**stören** to disturb *(interrupt)*; **bitte nicht stören** do not disturb
**stornieren** to cancel
**Störung** *f* hold-up; fault; disorder *(medical)*
**Stoßdämpfer** *m* shock absorber
**Stoßstange** *f* bumper *(on car)*
**Stoßzeit** *f* rush hour
**Strafe** *f* punishment; fine
**Strafmandat** *nt* /**Strafzettel** *m* parking ticket
**stramm: strammer Max** *m* smoked ham on bread topped with a fried egg
**Strand** *m* shore *(of sea)*; beach

**Strandkorb** *m* wicker beach chair with a hood
**Straße** *f* road; street; **Straße gesperrt** road closed
**Straßenbahn** *f* tram(car)
**Straßenbauarbeiten** *pl* road works
**Straßenglätte** *f* slippery road surface
**Straßenkarte** *f* road map
**Straßenschaden** *pl* damage to the road
**Straßensperre** *f* road block
**Straßenverkehrsordnung** *f* Highway Code
**Straßenzustand** *m* road conditions
**Straßenzustandsbericht** *m* road report
**Strecke** *f* route, distance
**Streichholzschachtel** *f* matchbox
**Streichkäse** *m* cheese spread
**Streik** *m* strike *(industrial)*
**Streuselkuchen** *m* sponge cake with crumble topping
**Strickwaren** *pl* knitwear
**Strom** *m* power *(electricity)*
**Stromanschluß** *m* electric points
**Strömung** *f* current *(of water, air)*
**Strümpfe** *pl* stockings
**Strumpfhose** *f* tights
**Strumpfwaren** *pl* hosiery
**Stück** *nt* piece; cut *(of meat)*
**Stufe** *f* step *(stair)*
**Stunde** *f* hour; lesson
**stündlich** hourly
**Sturzhelm** *m* crash helmet
**Süden** *m* south
**südlich** southern

**Sultaninen** *pl* sultanas
**Sülze** *f* brawn *(food)*
**Summe** *f* sum *(total amount)*
**Super(benzin)** *nt* four-star petrol
**Suppe** *f* soup
**Suppenhuhn** *nt* boiling fowl
**surfen: surfen gehen** to go surfing
**süß** sweet
**Süßigkeiten** *pl* sweets
**Süßstoff** *m* sweetener
**Süßwaren** *pl* confectionery
**Süßwasserfische** *pl* freshwater fish
**Sylvaner** *m* medium-dry white wine

**Tabak** *m* tobacco
**Tabakladen** *m* tobacconist's (shop)
**Tabelle** *f* chart *(diagram, table)*
**Tablette(n)** *f* tablet(s); pill(s)
**Tachometer** *m* speedometer
**Tafel** *f* table; board; **eine Tafel Schokolade** a bar of chocolate
**Tafelwein** *m* table wine
**Tag** *m* day; **jeden Tag** every day
**Tagesanzeiger** *m* daily information guide
**Tagesfestpreis** *m* rental price per day
**Tageskarte** *f* day ticket; menu of the day
**Tagespauschale** *f* daily unlimited rate *(for rented car)*
**Tagesrückfahrkarte** *f* day return
**Tagessuppe** *f* soup of the day
**täglich** daily
**tagsüber** during the day
**Tal** *nt* valley

**Tankanzeige** *m* fuel gauge
**tanken** to get petrol
**Tankfüllmenge** *f* tank capacity
**Tanksäule** *f* petrol pump
**Tankstelle** *f* filling station; **Tankstelle und Raststätte** service area
**Tanz** *m* dance
**Tarif** *m* rate; tariff
**Tarifzone** *f* tariff zone
**Taschenbuch** *nt* paperback
**Taschendieb** *m* pickpocket
**Taschenlampe** *f* torch
**Taschenmesser** *nt* pocketknife
**Taschentuch** *nt* handkerchief
**Tasse** *f* cup
**Taste** *f* : **Taste drücken** push button
**Tatar** *nt* steak tartare
**Tätigkeit** *f* activity; occupation
**Taube** *f* pigeon
**Taucherausrüstung** *f* diving equipment
**tausend** thousand
**Tauwetter** *nt* thaw
**Taxistand** *m* taxi rank
**technisch** technical; **technische Daten** technical data
**Tee** *m* tea
**Teebeutel** *m* tea bag
**Teich** *m* pond
**Teig** *m* dough; pastry
**Teil** *m* part
**teilen** to divide; to share
**Teilkaskoversicherung** *f* ≈ third party, fire and theft
**Teilnahme** *f* participation
**teilnehmen** to participate
**teilweise** partly

# TEL – TRA

**Telefonansagen** *pl* telephone information services
**Telefonauskunft** *f* directory enquiries
**Telefonbuch** *nt* telephone directory
**Telefongespräch** *nt* phone call
**telefonisch** by telephone
**Telefonkarte** *f* **(mit Guthaben)** phonecard
**Telefonnummer** *f* telephone number
**Telefonverzeichnis** *nt* telephone directory
**Telefonzelle** *f* telephone booth
**Teleobjektiv** *nt* telephoto lens
**Teller** *m* plate
**Temperaturanzeige** *f* temperature gauge
**Tempo** *nt* pace (speed)
**Tennishalle** *f* indoor tennis courts
**Tennisplatz** *m* tennis court
**Tennisschläger** *m* tennis racket
**Termin** *m* date; deadline; appointment
**Terrasse** *f* patio; terrace (of café)
**teuer** expensive
**Theater** *nt* theatre; fuss
**Theaterveranstaltungen** *pl* theatre programme
**Theke** *f* bar (counter)
**Thunfisch** *m* tuna(-fish)
**Thymian** *m* thyme
**tief** deep; low (in pitch)
**Tiefgarage** *f* underground car park
**Tier** *nt* animal
**Tilsiter** *m* smooth, mild cheese with a slightly sharp taste

**Tinte** *f* ink
**Tintenfisch** *m* cuttlefish; squid
**Tiroler Eierspeise** *f* eggs, potatoes, anchovies, cream, topped with breadcrumbs and oven baked
**Tisch** *m* table
**Tischdame** *f* hostess (in night club)
**Tischtennis** *nt* table tennis
**Tischwein** *m* table wine
**Toastbrot** *nt* sliced white bread for toasting
**tödlich** fatal
**Toiletten** *pl* public conveniences
**Toilettenartikel** *pl* toiletries
**Toilettenpapier** *nt* toilet paper
**Tollwut** *f* rabies
**Tomate** *f* tomato
**Tomatenmark** *nt* tomato purée
**Tomatensaft** *m* tomato juice
**Ton** *m* sound; tone; clay
**Tonband** *nt* tape (magnetic)
**Tonbandbegleiter** *m* audio-guide
**Tönung** *f* semi-permanent tint
**Topfen** *m* curd cheese (Austria)
**Töpferei** *f* pottery (workshop)
**Tor** *nt* gate; goal (sport)
**Torte** *f* gâteau; tart
**Tortelett** *nt* pie
**tot** dead
**Tourismus** *m* tourism
**Touristenklasse** *f* economy class
**Touristikschalter** *m* tourist desk
**Tracht** *f* costume
**tragbar** portable
**trampen** to hitchhike
**Trauben** *pl* grapes
**Traubenzucker** *m* dextrose

**treffen** to meet
**Treffpunkt** *m* meeting-place
**trennen** to divide *(separate)*
**Treppe** *f* flight of steps; stairs
**Treppenhaus** *nt* staircase
**Tresor** *m* safe
**Tretboot** *nt* pedalo
**treten** to step; to kick
**Trimmdichpfad** *m* keep-fit trail
**trinkbar** drinkable
**trinken** to drink
**Trinkgeld** *nt* tip *(money given)*
**Trinkwasser** *nt* drinking water
**trocken** dry
**tropfnaß: tropfnaß aufhängen** to drip-dry
**Trüffel** *f* truffle *(fungus)*
**Truthahn** *m* turkey
**tschüs** cheerio
**Tube** *f* tube
**Tuch** *nt* cloth; scarf; towel; shawl
**tun** to do; to put; **das tut nichts** that doesn't matter
**Tür** *f* door; **Tür weit öffnen/zumachen** open door wide/close door
**Turm** *m* tower
**Turnhalle** *f* gym(nasium)
**Turnschuhe** *pl* plimsolls
**Tüte** *f* bag *(paper)*

**u.A.w.g.** RSVP
**U-Bahn** *f* underground railway
**Übelkeit** *f* sickness *(nausea)*
**über** over; above; **über London fahren** to go via London
**überall** everywhere

**überbacken** au gratin
**überbelichtet** overexposed *(photo)*
**Überfahrt** *f* crossing *(voyage)*
**überfällig** overdue
**Überführung** *f* overpass
**überfüllt** crowded
**Übergabe** *f* handing over; delivery
**übergeben** to hand over; to present *(give)*; **sich übergeben** to vomit
**Übergewicht** *nt* excess baggage
**Überholspur** *f* outside lane
**Überholverbot** *nt* no overtaking
**übermorgen** the day after tomorrow
**übernachten** to stay the night
**Übernachtung** *f* overnight stay; **Übernachtung und Frühstück** bed and breakfast
**Übernachtungsmöglichkeit** *f* accommodation
**überprüfen** to check
**Übersetzung** *f* translation
**übertragbar** transferable
**überweisen** to transfer *(money)*; to refer *(patient)*
**Überweisung** *f* remittance; referral
**Überzelt** *nt* fly sheet
**übrig** left over
**Ufer** *nt* bank *(of river)*; shore
**Uhr** *f* clock; watch; **um 3 Uhr** at 3 o'clock; **es ist 4 Uhr** it's 4 o'clock
**um** around; **um 4 Uhr** at 4 o'clock
**umadressieren** to readdress
**umbuchen** to alter one's booking
**Umgebung** *f* surroundings; neighbourhood
**Umgehungsstraße** *f* bypass; ring

road

**umgekehrt** vice versa; reversed; **in umgekehrter Richtung** in the opposite direction

**Umkleidekabine** *f* cubicle

**umleiten** to divert; to reroute

**Umleitung** *f* diversion *(traffic)*

**umrandet: stark umrandetes Feld** *nt* area outlined in bold

**Umrechnungskurs** *m* rate of exchange

**Umschlag** *m* envelope

**umsonst** free of charge; in vain

**Umsteigebahnhof** *m* interchange station

**umsteigen** to change; **in Bonn umsteigen** to change trains at Bonn

**umtauschen** to (ex)change

**Umweg** *m* detour

**Umwelt** *f* environment

**Umweltverschmutzung** *f* pollution

**Umzug** *m* parade

**unaufgefordert** without being asked

**unbedingt** absolutely

**Unbefugte(r)** *m/f* unauthorized person

**unbegrenzt** unlimited, **unbegrenzte Kilometer** unlimited mileage

**unbewirtschaftet: unbewirtschaftete Hütte** *f* unserviced mountain shelter

**und** and

**uneben: unebene Fahrbahn** *f* uneven road surface

**unerläßlich** vital

**unerwünscht** unwelcome;

unwanted

**Unfall** *m* accident

**Unfallhilfsstelle** *f* first-aid station

**Unfallschäden** *pl* damages

**ungefähr** approximate; **ungefähr £10** about £10

**Unglück** *nt* accident

**ungültig** invalid; **ungültig werden** to expire

**Unkosten** *pl* costs

**unmöglich** impossible

**unregelmäßig** irregular

**unreif** unripe

**unsicher** uncertain *(fact)*

**unten** downstairs; below; **nach unten** downward(s); downstairs

**unter** under(neath)

**unterbelichtet** underexposed

**Unterbodenschutz** *m* underseal

**unterbrechen** to interrupt

**Unterbrecherkontakt** *m* contact-breaker point

**unterbringen** to accommodate

**untere(r/s)** lower; bottom

**Unterführung** *f* subway; underpass *(for pedestrians)*

**Untergeschoß** *nt* basement

**Unterhaltung** *f* entertainment

**Unterkunft** *f* accommodation

**Unterschied** *m* difference

**unterschreiben** to sign

**Unterschrift** *f* signature

**unterste(r/s)** bottom

**unterstreichen** to underline

**Untersuchung** *f* test; examination *(medical)*

**Untertitel** *m* subtitle *(of film)*

**unterwegs** on the way
**unterzeichnen** to sign *(document)*
**Unterzeichnete(r)** *m/f* undersigned
**unverbindlich** without obligation
**unwohl** unwell; **sich unwohl fühlen** not to feel at ease
**Urlaub** *m* leave; holiday; **auf Urlaub** on holiday; on leave
**Urlauber** *m* holiday-maker
**Urlaubsort** *m* resort
**Ursache** *f* cause
**Ursprung** *m* origin
**ursprünglich** originally *(at first)*
**Ursprungsland** *nt* country of origin

**Vanilleeis** *nt* vanilla ice cream
**Varietévorführung** *f* variety show
**Vater** *m* father
**vegetarisch** vegetarian
**Veitshoechheimer** *m* quality wine from Franken region
**Ventil** *nt* valve
**Venusmuschel(n)** *f* clam(s)
**Verabredung** *f* date *(appointment)*
**Veränderung** *f* change
**veranlassen** to cause
**Veranstalter** *m* organizer
**Veranstaltungen** *pl* events
**Veranstaltungskalender** *m* diary of events
**Veranstaltungsprogramm** *nt* entertainment guide
**verantwortlich** responsible
**Verband** *m* association; bandage
**Verbandskasten** *m* /**Verbandszeug** *nt* first-aid box
**verbieten** to ban; to prohibit

**verbinden** to connect *(join)*
**Verbindung** *f* service *(bus etc)*; line *(telephone)*; **sich in Verbindung setzen mit** to contact
**verbleit** leaded
**Verbot** *nt* ban
**verboten** forbidden
**Verbrauch** *m* consumption
**Verbrennung** *f* burn
**verbringen** to spend *(time)*
**Verbundfahrausweis** *m* combined ticket for use on local public transport services
**verdaulich** digestible
**verderben** to go bad *(food)*; to spoil
**verdienen** to deserve; to earn
**verdorben** spoilt
**verdünnen** to dilute
**Verein** *m* society *(club)*
**vereinbaren** to agree upon
**Vereinigtes Königreich** *nt* United Kingdom
**Vereinigte Staaten (von Amerika)** *pl* United States (of America)
**Verfallsdatum** *nt* expiry date; eat-by date
**Verfassung** *f* state *(health)*
**Verfügung** *f* disposal; **zur Verfügung** at one's disposal
**Vergangenheit** *f* past
**vergessen** to forget
**Vergnügen** *nt* enjoyment; pleasure; **viel Vergnügen!** have a good time!
**Vergnügungsdampfer** *m* pleasure boat
**Vergnügungspark** *m* amusement park
**vergoldet** gold-plated

**Vergrößerung** f enlargement
**verheiratet** married
**verhindern** to prevent
**Verhütungsmittel** nt contraceptive
**Verkauf** m sale
**verkaufen** to sell
**Verkäufer(in)** m(f) sales assistant
**verkäuflich** negotiable
**Verkaufsautomat** m vending machine
**Verkehr** m traffic
**verkehren** to run; to fly
**Verkehrsbüro** nt tourist information office
**Verkehrsführung** f: **Verkehrsführung geändert** diversion ahead
**Verkehrsfunkdecoder** m traffic broadcast selector
**Verkehrspolizist** m traffic warden
**Verkehrszeichen** nt road sign
**verkehrt** wrong; **verkehrt herum** upside down; **verkehrt nicht täglich** not daily
**verlangen** to demand
**verlängern** to renew
**Verleih** m rental company; hire company
**Verletzung** f injury
**verlieren** to lose
**verlobt** engaged (betrothed)
**Verlust** m loss
**vermeiden** to avoid
**Vermerk** m remark
**vermieten** to rent; **zu vermieten** to let
**Vermittlung** f telephone exchange; operator
**Verpackung** f wrapper; packing

**Verpflegung** f food
**Verrechnungsscheck** m crossed cheque
**verreisen** to go on a journey
**Verrenkung** f sprain
**verschieben** to postpone
**verschieden** various; different
**Verschleiß** m wear and tear
**verschreiben** to prescribe
**verschreibungspflichtig** available only on prescription
**Versicherer** m underwriter
**versichern** to insure
**Versicherung** f insurance
**Versicherungsbedingungen** pl insurance conditions
**Versicherungskarte** f insurance card; **grüne Versicherungskarte** green card
**versilbert** silver-plated
**versorgen** to keep (feed and clothe); **jemanden mit etwas versorgen** to provide someone with something
**verspäten: sich verspäten** to be late
**Verspätung** f delay; **der Zug hat Verspätung** the train has been delayed
**verstauchen** to sprain
**verstehen** to understand
**Verstopfung** f blockage; **Verstopfung haben** to be constipated
**Vertrag** m contract
**verunglücken** to have an accident
**Verwandte(r)** m/f relative
**verwechseln** to confuse
**verwenden** to use
**Verwendung** f use
**verwitwet** widowed

**verzehren** to consume
**Verzeichnis** *nt* list
**Verzeihung!** sorry; excuse me
**verzögern** to delay
**verzollen** to declare *(customs)*;
**nichts zu verzollen** nothing to
declare
**viel** much
**viele** many
**vielleicht** perhaps; possibly
**vier** four
**Viertel** *nt* quarter
**Viertelstunde** *f* quarter of an hour
**vierzehn** fourteen; **vierzehn Tage** a
fortnight
**Visum** *nt* visa
**Völkerkundemuseum** *nt* museum
of ethnology
**Volkslied** *nt* folk song
**Volkstanz** *m* folk dance
**voll** full
**vollendet** completed; **nach
vollendetem 6. Lebensjahr** from
one's 6th birthday
**Vollkaskoversicherung** *f*
comprehensive insurance
**Vollkornbrot** *nt* wholemeal bread
**Vollmacht** *f* power of attorney
**Vollmilchschokolade** *f* milk
chocolate
**Vollpension** *f* full board
**vollständig** complete
**volltanken** to fill up *(car)*
**Vollwaschmittel** *nt* washing
powder for all temperatures
**von** from
**vor** before; **vor 4 Jahren** 4 years ago
**Voranzeige** *f* preview

**voraus** ahead; **im voraus** in advance
**voraussichtlich** probably
**vorbei** past
**vorbestellen** to reserve *(seat, room)*
**Vorbestellung** *f* reservation
**Vorder-** front
**Vorderradantrieb** *m* front-wheel
drive
**Vorderseite** *f* front *(foremost part)*
**Vordruck** *m* form *(document)*
**Vorfahrt** *f* right of way *(on road)*;
**Vorfahrt achten** give way; **die
Vorfahrt beachten** to give way
**Vorfahrtsstraße** *f* priority road;
you have priority
**Vorführung** *f* demonstration;
presentation; showing *(of film)*
**vorgekocht** ready-cooked
**vorgestern** the day before
yesterday
**vorhanden** available
**vorher** before
**Vorhersage** *f* forecast
**vorläufig** temporarily
**vorletzte(r/s)** last but one
**vormittags** a.m.
**vorn** at the front
**Vorname** *m* first name
**vorne** in front
**Vorortbahn** *f* suburban line
**Vorrat** *m* provisions
**Vorsaison** *f* early season
**Vorschau** *f* preview
**Vorschlag** *m* proposal; suggestion
**Vorschrift** *f* regulation *(rule)*
**Vorsicht** *f* care; caution; **Vorsicht!**
look out!; be careful!; **Vorsicht!
Stufe!** mind the step

**Vorspeise** f hors d'oeuvre
**Vorstellung** f introduction (social); performance (of play)
**Vorteil** m advantage; benefit
**vorübergehend** temporarily
**Vor- und Zuname** m first name and surname
**Vorverkauf** m advance booking
**Vorverkaufskasse/Vorverkaufsstelle** f advance booking office
**Vorwahl(nummer)** f dialling code
**vorwärts** forward(s)

**Wacholder** m juniper
**Wachs** nt wax
**Wachsbohnen** pl butter beans
**Wachtel** f quail
**Wackelpeter** m jelly
**Waffel** f wafer; waffle
**Wagen** m car; carriage (railway)
**Wagenheber** m jack (for car)
**Wagenrückgabe** f check-in
**Wagentyp** m type of car
**Wagenübernahme** f rental
**Wagenwäsche** f car wash
**Wahl** f choice; election; **engere Wahl** short list
**wählen** to dial (number); to choose
**während** during; while
**wahrscheinlich** likely; probable
**Währung** f currency
**Wahrzeichen** nt landmark
**Wald** m wood; forest
**Waldlehrpfad** m nature trail
**Waldorfsalat** m Waldorf salad
**Waldpilze** pl wild mushrooms
**Waldsportpfad** m keep-fit trail

through forest
**Walnuß(-nüsse)** f walnut(s)
**Wandern** nt hiking
**Wanderung** f hike
**Wanderweg** m trail for ramblers
**wann** when (in questions)
**Ware** f commodity; **Waren** goods
**Warenmuster** nt /**Warenprobe** f trade sample
**Warensendung** f sample of goods
**warm** warm; **warme Getränke** hot drinks
**Warndreieck** nt warning triangle
**Warnlichtanlage** f hazard warning lights
**Warnung** f warning
**Wartehalle** f lounge (at airport)
**Warteliste** f waiting list
**warten** to wait
**Wartesaal** m waiting room
**Wartung** f maintenance
**warum** why
**was** what
**waschbar** washable
**Waschbecken** nt washbasin
**Wäsche** f linen; washing (clothes); **schmutzige Wäsche** laundry
**waschecht** colourfast
**waschen** to wash; **Waschen und Legen** shampoo and set
**Waschgelegenheit** f washing facilities
**Waschmittel** nt detergent
**Waschraum** m washroom
**Waschsalon** m launderette
**Waschstrasse** f car wash
**Wasser** nt water; **destilliertes Wasser**

distilled water

**Wasseranschluß** *m* water point

**wasserdicht** waterproof

**Wassermelone** *f* water melon

**Wasserski** *m* : **Wasserski laufen** to go water-skiing

**wasserundurchlässig** waterproof

**Watte** *f* cotton wool

**Wechsel** *m* bureau de change

**Wechselgeld** *nt* change

**Wechselkurs** *m* exchange rate

**wechseln** to change; to give change

**Weckdienst** *m* early morning call

**Wecker** *m* alarm (clock)

**Weckklöße** *pl* bread dumplings

**weder ... noch** neither ... nor

**weg** away

**Weg** *m* path; lane *(in country)*; **auf dem Weg nach** bound for *(ship)*

**wegen** because of

**Wegweiser** *m* signpost

**weh: weh tun** to ache; to hurt; **sich weh tun** to hurt oneself

**weiblich** female; feminine

**Weichkäse** *m* soft cheese

**Weihnachten** *nt* Christmas

**Weihnachts(feier)tag** *m* : **der erste Weihnachtstag** Christmas Day; **der zweite Weihnachtstag** Boxing Day

**weil** because

**Wein** *m* wine

**Weinberg** *m* vineyard

**Weinbergschnecken** *pl* escargots

**Weinbrand** *m* brandy

**Weinkeller** *m* wine cellar

**Weinkraut** *nt* sauerkraut

**Weinprobe** *f* wine-tasting

**Weinstube** *f* wine tavern

**Weintrauben** *pl* grapes

**weiß** white

**Weißbier** *nt* light, fizzy beer made using top-fermentation yeast

**Weißbrot** *nt* white bread

**Weißkohl** *m* /**Weißkraut** *nt* white cabbage

**Weißwein** *m* white wine

**Weißwurst** *f* veal sausage

**weit** far; loose *(clothing)*; **bei weitem** far *(much)*

**weiter** farther; further; **weitere Fahrer** additional drivers

**Weiterflug** *m* transit

**Weizen** *m* wheat

**Weizenbier** *nt* light, fizzy beer made using top-fermentation yeast

**welche(r/s)** which; what; which one

**wem** to whom

**Wende** *f* U-turn *(in car)*

**wenden** to turn; **wenden Sie sich an ...** turn to ...; consult ...

**Wendeplatz** *m* /**Wendefläche** *f* turning area

**wenig** little; **ein wenig** a little

**wenige** few

**wenigstens** at least

**wenn** if; when *(with present tense)*

**wer** who

**werden** to become; **schlecht werden** to go bad

**werfen** to throw

**Werft** *f* shipyard

**Werk** *nt* plant *(factory)*; work *(of art)*

**Werkstatt** *f* workshop
**werktags** on workdays
**Werkzeug** *nt* tool; tool kit
**wert** worth
**Wert** *m* value
**Wertangabe** *f* declaration of value;
  **Sendung mit Wertangabe** registered
  parcel; registered letter etc
**Wertbrief** *m* registered letter
**Wertgegenstände** *pl* valuables
**Wertzeichen** *nt* postage stamp
**Westen** *m* west
**westlich** western
**Wetter** *nt* weather
**Wetterbericht** *m/*
**Wettervorhersage** *f* weather
  forecast
**wichtig** important
**Wickelraum** *m* mother and baby
  room
**widerrechtlich: widerrechtlich
  geparkte Fahrzeuge werden
  kostenpflichtig abgeschleppt**
  vehicles parked illegally will be
  towed away at owner's expense
**wie** like; how
**wieder** again
**wiederholen** to repeat
**Wiederholung** *f* repetition
**Wiedersehen** *nt* : **auf Wiedersehen**
  goodbye
**wiegen** to weigh
**Wien** *nt* Vienna
**Wiener Fischfilets** *pl* fish fillets
  baked in sour cream sauce
**Wiener Schnitzel** *nt* veal
  escalope, fried in breadcrumbs
**Wiener Würstchen** *nt* frankfurter

**Wiese** *f* lawn
**wieviel** how much
**Wild** *nt* game *(hunting)*; venison
**Wildbraten** *m* roast venison
**Wildgulasch** *nt* game stew
**Wildleder** *nt* suede
**Wildsuppe** *f* game soup
**willkommen** welcome
**Windbeutel** *m* cream puff
**Windel** *f* nappy
**Windschutzscheibe** *f* windscreen
**Windstärke** *f* wind force
**windsurfen** to go windsurfing
**Winter** *m* winter
**Winterausrüstung** *f* winter tyres
  and snow chains
**Winterfahrplan** *m* winter railway
  timetable
**Winterreifen** *pl* snow tyres
**Wintersport** *m* winter sports
**Wintersportwetterbericht** *m*
  weather report for skiers
**wir** we
**wirksam** effective *(remedy etc)*
**Wirkung** *f* effect
**Wirt** *m* landlord
**Wirtin** *f* landlady
**Wirtschaft** *f* pub; inn
**Wirtshaus** *nt* inn
**wissen** to know *(fact)*
**wo** where
**Woche** *f* week
**Wochenende** *nt* weekend
**Wochenendpauschale** *f* weekend
  rate with unlimited mileage
**Wochenendtarif** *m* weekend tariff
**Wochenpauschale** *f* weekly

unlimited rate
**Wochentag** *m* weekday
**wöchentlich** weekly
**woher** where ... from
**wohin** where
**Wohnadresse** *f* home address
**wohnen** to stay; to live
**Wohnheim** *nt* residence (of college)
**Wohnmobil** *nt* dormobile
**Wohnort/Wohnsitz** *m* place of residence
**Wohnung** *f* flat; residence
**Wohnwagen** *m* caravan
**wolkig** cloudy
**Woll-** woollen
**Wolldecke** *f* blanket
**Wolle** *f* wool
**wollen** to want (wish for)
**Wollwaschmittel** *nt* detergent for woollens
**Wörterbuch** *nt* dictionary
**Wunde** *f* wound (injury)
**Würfel** *m* dice; cube
**Wurst** *f* sausage; **rote Wurst** sausage for frying
**Würstchen** *nt* sausage (for boiling); frankfurter
**Wurstplatte** *f* (plate of) assorted cold meats
**Wurstsalat** *m* sausage salad (with onions and vinaigrette)
**Württemberger Wein** *m* wine from the area around Stuttgart
**würzen** to season
**würzig** spicy
**Würzmischung** *f* seasoning

**Yachthafen** *m* marina

**Zahl** *f* number (figure)
**zahlbar** payable
**zahlen** to pay
**zählen** to count (objects, people)
**Zähler** *m* meter
**Zahlkarte** *f* giro transfer form
**Zahlung** *f* payment
**Zahn** *m* tooth
**Zahnarzt** *m* dentist
**Zahnbürste** *f* toothbrush
**Zahncreme** *f* toothpaste
**Zähne** *pl* teeth
**Zahnfleischbluten** *nt* bleeding gums
**Zahnschmerzen** *pl* toothache
**Zahnstocher** *m* toothpick
**Zange** *f* pliers
**Zäpfchen** *nt* suppository
**Zapfsäule** *f* petrol pump
**zart** tender (meat); delicate
**z.B.** e.g.
**zehn** ten
**Zeichen** *nt* sign, mark
**Zeichenerklärung** *f* key to the symbols
**Zeichentrickfilm** *m* cartoon
**zeigen** to show; **auf etwas zeigen** to point at something
**Zeit** *f* time; **Zeit und Kilometer** time and mileage
**Zeitansage** *f* speaking clock
**Zeitkarte** *f* season ticket
**Zeitraum** *m* period (of time)
**Zeitschrift** *f* magazine
**Zeitung** *f* (news)paper

**Zelt** nt tent
**Zeltboden** m groundsheet
**zelten** to camp
**Zeltplatz** m camp(ing) site
**Zentrale** f head office; switchboard
**Zentrum** nt centre
**zerbrechlich** fragile
**zerlassen: zerlassene Butter** f melted butter
**zerstören** to destroy
**Zeug** nt stuff (substance)
**Zeugnis** nt certificate
**Ziegenleder** nt kid (leather)
**ziehen** to tow (trailer); to pull
**Ziel** nt destination; goal; target; **Ziel suchen** select destination
**Zielbahnhof** m destination
**Zieltaste** f button to select destination
**ziemlich** quite; fairly
**Ziffer(n)** f figure(s)
**Zigarette(n)** f cigarette(s)
**Zigarettenpapiere** pl cigarette papers
**Zigarre(n)** f cigar(s)
**Zigeunersteak** nt steak with peppers
**Zimmer** nt room; **freies Zimmer** vacancy (in hotel etc)
**Zimmer-** indoor (games)
**Zimmermädchen** nt chambermaid
**Zimmernachweis** m accommodation directory
**Zimmerservice** m room service
**Zimt** m cinnamon
**Zinn** nt tin (substance); pewter
**Zirkus** m circus
**Zitrone** f lemon

**Zitronensaft** m lemon juice
**Zoll** m customs; customs duty; toll
**Zollabfertigung** f customs clearance
**Zollamt** nt customs office
**Zollbeamte(r)** m customs officer
**zollfrei** duty-free (goods)
**Zollgebühren** pl customs duties
**Zoll(inhalts)erklärung** f customs declaration
**Zollkontrolle** f customs check
**zollpflichtig** dutiable
**zu** to; off (water supply); too; **zu mieten** for hire; **zu verkaufen** for sale; **zu den Zügen** to the trains
**Zubehör** nt accessories
**Zubringerdienste** pl shuttle service; airport bus/train/taxi services
**Zucchini** pl courgettes
**Zucker** m sugar
**Zuckerguß** m icing (on cake)
**Zuckerkrankheit** f diabetes
**zuerst** at first; first
**zufrieden** pleased; content(ed)
**Zug** m train
**Zugang** m access
**Zugbegleiter** m guard (on train); train timetable
**Zugbegleitpersonal** nt staff on train
**Zugrestaurant** nt restaurant on train
**zulässig** permissible; **zulässiges Gesamtgewicht** maximum laden weight; **zulässige Höchstgeschwindigkeit** (upper) speed limit
**Zuname** m surname

**Zündhölzer** *pl* matches
**Zündkerze(n)** *f* sparking plug(s)
**Zündschloß** *nt* ignition lock
**Zündschlüssel** *m* ignition key
**Zündung** *f* ignition
**Zunge** *f* tongue
**zurück** backward *(glance)*
**zurückgeben** to give back; to check in *(car)*
**zurücklegen** to travel; to replace
**zurückrufen** to ring back
**zurückzahlen** to pay back *(money)*
**zusammen** together
**zusätzlich** extra; additional
**Zusatztag** *m* additional day
**Zuschauer** *pl* audience *(in theatre)*
**Zuschauerterrasse** *f* observation deck
**Zuschlag** *m* surcharge; supplement; **Zuschlag erforderlich** subject to a supplement(ary charge)
**zuschlagpflichtig** subject to a supplement(ary charge)
**zuschließen** to lock
**Zustand** *m* state *(condition)*
**zuständig** responsible
**Zusteigebahnhof** *m* station of departure
**Zustellung** *f* delivery *(of mail)*
**Zutaten** *pl* ingredients
**Zutritt** *m* admission
**zuverläßig** reliable
**zuviel** too much
**zuzüglich** extra
**zwanglos: zwanglose Kleidung** dress: informal
**Zweck** *m* purpose; **es hat keinen Zweck** it's no use
**zwei** two
**Zweibettabteil** *nt* two-berth compartment
**Zweibettkabine** *f* double cabin
**Zweigstelle** *f* branch (office)
**zweimal** twice
**zweite(r/s)** second; **zweiter Stock** second floor
**Zwetschge(n)** *f* plum(s)
**Zwetschgenwasser** *nt* plum brandy
**Zwetschkenknödel** *pl* boiled plum dumplings, served hot, sprinkled with sugar *(Austria)*
**Zwieback** *m* rusk
**Zwiebel(n)** *f* bulb(s); onion(s)
**Zwiebelsuppe** *f* onion soup
**zwischen** between
**Zwischenlandung** *f* stopover
**Zwischenrippenstück** *nt* sirloin steak
**Zwischenstecker** *m* adaptor
**Zwischenstop** *m* brief stop-off
**Zwischensumme** *f* subtotal